URBAN DESIGN:
GREEN DIMENSIONS

To Kate

URBAN DESIGN: GREEN DIMENSIONS

Cliff Moughtin

Department of Urban Planning
University of Nottingham

Architectural Press

OXFORD AMSTERDAM BOSTON LONDON NEW YORK PARIS
SAN DIEGO SAN FRANCISCO SINGAPORE SYDNEY TOKYO

Architectural Press
An imprint of Elsevier Science
Linacre House, Jordan Hill, Oxford OX2 8DP

First published 1996
Reprinted 1997, 2002

British Library Cataloguing in Publication Data
A catalogue record for this book is available from
the British Library

Library of Congress Cataloguing in Publication Data
A catalogue record for this book is available from
the Library of Congress

ISBN 0 7506 2659 3

For information on all Architectural Press publications visit
our website at www.architecturalpress.com

Composition by Scribe Design, Gillingham, Kent
Printed in Great Britain

CONTENTS

PREFACE

The subject matter of this book is sustainable city development. Any discussion of urban design which does not address environmental issues has little meaning at a time of declining natural resources, ozone layer destruction, increasing pollution and fears of the greenhouse effect. The long-term survival of the planet as a hostess for sustained human occupation in anything other than a degraded lifestyle is in some doubt. In these circumstances any discussion of aesthetics in a pure or abstract form unrelated to environmental concerns could be thought to be superficial. This book considers architecture and its sister art, urban design, to consist of: 'Commodotie, Firmness and Delight' (Wotton, 1969; Moughtin, 1992). One aspect of 'Commodotie' in urban development is sustainability, that is a development which is non-damaging to the environment and which contributes to the city's ability to sustain its social and economic structures.

The requirements of sustainable development closely mirror the current agenda in urban design. The reactions to modern architecture and modern planning have led to a new appreciation of the traditional European city and its urban form. The current preoccupations of urban designers with the form of urban space, the vitality and identity of urban areas, qualities of urbanity, respect for tradition, and preferences for developments of human scale can all be encompassed within the schema of sustainable development. The two movements – Sustainable Development and Post Modern Urban Design – are mutually supportive. Post Modern Urban Design gives form to the menu of ideas subsumed under the title of Sustainable Development; in return it is given functional legitimacy. Without this functional legitimacy and the discipline a functional dimension imposes on the design process, Post Modern Urban Design may develop into just another esoteric aesthetic. The foundation of urban design is rooted in social necessity: society today is faced with an environmental crisis of global proportions and it is coming to terms with the effects of this crisis on the world's cities which gives purpose and meaning to urban design.

Pursuit of sustainable city structures presupposes also the development of a built environment of quality. The pursuit of environmental quality in the city requires attention to aesthetics and the definition of criteria by which visual quality or delight is judged. This book explores the problems of defining quality in urban design but seen against a backcloth of the current concerns about the global environment. It is the third volume in this series and builds upon the ideas contained in the first two volumes. The first volume outlined the meaning and role played by the main elements of urban design; discussing, in particular, the form and function of street and square. The second volume dealt in more detail with the ways in which the elements of the public realm are decorated. It outlined the general principles for the embellishment of: floor plane; the walls of streets and squares, corners, roofline, roofscape and skyline, corners; together with a discussion of the design and distribution of the three-dimensional ornaments that are placed in streets and squares. The present book aims to relate the main components of urban design to a general theory of urban structuring, paying particular attention to the city and its form, the urban quarter or district and the street block or insulae. This book, like the previous volumes,

explores the lessons for urban design which can be learnt from the past. However, like *Urban Design: Street and Square* and *Urban Design: Ornament and Decoration* this book does not advocate a process of simply copying from the past: it is not an apologia nor a support for wholesale pastiche in the public realm. The book attempts to come to terms with the logic of sustainable development and then to formulate principles of urban design based upon the acceptance of this particular environmental code. In the final chapter of the book the ideas of sustainable development are confronted with the reality of the modern, largely unsustainable city which has an extensive physical infrastructure and which will change only slowly. The last chapter, therefore, examines those elements within the range of ideas which are subsumed under the umbrella title of sustainable development which may in favourable circumstances be implemented in the foreseeable future.

March 1996

ACKNOWLEDGEMENTS

I wish to acknowledge my debt to two former students: to Bob Overy who, while I was teaching at The Queen's University of Belfast, introduced me to the role of public participation in planning; and to Steve Charter who encouraged me to start courses in sustainable development at the Institute of Planning Studies in the University of Nottingham. Both of these ideas, sustainable development and participation, are, in my view, critical for the development of a discipline of urban design. I have also had the pleasure in recent years of working in the same department as Brenda and Robert Vale. Their work in the field of Green Architecture is inspirational. The manuscript of this book, as in the case of the other two volumes in the series, was read by my wife Kate McMahon Moughtin who ensured that it made sense and that it could be read easily. The fine drawings, which help to clarify the meaning of the text, were once again made by Peter Whitehouse while Glyn Halls turned my negatives into photographs which illustrate the text. My thanks go also to Patricia Hulme who typed the final manuscript.

I am also greatly indebted to the Leverhulme Trust who have given generous financial support for the preparation of this book.

SUSTAINABLE DEVELOPMENT

1

INTRODUCTION

The subject matter of this book is urban design or the art of city building: the book is concerned with the method and process of structuring public space in cities. It is concerned in particular with the green dimensions of city building, that is, with the pursuit of sustainable urban form. Any discussion of urban design which does not address environmental issues has little meaning at a time of declining natural resources, ozone layer destruction, increasing pollution and fears of the greenhouse effect. The long-term survival of the planet as a vehicle for sustained human occupation in anything other than a degraded lifestyle is in some doubt. In these circumstances any discussion of the aesthetics of city design in a pure or abstract form unrelated to environmental concerns could be described as superficial and rather like rearranging the deckchairs on the Titanic. Architecture and its sister art, urban design, are often said to consist of: 'Commodotie, Firmness and Delight' (Wotton, 1969; Moughtin, 1992). One aspect of 'Commodotie' in urban development is sustainability, that is a development which is non-damaging to the environment and which contributes to the city's ability to sustain its

social and economic structure. Pursuit of sustainable city structures presupposes also the development of a built environment of quality. Environmental quality in the city, in part, is determined by aesthetic values and the definition of criteria by which visual quality or delight is judged. This book aims to explore the problems of defining quality in urban design but seen against a backcloth of the current concerns about the global environment.

The requirements of sustainable development are compatible with, and closely mirror, the Post Modern agenda in urban design. The current preoccupations of urban designers are with the form of urban space, the vitality and identity of urban areas, qualities of urbanity, respect for tradition and preference for medium rise development of human scale. These and other features in the best of Post Modern Urban Design can be absorbed within the schema of sustainable development. The two movements - Sustainable Development and Post Modern Urban Design - are mutually supportive: indeed, they are both expressions of current philosophy which has rejected the grand development strategies of the 1950s, 1960s and 1970s together with the modernist architecture which gave those strategies form. Post Modern Urban Design gives form to the ideas of sustainable development while in return it is given functional legitimacy. Without this functional legitimacy and the discipline it imposes on the design process, Post Modern Urban Design, like some of the buildings of post modernism, may develop into the whimsy of another esoteric aesthetic. The foundation of urban design is social necessity. The social imperative of today is an environmental crisis of global proportions and it is coming to terms with the effects of this crisis on cities which gives purpose and meaning to urban design.

ENVIRONMENTAL PROBLEMS

It has been suggested that the publication of *Silent Spring* by Rachel Carson (1962), is the start of the modern environmental movement (Dobson, 1991). The book outlines the inevitable damage caused by the large-scale and indiscriminate use of chemical pesticides, fungicides and herbicides. Carson's influence was widespread, affecting pressure groups such as Friends of the Earth in addition to giving a more general stimulus to the development of green politics and philosophy. *Small is Beautiful* by Schumacher (1974) is another milestone in the analysis of the causes of environmental problems and in the development of green principles. One such principle recognizes as an illusion the notion that we can continue to produce and consume at ever-increasing rates in a finite planet. Schumacher warned that the planet which is our stock of capital is being threatened by overproduction: in effect, the human race is consuming its capital at an alarming rate, endangering the tolerance margins of nature, and so threatening the life support systems that nurture mankind. A further landmark in green analysis was 'The Tragedy of the Commons' (Hardin, 1977). Hardin argued that if everyone maximized his or her own gain from commonly held property, whether land, sea or air (the commons) the result would be the destruction of those commons. Where populations are comparatively small, the 'commons'

now under threat include the air we breathe, the ozone layer that protects us and the ecological systems that deal with the waste we cause. How far *The Limits to Growth* (Meadows *et al.*, 1972) for the Club of Rome's Project on the Predicament of Mankind progressed the aims of the environmental movement is problematical. It attempted to plot the depletion of resources and to warn of the danger of exponential growth leading, it was argued, to the ultimate destruction of a global environment fit for human occupation. The book has been described as mechanistic and non-scientific. It has also been criticized for overstating the case and therefore of damaging the environmental or green cause. To some extent these criticisms have been addressed in *Beyond the Limits* (Meadows *et al.*, 1992). *The Limits to Growth* did, however, attempt to study some aspects of the global environment holistically, concentrating on linkages and adopting a systems approach to environmental analysis, all being common features of a green method.

An important contributory factor affecting the deterioration of the environment is population growth. The population of the planet was approximately 0.5 billion in the mid-seventeenth century. It was then growing at approximately 0.3 per cent per annum, which represented a doubling of population every 250 years. By the beginning of the twentieth century the population was 1.6 billion but growing at a rate of 0.5 per cent per annum, which corresponds to a doubling time of 140 years. In 1970 the global population was 3.6 billion with a growth rate of 2.1 per cent per annum. Not only was the population growing exponentially but the rate of growth itself was increasing. However, for the twenty years from 1971 to 1991 while the population was still growing from 3.6 to 5.4 billion the growth rate fell from 2.1 per cent to 1.7 per cent per annum. For this short period death rates fell but birth rates, on average, fell faster. This change in population growth rate is a significant improvement and means a reduction in the rate at which total world population grows. Nevertheless the popula-

Table 1.1
Projected population size and growth rate*. (As assessed in 1984)

Region	Population (billion)		Annual Growth Rate (per cent)		
	2000	2025	1950 to 1985	1985 to 2000	2000 to 2025
World	6.1	8.2	1.9	1.6	1.2
Africa	0.87	1.62	2.6	3.1	2.5
Latin America	0.55	0.78	2.6	2.0	1.4
Asia	3.55	4.54	2.1	1.6	1.0
North America	0.30	0.35	1.3	0.8	0.6
Europe	0.51	0.52	0.7	0.3	0.1
USSR	0.31	0.37	1.3	0.8	0.6
Oceania	0.03	0.04	1.9	1.4	0.9

*Medium-variant projections.
Source: World Commission on Environment and Development, *Our Common Future*, Oxford University Press, Oxford, 1987

tion growth is not close to levelling off (Table 1.1). It is estimated that the global population will be 8.2 billion by 2025, with 83 per cent of this population being in developing countries. Demand for feeding this extra population will increase by 50 per cent before the end of the millennium: 'The ability of agriculturalists to meet this challenge remains uncertain' (UN Conference on Environment and Development, 1992).

At least 1 billion people do not have access to safe and healthy shelter. It is estimated that by the year 2000, 2 billion people will be without sanitation. Furthermore, 5.2 million people, of which 4 million are children, die each year from waste-related diseases. According to the Earth Summit: 'Poverty and environmental degradation are closely interrelated. While poverty results in environmental stress, the major cause of environmental deterioration is an unsustainable pattern of consumption and production, particularly in the industrialised countries, which aggravates poverty and imbalances' (UN, 1992). The problems are: . . .'increasingly international, global and potentially more life-threatening than in the past' (Pearce, 1989). A reduction in population growth rates through education and family planning, while of great importance in establishing a sustainable future for mankind, alone is insufficient: sustainable patterns of consumption and production in the developed world are critical for the development of a global environment of quality.

The nature and extent of global environmental problems have been discussed fully in many texts so they will be dealt with only in summary here. One major threat to the quality of life is global pollution and the damage it causes to the ozone layer. Depletion of the earth's protective stratospheric ozone layer allows dangerous ultraviolet light from the sun to penetrate to the surface of the planet. This increase in radiation has the potential to cause adverse effects upon plants and animals, including man. Current economic policies and some land use practices can increase atmospheric emissions, particularly the greenhouse gases. The resulting global warming may cause a sea level rise which could be catastrophic for some countries. There is also danger that losses to biodiversity resulting from man's activities could: 'reduce the resilience of ecosystems to withstand climatic variations and air pollution damage. Atmospheric changes can affect

forests, biodiversity, freshwater and marine ecosystems, and economic activity such as agriculture'
(UN, 1992).

As Pearce (1989) points out, there is uncertainty
about the nature and effect of these changes to
climate. For example, there is uncertainty about
both the exact trace gas emissions which will enter
the atmosphere and precise fuel mix which will be
used in the future. There is also uncertainty about
the nature and extent of the ecological changes
which will be brought about by pollution; in particular, there is no certainty about the ways in which
the climate will respond either at a global level or
in a regional context. There is also uncertainty
about environmental thresholds, that is, points at
which an environmental catastrophe occurs or
where particular processes cannot be reversed.
Above all there is great uncertainty about the ways
in which man will respond to any changes to the
environment that may occur. Human response to a
real or perceived environmental threat may be part
of a natural adaptation process and include
responses at a personal, institutional or governmental level. The response may be as small-scale as the
installation of more thermal insulation in the home
to a process of mass migration from areas of
drought or flooding.

Where such uncertainty exists it is wise to
approach the problem with caution and plan for the
worst outcome. If this view is taken then it is difficult to argue with Pearce (1989) when he suggests
that: 'International cooperation to contain greenhouse effects to an "acceptable level" is vital and
urgent. The urgency arises because of the nature of
the risks if the worst outcome occurs; because the
longer the delay the more the world is "committed"
to increased warming and hence increased damage;
because future adjustment is likely to be expensive;
and because the only form of containment is
through international cooperation which will be
complex and difficult to secure. Global pollution
problems underline the need for anticipatory
policy.'

SUSTAINABLE DEVELOPMENT: DEFINITIONS

There seems to be widespread agreement that
solving the global problems means the adoption of
policies and programmes that lead to sustainable
development. Sustainable development, however,
has many different meanings (Pearce *et al.*, 1989).
There is a danger that the concept will become
meaningless or simply used as the latest panacea for
the environmental ills that befall the planet. The
pursuit of a sustainable future for mankind in an
environment of quality will require the design of
hard-edged and effective policies and programmes
which directly address the related problems of
unsustainability and environmental degradation. If
these policies and programmes are grouped beneath
the generic term 'sustainable development' then that
term must have a generally accepted meaning which
does not reduce it to an anodyne instrument for
political obfuscation.

A generally accepted definition of sustainable
development and a good point to begin an exploration of this concept is from the Brundtland
Report: 'Sustainable development is development
that meets the needs of the present generation
without compromising the ability of future generations to meet their own needs' (World Commission
on Environment and Development, 1987). This
definition contains three key ideas: development,
needs and future generations. According to
Blowers (1993) development should not be
confused with growth. Growth is a physical or
quantitative expansion of the economic system
while development is a qualitative concept: it is
concerned with improvement, progress, including
cultural, social and economic dimensions. The term
'needs' introduces the ideas of distribution of
resources: 'meeting the basic needs of all and
extending to all the opportunity to satisfy their
aspirations of a better life' (World Commission on
Environment and Development, 1987). These are
fine sentiments but in reality the world's poor are
unable to achieve their basic needs of life while

the more affluent effectively pursue their aspirations, many luxuries being defined by affluent groups as needs. There will naturally be environmental costs if the standards of the wealthy are maintained while at the same time meeting the needs of the poor. A choice may be inevitable: meeting needs is therefore a political, moral and ethical issue. It concerns the redistribution of resources both within and between nations. Sustainable development means a movement towards greater social equity both for moral and practical reasons. An environmental *cordon sanitaire* cannot be erected around the poor south: it is one earth we inhabit and its environmental problems have no borders. The third idea, 'future generations' introduces the concept of inter-generational equity: 'We have a moral duty to look after our planet and to hand it on in good order to future generations' (Department of the Environment, 1990). Stewardship was fostered by the United Nations Conference on the Human Environment in 1972. Stewardship implies that mankind's role on this planet is one of caring for the earth and steering a path which as far as possible benefits the human and natural systems of the world. Mankind is viewed as the custodian of the earth for future generations. This attitude is best summed up by a quotation attributed to the North American Indian: 'We have not inherited the earth from our parents, we have borrowed it from our children.' Following this line of argument the aim is not to maintain the status quo but for each generation to hand on a better environment particularly where it is degraded or socially deprived. It requires of any particular generation the wisdom: to avoid irreversible damage; to restrict the development of environmental assets; to protect important habitats, high quality landscapes, forests and non-renewable resources. In summary the definition from Brundtland implies both inter- and intra-generational equity within a framework of development which does not destroy the planet's environmental support system.

Elkin *et al.* in *Reviving the City* (1991a) appear to be in broad agreement with the ideas expressed in the last paragraph. They, however, note four principles of sustainable development: futurity, environment, equity and participation. The principle of futurity is seen as maintaining a minimum of environmental capital including the major environmental support systems of the planet together with the conservation of more conventional renewable resources such as forests. This is to meet the Brundtland requirement that human activity should be limited by consideration of the effect that activity may have on the ability of future generations to meet their needs and aspirations. The second principle is concerned with costing the environment. The true cost of all activities, whether they take place in the market or not, should be paid for by the particular development through regulation, and/or market-based incentives. While it is difficult to identify the minimum environmental stock necessary to fulfil this principle it is clear that: 'current rates of environmental degradation and resource depletion are likely to carry us beyond that level' (Elkin, 1991a). Sustainability constraints may be difficult to define with any precision. It is possible, however, to identify the direction of changes in consumption patterns which are necessary to avoid breaching environmental thresholds. By applying the precautionary principle, where doubt and uncertainty exist, it may be possible to outline the type of urban development and designs which are more sustainable or possibly less unsustainable.

Elkin (1991a) distinguishes two secondary principles of sustainable development which combine with and support the main principles: he stresses inter- and intra-generational equity, as indeed do many others writing on this subject. Elkin includes a further principle, that of participation. He notes: 'The problems of "economic development" without democratic participation have been made manifest time after time. Unless individuals are able to share both in decision-making and in the actual process of development, it is bound to fail.'

SUSTAINABLE DEVELOPMENT: OFFICIAL RESPONSES

Sustainable development was placed on the political agenda in 1987 with the publication of the Brundtland Report, *Our Common Future*. The pioneering work of Carson (1962), Schumacher (1974), Hardin (1977) and Meadows *et al.* (1972), had finally received global recognition. In Britain the Government commissioned a report by Pearce *et al.* (1989) called *Blueprint for a Green Economy*. Pearce suggested ways in which the constraints of sustainable development could be introduced into the economic system of the United Kingdom. Later the United Kingdom government published a White Paper called *This Common Inheritance* (Department of the Environment, 1990). While full of fine sentiment the White Paper paid little attention to the argument of the Pearce report. Consequently it gave no lead in this policy area, merely repeating existing policies on economic and urban developments. The environmental movement was given a European dimension when the European Commission published its *Green Paper on the Urban Environment* (Commission of the Economic Communities, 1990). The paper considered policies to deal with the underlying causes of environmental problems and called for research to explore ways in which urban management could serve the needs of sustainable development.

The early 1990s in Britain saw the publication of a number of official documents addressing environmental issues. *Development Plans: A Good Practice Guide* (Department of the Environment, 1992a) has a section on Environmental Issues which attempts to show how concerns about environmental issues can be reflected in the Development Plan. It discusses: 'achieving a balance between economic growth and technological development and environmental considerations.' It does not attempt to define the point of balance nor does it enter the thorny argument about development and growth. The

section on energy goes a little further, incorporating some of the ideas on energy-efficient urban form that appear in *Energy Conscious Planning* (Owens, 1991), a report prepared for the Council for the Protection of Rural England. 1992 saw the publication of *Planning Pollution and Waste Management*, which formed the basis of planning guidance (Department of the Environment, 1992b), while in 1993 *Reducing Transport Emissions Through Planning* was published: this was a document prepared jointly by the Department of the Environment and the Department of Transport (1993a). The document states that:

> In recognition of the problem of global warming the UK Government has signed the Climate Change Convention. This calls for measures to reduce CO_2 emissions to 1990 levels by 2000. If the transport sector is to contribute to this reduction there are three mechanisms through which this could be achieved:
>
> (1) through reductions in overall travel demand;
> (2) through encouraging the use of more emissions-efficient modes of travel; and
> (3) through changes in the emissions efficiency of transport.

Item (1) reinforces many of the points made by Owens (1991) emphasizing the relationship of land use, density and urban structure upon travel demand and advocating more energy-efficient urban form. Item (3) is a straightforward advocacy of improvements in transport technology – a suggestion without too much political pain. Item (2) is probably the area which has the greatest potential for the reduction of CO_2 emissions. This course of action, however, causes the most difficulty for a Conservative government with a prejudice in favour of the road lobby and a propensity to support a roads solution to transport problems. There are, however, changes in government rhetoric about transport which may indicate a move towards policies giving greater weight to public transport.

1993 also saw the publication of *A Framework for Local Sustainability*. This was a response by UK local government to the UK government's first strategy for sustainable development. The report was prepared by the Local Government Management Board setting a framework for considering Local Agenda 21 for the United Kingdom. It is an attempt, amongst other things, to follow the exhortation 'to think globally but act locally'. It also builds upon Agenda 21 signed by 178 Nations including the UK at the United Nations Conference on Environmental Development, Rio de Janeiro in 1992. The report prepared by the Local Government Management Board is closer in its approach to both Brundtland and Agenda 21 than the earlier documents originating from the UK government. For example, it discusses equity in these terms:

> The poor are the worst affected by environmental problems and least able to solve them. Poverty often forces people to unsustainable behaviour while the wealthy can afford to ignore or escape the environmental consequences of their actions. So inequitable distribution of wealth both causes unsustainable behaviour and makes it harder to change. Fairness to people now living must accompany sustainability's concern for fairness to future generations.

The report also discusses the green economy in terms close to those in the Pearce report (Pearce *et al.*, 1989): 'Economic growth is neither necessary for sustainability nor incompatible with it: there is no necessary connection between them, or, for that matter, between growth and quality of life' (Local Government Management Board, 1993). In addition, the report makes a strong case for the use of the planning system in the pursuit of sustainable development: 'The planning system is an important mechanism for making decisions about sustainable resource use. It operates at scales to match the issues, it is open and democratic, and it allows general principles of environmental management to

be adopted then applied.' While this report welcomes existing government advice it recommends a strengthening and extension of the planning system.

In 1994 four further official documents appeared: *Climate Change: The UK Programme, Biodiversity: The UK Action Plan, Sustainable Forestry: The UK Programme* and *Sustainable Development: The UK Strategy* (Department of the Environment, 1994a–d). *Climate Change* outlines the UK's programme of measures to implement the Framework Convention on Climate Change signed by the British Prime Minister at the Earth Summit in Rio in June 1992. The programme includes inventories of emissions and their possible future trends: it sets out measures aimed at returning emissions of the main greenhouse gases to 1990 levels by the year 2000. The report also outlines the commitment to enhance carbon sinks in soils and vegetation. The section on transport reveals the philosophy behind the government's strategy: 'As in other sectors a market based approach is being used, and a key element of the programme is providing the right price incentives' (Department of the Environment, 1994a). For example, transport fuel duties will be increased by at least 5 per cent per annum, on average above the rate of inflation, while road pricing and motorway charging will receive careful consideration. Whether market mechanisms alone will be enough to change energy patterns of consumption to those that do not damage the environment for future generations remains to be seen. The side-effects of such mechanisms may also be to undermine any pretence at pursuing equity, one of the philosophical supports of sustainable development.

An important recommendation of the Earth Summit in 1992 was that each country should prepare its own strategy and action plans showing how it intended to implement Agenda 21 and the agreements in 'Rio'. The UK government prepared separate documents on each of the four 'Rio' agreements in the fields of: climate change, biodiversity, sustainable forestry and Agenda 21. *Sustainable Development: The UK Strategy* (Department of the Environment, 1994d) is the UK's response to Agenda 21. Section 1 of the report considers and restates the general principles of sustainable development. The report goes on in Section 2 to identify key trends and possible pressure points over the following 20 years. In Section 3 the economy is reviewed with particular regard to the areas where new policy may be required to secure sustainable development and also those areas where securing environmental improvements may provide market opportunities or points of possible growth in the economy. Section 4 deals with implementation: 'Sustainable development does not mean having less economic development: on the contrary, a healthy economy is better able to generate the resources to meet people's needs, and new investment and environmental improvement often go hand in hand'. For those working in the field of sustainable development this report is one of the fundamental sources. There are specific chapters which deal with the development in Town and Country, Construction of the Built Environment, Transport and the Land Use Planning System which are of great relevance for urban design.

The report of the Royal Commission on Environmental Pollution (1994) is a seminal work in the field of sustainable development: it spells out in great detail the relationship between energy use, pollution and the built environment. It makes a number of practical recommendations pertinent to city development. The ideas about sustainable development have also begun to affect the drafting of Planning Policy Guidance issued by the Department of the Environment to Local Authorities. Of particular relevance are *PPG 13, Transport* (Department of the Environment, 1994e) and *PPG 6, Town Centres and Retail Developments* (Department of the Environment, 1993c), which is currently being redrafted strengthening policies to revitalize town centres.

POLITICS AND SUSTAINABLE DEVELOPMENT

The meaning of the term 'sustainable development' is largely determined by an individual's ideological viewpoint. As Dobson points out: 'The Conservative Party, like the other major political parties and along with the countless individuals, groups and organizations who are discovering the environment as a political issue towards the end of the twentieth century, now publicly considers itself as a steward, rather than master' (Dobson, 1990). This view of the environment and the difficulties the world community faces is shared by the United Nations, the Economic Union and most of the scientific community including many in the planning profession. The stewardship perspective is the one that, in the main, has been presented in this chapter. It represents the views of those who believe that environmental problems can be solved within the present political and economic system. It is not the only viewpoint. Dobson (1990) distinguishes two diametrically opposed views on sustainability and the environment. The establishment viewpoint he labels 'green' with a lower case 'g' while those who believe sustainability depends upon the system being fundamentally changed he describes as 'Green' with a capital 'G'.

The ideology of all those shades along the spectrum of greenness is determined by their attitude to the environment. The 'Green' ideology or 'ecologism' takes *The Limits to Growth* (Meadows, 1972) as an axiom: 'Greens will admit that the report's estimates as to the likely life expectancy of various resources are over-pessimistic and they will agree that the Club of Rome's world computer models were crude, but they will subscribe to the report's conclusion that the days of uncontrolled growth . . . are numbered' (Dobson, 1991). Green ideology also questions the current dominant paradigm with its foundation in the Enlightenment, science, technology and the objectivity of rational analysis (Capra, 1985). The Greens' world view removes man from centre stage:

> Green politics explicitly seeks to decentre the human being, to question mechanistic science and its technological consequences, to refuse to believe that the world was made for human beings - and it does this because it has been led to wonder whether dominant post-industrialism's project of material affluence is either desirable or sustainable. (Dobson, 1990)

Ecologism goes beyond human-instrumental or paternalistic care for the natural world and argues that the environment has an independent value that should guarantee its existence. Green ideology puts forward the idea that a new paradigm is necessary for solving the problems now faced by mankind. Such a paradigm should be based upon holism, a systems view of the world and interconnectedness rather than the present mechanistic and reductionist view of nature.

If politics, as is often asserted, is the art of the possible, then the approach to sustainable development will vary from place to place and from time to time in any given place. Sustainable development policies must be politically acceptable, which in a democracy means welcomed by the electorate. In Britain neither main political party is advocating radical redistribution of wealth while both parties are committed to economic growth. Clearly a pragmatic environmentalist in this political situation would be advocating policies which by 'Green' definitions, would be 'more or less unsustainable'. While from time to time, in this book, ideals of sustainability may be advocated or 'Green' experiments reported, in the main it will be informed by political realism rather than Utopian idealism.

SUSTAINABLE DEVELOPMENT AND ECONOMICS

Pearce and his colleagues attempt to integrate ideas of sustainable development within the current establishment viewpoint and the general political consensus in this country for policies aimed at economic growth:

> The call for lifestyle changes usually confuses two things: the growth of an economy, and the growth of the resources used to sustain that economic growth. It is possible to have economic growth (more Gross National Product - GNP) *and* to use up fewer resources. There are very good reasons as to why we should prefer this solution to the problem to one in which 'lifestyle change' means reducing GNP per capita. The first is that GNP and human well-beings are inextricably linked for the vast majority of the world's population. Failure to keep GNP high shows up in the misery of unemployment and in poverty. Anti-growth advocates are embarrassingly silent or unrealistic on how they would solve problems of unemployment and poverty. (Pearce, 1989)

Traditional forestry and fishing industries have long practice in the art of maintaining sustainable yields from the environment by harvesting at a rate which is equal to or less than the regenerative capacity of the crop. Failure of the industry to conserve its capital stock would result in the disappearance of the resource and with it the industry. This analogy is appropriate in some ways for the present discussion: it emphasizes a concern for the future and the value of good husbandry, or living within the capacity of the supporting environment. National economies, however, do not rely entirely upon renewable resources, nor does the analogy apply comfortably to economies which aim to grow or increase output. Non-renewable resources such as oil or natural gas when used for human well-being must, if sustainable development is a goal, be capable of being replaced by other renewable resources. For example, the use of fossil fuels should be accompanied by the development of alternative sources of renewable energy such as wind, water and solar power. Interesting experiments, not always welcomed by the local population, are being implemented throughout Europe.

1.1

1.2

Figure 1.1 Wind farm, Bellacorick, County Mayo, Ireland. The wind farm is sited on 'cut-away-bog'
Figure 1.2 Power Station, Bellacorick, County Mayo, Ireland. The power station is fed by local peat bogs

For example, in Bellacorick, Mayo, Ireland, an experimental wind farm has been established on cut-away bog land: it is far less damaging to the landscape than its near neighbour, a more traditional generator (Figures 1.1 and 1.2). Examples of this type illustrate Pearce's line of reasoning which leads him to develop a further definition of sustainability: 'So, sustainability means making sure that substitute resources are made available as non-renewable resources become physically scarce, and it means ensuring that the environmental impacts of using those resources are kept within the Earth's carrying capacity to assimilate those impacts' (Pearce *et al.*, 1993).

Clearly sustainable development without the political pain which would accompany a redistribution of existing or reduced resources requires some level of growth. Two associated problems are the methods of measuring that growth in order to present an accurate view of well-being and a true reflection of environmental depreciation. There seem to be two main adjustments required to the tools for economic management. The first is the method by which economic growth or well-being is measured. The second concerns how we measure the use and abuse of environmental resources, that is, the value attributed to the environment. 'Economic growth' in the past has been measured using some misleading indicators. GNP is constructed in such a manner that it does not fully express the standard of living of the population: for example, if pollution damages health and the cost of health care rises it results in an increase in GNP. A rise in GNP of this nature would seem to indicate an improvement in the standard of living and not a decrease in the quality of life. In national accounting the depreciation of man-made capital is costed but the degradation of the environment or the depreciation of 'environmental capital' is not recorded. Using up natural resources is equivalent to the capital depreciation of machines and infrastructure and as such should count as a cost to the nation. Just how environmental costs are quantified and how GNP is amended to take into consideration such costs or how it is to be adjusted to reflect more closely the development of human well-being is debatable:

> Better decisions about sustainability could be taken within government and in industry if the full economic costs of environmental considerations were taken into account. Research into environmental accounting is being promoted in many countries. There are major difficulties, however, including fundamental questions of methodology. The best hope in the short term lies in making better measurements of the quantities of environmental pollution or the use of resources, whether or not costs can be added. Nonetheless the Government will take forward work on constructing environmental accounts for the UK (Department of the Environment, 1994d).

The debate depicted as 'growth versus environment' is still very much a live issue in the context of sustainable development. In some cases growth may involve a loss of environmental quality or a decrease in non-renewable resources. In other situations conservation of the environment may mean the loss of the possibility of economic growth but: 'sustainable development attempts to shift the focus to the opportunities for income and employment opportunities from conservation, and to ensuring that any trade-off decision reflects the full value of the environment' (Pearce *et al.*, 1989).

1.3

Figure 1.3 Cushendun, Northern Ireland. Conservation area
Figures 1.4 and **1.5** Cushendun, Northern Ireland. Group of buildings designed by Clough Williams-Ellis

URBAN DESIGN AND SUSTAINABLE DEVELOPMENT

The objectives for a framework of urban design in a regime of sustainable development would emphasize conservation of both the natural and built environments. There is a need to use already developed areas in the most efficient way while making them more attractive places to live and work. Principles of sustainable urban design would place priority on the adaption and reuse of existing buildings, infrastructure and roads together with the reuse of recycled materials and components. There would be a presumption in favour of conservation: the onus of proof of the need for development would be placed squarely upon the developer. The concept of the conservation area, so successful in the past in towns such as Cushendun and Cushendall in Northern Ireland or in Wirksworth, Derbyshire, may need to be strengthened and its use extended to less noteworthy traditional areas of cities and towns. (Figures 1.3 to 1.10). Secondly, sustainable development places a premium on the conservation of natural resources, wildlife and landscape. Any new materials for building purposes should be obtained from sustainable sources such as timber from well managed sustainable forests. Thirdly, where new development is necessary the patterns and constructions should minimize the use of energy consumed

1.4

1.5

in travel between dispersed activities and also in the operation of the buildings.

Future developments have to provide for the nation's need for food products, mineral extraction, new homes and other buildings. It is important,

Figure 1.6 Cushendun, Northern Ireland. Group of buildings designed by Clough Williams-Ellis
Figure 1.7 Cushendall, a model for Clough Williams Ellis
Figures 1.8 and **1.9** Wirksworth, Derbyshire. Conservation area

1.6

1.9

1.8

however, that such developments respect environmental objectives and meet the criteria laid down by the principles of sustainable developments. Any new buildings should be flexibly planned so that they can be adapted for different uses over their lifespan. The transport system serving the new urban structures will have to: '. . . strike the right balance between the ability of transport to serve economic development and the ability to protect the environment and sustain future quality of life' (Department of the Environment, 1994d).

The prospect of restructuring the built environment in a way that serves the needs of sustainable development is a unique challenge to the urban design profession. It also offers the prospect of economic growth in the development industry while

1.10

Figure 1.10 Wirksworth, Derbyshire. Conservation area

at the same time enhancing the quality of life and making cities more sustainable.

ENERGY AND THE BUILT ENVIRONMENT

2

INTRODUCTION

The theme of this chapter is the design of energy-efficient buildings: it is concerned with the development of a building process which minimizes pollution. A discussion of conservation and the traditions of a 'timeless way of building' is followed by an analysis of adaptable building shapes and the development of a robust and flexible built environment adapted to its regional context.

It is generally accepted that global warming is happening and that the depletion of the ozone layer is proceeding at a rapid rate. The greenhouse effect and the hole in the ozone layer are two of the most threatening effects of pollution for mankind. Much of this atmospheric pollution is caused by the burning of fossil fuels in the creation of energy to support city life. While startlingly apparent, these are not the only environmental hazards directly stemming from current lifestyles on the planet. Other hazards include: contamination of water sources, overloading of environmental sinks such as the great river estuaries, acid rain and air pollution in cities. Much of the pollution causing environmental damage can be attributed directly to the building process. Approximately half of the

CFCs (chlorofluorocarbons) produced throughout the world are used in buildings, as part of the air conditioning, refrigeration and fire extinguishing systems, while some insulation materials are dependent upon CFCs for their manufacture. Fifty per cent of the world's fossil fuel consumption is directly related to the servicing and use of buildings. In addition energy is used to make building materials, to transport them to the site, and in their erection as part of the building. The servicing and use of buildings, alone, results in the production of fifty per cent of the world's output of carbon dioxide, amounting to about one-quarter of the greenhouse gases. The designers, developers and users of buildings, however, through careful choice of environmentally friendly material, the use of an intelligent design approach, sensible care and use of the building, which together with sensitive planning control, could reduce considerably the quantity of pollutants entering the environment.

Energy in the building industry is consumed in two main ways: energy capital and energy revenue (Vale and Vale, 1993). Energy capital is the energy used to construct both buildings and urban infrastructure while energy revenue is the energy consumed throughout the lifetime of the building.

a

b

c

Figure 2.1 Pollution caused by the car. (a) Quarry to provide the materials for road construction; (b) estaleiro: storage of materials for road building and infrastructure development, once the site of an extensive vineyard; (c) dump for used cars

Building operations affect the environment in another important manner. The extraction and processing of raw building materials has an immediate and clearly visible effect on the landscape. The quarries necessary for the production of aggregate for concrete and clay for brick-making have a particularly devastating effect on the environment. They can remain eyesores for decades, often in the most impressive landscapes. The routes to and from such quarries expand the devastation into surrounding areas. In considering the design and construction of a building for a sustainable world these three factors have to be balanced in order to come to a considered view of the impact of the construction on the natural environment (Figure 2.1).

A TIMELESS WAY OF BUILDING

We do not have to search far for ideas for sustainable building: they are all-pervasive in our lost constructional traditions. The solutions to present environmental problems, however, are probably not to be found in the traditions of 'great architecture'; it is more likely that they will be associated with the 'prose of architecture' as Summerson called the everyday buildings that have always formed the greater part of towns and cities. Monumental architecture of the past with its profligate use of resources does not provide a model for a Green Architecture for today and tomorrow (Vale and Vale, 1991). It is the vernacular or 'A Timeless Way of Building' to which the urbanist must turn for inspiration and guidance (Alexander, 1979). Monumental buildings, however, have always been part of the urban scene. The Hellenic Temple, great Medieval Cathedral or Renaissance Palace have dominated city, town and even village but the vast majority of the built environment comprises the lesser structures of the ordinary citizen. Good urban design, that is the organization of public space, results not necessarily from the juxtaposition of great works of architecture but often from the pleasant arrangement of the homes of the not so powerful, together with the structures that house commercial, educational and other institutions which make the city function. Societies in the past have attempted to symbolize solidarity, power and position by adorning their cities with great works of architecture. Such buildings were the result of the surplus wealth created by society from economic activity, agriculture or conquest and exploitation. In the frugal world of sustainability it may seem an anachronism to suggest that a 'Green Society' may find some way to symbolize with architecture its philosophy and *raison d'être*. Unless mankind is reduced to some form of troglodyte existence then a time, place and resources will be found for higher forms of art,

Figure 2.3 (a) The Guildhall of the Holy Trinity, King's Lynn; (b) Steep Hill, Lincoln

Figure 2.4 (a) Derbyshire; (b) Kettlewell, Yorkshire

Figure 2.2 Vernacular architecture. (a) Cottage in Chipping Campden; (b) Chipping Campden

2.3a

2.3b

2.2a

2.4a

2.4b

2.2b

music and architecture. This book, however, does not aim to discuss the place or form of monumental architecture in the Green City of the future: it is only noted that it is likely to persist. The intention of this chapter is to suggest the lessons that can be learnt from native building traditions (Figures 2.2 to 2.5). Such building traditions in the past have produced many delightful urban environments: this therefore is not a treatise in pursuit only of a functional philosophy, important though that may be. It follows the Renaissance prescription for good architecture and indeed its sister art of urban design, as consisting of 'commodotie, firmness and delight' (Wotton, 1969).

2.5a

Figure 2.5 (a) Hawkshead, Cumbria; (b) Speke Hall, Liverpool

2.5b

CONSERVATION

In pre-industrial society, with the exception of the monumental building of political, civic or religious importance, construction work was carried out very much as a case of necessity. A new structure, the replacement of an existing structure or its extension was a development not undertaken lightly. This seems to contrast markedly with conditions prevailing today or in the recent past. Built-in obsolescence appears to be a feature of the current ethos of a society which changes its buildings and their styles with as much ease as it changes its clothes for the latest fashion. To a degree, construction work still requires a perceived need and an economic justification before it will be undertaken. Nevertheless in the consumer society the growth in the economy, to some extent, is based upon the individual's desire and ability to acquire the most fashionable artifacts, whether it is the latest model in cars or higher space standards and equipment in the home. 'Keeping up with the Joneses' ensures a rapid replacement of comparatively new equipment, last year's model being confined to the dustbin of recent history, often when it still has many years of useful life. This attitude permeates the construction and development industry where buildings are designed to meet immediate needs and are located on the most convenient and easily developed greenfield site which has easy access for the motor car. The economic appraisal of such disposable buildings presently does not include a full environmental evaluation of the project in terms of energy needs and energy use over the buildings' life or the damage a particular development will inflict upon the global ecosystem: the future is 'discounted' both in accounting and environmental terms.

A principle of Green Urban Design is: do not build unless it is absolutely necessary - examine other ways of meeting needs. It follows that the first rule for any development control officer should be to make a presumption of planning refusal for any 'new build', particularly on a greenfield site. The onus for proving the desirability of new development in a sustainable city is on the developer. Conservation in these circumstances is the natural outcome of a development philosophy which has sustainability as its ultimate goal. Conservation includes extending, adapting and finding new uses for existing buildings: demolition would occur only after detailed environmental appraisal (Figures 2.6 and 2.7). The reason for giving priority to conservation as opposed to demolition and replacement is the pursuit of policies for the efficient and frugal use of resources, particularly energy from non-renewable sources.

The answers to the questions: 'to build or not to build?' and 'to conserve, or demolish and reconstruct?' are not as straightforward as they would appear from the last paragraph. Existing structures embody quantities of energy capital: their demolition usually means the loss of that capital, unless some of the material can be reused, usually in a low grade capacity as hardcore or land fill. An existing building, however, may require energy capital inputs in terms of maintenance, new equipment and insulation, or it may consume costly energy revenue to keep an outworn structure operating. Any new structure replacing an old building requires energy capital for demolition and energy capital for its

building. A resulting super-insulated new building served by passive or solar heating may, however, use little or no energy revenue from non-renewable sources. A requirement of Green Urban Design is an energy impact statement covering the lifespan of any proposed development. From the analysis of such a statement it is then possible to judge more clearly the development most in tune with the public good rather than private gain. An energy impact statement should therefore be a standard technique of urban design method.

Numerous examples of the reuse, refurbishment and extension of structures can be cited from the past. In the pre-industrial city a building, however renowned, was remodelled for its new purpose without the sentiment we now attach to this process. An examination of many English parish churches, for example, reveals a mixture of many styles developed over many centuries. Old walls, details and materials were reused while extensions, in the then latest style, were woven into the existing fabric without regard to the destruction of the architectural integrity of the original building. The result is often a fine building much admired by succeeding generations. The most common feature of the medieval city, the dwelling, was recycled in a number of ways. Parts of a timber structure from an

2.6

Figure 2.6 The Lace Hall, Church conversion, Nottingham
Figure 2.7 Church conversion to shops, Stamford
Figure 2.8 Eighteenth century façade, Stamford

2.7a

2.7b

2.8

2.9

Figure 2.9 Façade
conservation, Amsterdam
Figure 2.10 Façade
conservation, Nottingham
Figure 2.11 Façade
conservation, Nottingham

2.10a

2.11a

2.11b

earlier building were commonly used again when a replacement was necessary, while in towns like Stamford whole medieval structures lie buried beneath a later façade dating from the eighteenth century (Figure 2.8). Even in that most classical of structures, the Parthenon, parts meant for an older temple were reused in the building that presently occupies the site on the Acropolis in Athens (Carpenter, 1970). The lessons that such examples teach is a respect not for aesthetic form, although the results are often great works of architecture, but a common-sense approach to the idea of the stewardship of property and the good husbanding of scarce resources: in the case of buildings, the scarce resource is the hard-won material from which the structure is made. How different this attitude is from that which underpins some of today's conservation projects. Often a façade of questionable aesthetic value is shored up at great expense in terms of time, money and energy inputs (Figures 2.19 to 2.11). Behind the protected shell the inner building is gutted and remodelled for its new purpose. Such is the sentimental approach to conservation and not one advocated here. If energy conservation suggests the external remodelling of a façade, which is often the case for the purpose of effective insulation, then in a sustainable society that factor would take priority over aesthetic considerations in any decision about the building's future. This process is in the same tradition, though for different reasons, as the remodelling of the houses in Stamford. Where can one find a better model for conservation?

BUILDING MATERIALS

All building materials originate in the earth. Some materials such as clay and mud require only man's effort to make a structure from them. Most people on this planet live in buildings made from earth (Moughtin, 1985). Earth building can reach great heights of structural achievement such as the

2.12

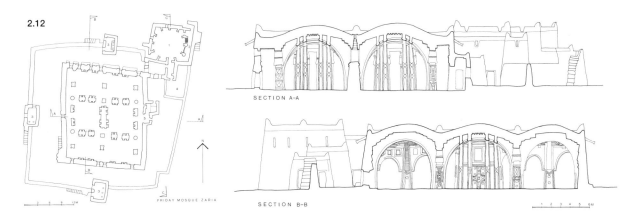

SECTION A-A

SECTION B-B

FRIDAY MOSQUE ZARIA

engineering feats of the Hausa people of Nigeria (Figures 2.12 to 2.14). Earth can be used in a variety of ways which encompasses a wide range of architectural styles and aesthetic appeal (Williams-Ellis *et al.*, 1947; Guidoni, 1975; Dethier, 1981). It is also true that earth has been used as a building material for low grade development to house the poor in the slums of the burgeoning cities of the developing world. Building from earth does the least damage to the environment: it is close to the building site so does not involve transport energy costs and when no longer required the building decomposes naturally and without pollution, returning to the earth from whence it came. Amongst the Hausa

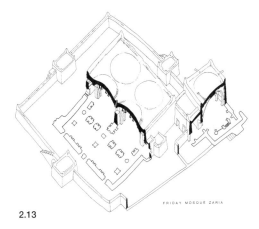

FRIDAY MOSQUE ZARIA

2.13

Figure 2.12 The Friday Mosque, Zaria: plan and sections
Figure 2.13 The Friday Mosque, Zaria: axonometric
Figure 2.14 The Friday Mosque, Zaria: interior

2.14

Figure 2.15 Kristiansand, Norway: timber building

Figure 2.16 Kristiansand, Norway: timber building

people it is customary for the occupier of a hut to be buried beneath it when he or she dies. The hut eventually collapses, forming the burial mound. This is possibly the ultimate form of sustainable building.

Timber is another building material that has served man well in the past and has been associated with great architecture and wonderful decorative effects. It is also a material eminently suited to recycling when the building, of which it forms a part, is defunct. Timber can be 'farmed', that is, it can be planted, grown, harvested and replaced. Once its useful life is complete, like clay and earth, it returns to the land without pollution. When used in medieval Britain, however, timber was a local, home-grown product. Now timber for construction

is imported into Britain at great cost in terms of the expenditure of energy for transportation. It will take some time to develop in Britain the native forests from which a sustainable harvest of timber can be obtained for the construction industry. Nevertheless if Britain is to boast the goal of a sustainable society this must be one of the country's long-term objectives. The prize for the development of a native timber industry would be the possibility of a modern equivalent of the half-timbered work in Tudor England or the delightful timber architecture of Scandinavia (Figures 2.15 and 2.16).

Most building materials are not as environmentally friendly as earth when unbaked, or timber taken from a local, sustainable source. Buildings damage the environment in a number of ways. Non-renewable energy is used and pollution results from the extraction, refining and fabrication of building materials, together with their transportation to the site, and in the construction process itself. Deciding which combination of building materials causes the least environmental damage is complex and a question of balance between competing requirements. All additions are *per se* damaging to the natural environment. The use of *in situ* earth and local timber from a sustainable source is least damaging and the most 'natural'. All other combinations of materials have a more deleterious effect. Those working in the field of Green Urban Design should attempt to reduce and mitigate the worst effects of development. In this sense Green Urban Design is the pursuit of more sustainable form.

In choosing a building material the first consideration is the amount of energy used in its manufacture. 'As a rough guide, however, the energy intensiveness of a building material will act as a guide to its greenness' (Vale and Vale, 1991). Building materials can be classified into three groups according to energy content: low, medium and high energy materials (see Table 2.1). The energy content of materials shown in that table is measured in kilowatt hours per kilogram. In construction work low energy materials such as

Table 2.1
Energy content of materials (Vale and Vale, 1991)

material	energy content: kWh/kg
Low energy materials	
sand, gravel	0.01
wood	0.1
concrete	0.2
sand-lime brickwork	0.4
lightweight concrete	0.5
Medium energy materials	
plasterboard	1.0
brickwork	1.2
lime	1.5
cement	2.2
mineral fibre insulation	3.9
glass	6.0
porcelain (sanitary ware)	6.1
High energy materials	
plastics	10
steel	10
lead	14
zinc	15
copper	16
aluminium	56

sand and gravel are used in bulk while high energy materials such as steel or plastic are used in small quantities, often precisely and economically dimensioned. It is therefore difficult to determine the energy content in the proposed structure without knowing the weights of each material used. Table 2.2 shows figures of estimated energy content for three building types. This analysis, if accurate, would seem to indicate that the small scale and

Table 2.2
Energy intensity of three building types (Szokolay, 1980; quoted in Vale and Vale, 1991)

	kWh/m²
domestic buildings	1000
office buildings	5000
industrial buildings	10000

largely traditional style of building is by far the least energy-intensive structure. This suggests a return to the traditional and more domestic scale of built form associated with the pre-industrial city, which comprised buildings with a general maximum height of about four storeys. Taller buildings in the pre-industrial city were unusual and confined to public buildings or those of a religious, political or military purpose.

The energy content of a building material is connected with the nature of the process of refinement, for example the energy content of earth, mud or clay is zero while in its burnt form as bricks the figure is 0.4 kWh/kg. The closer the material is to its natural form the lower will be its energy content. Generally speaking the low energy materials tend to be the least polluting since less energy has been involved in their manufacture. It could be argued that, if all other circumstances are the same, then low energy materials should be used rather than those of high energy content. This oversimplification requires the application of a strong proviso. Some forms of insulation are high in energy content but being light result in a lower energy density. More importantly these insulating materials when used in the correct manner reduce the energy demand during the lifetime of the building. In this case the savings in energy revenue are greater than the extra energy capital expended, since energy used in construction is a 'one-off' expenditure. It would appear that high levels of insulation in all new developments should not only be encouraged but specified in the building regulations and applied rigorously to all new buildings. The standards we should be aiming at in Europe are those of countries like Denmark and Sweden from whose experience of dealing with the long hard winter we have much to learn. In addition double or triple glazing should be the norm, while the traditional porch or large comfortable entrance hall should be standard features of all homes.

Another important consideration in the choice of green building materials is the energy involved in their transportation to the place of manufacture and from there to the building site. Timber, for example, a potentially green building product, has to be imported into this country, resulting in environmental costs owing to the energy used for transportation. It may be useful to turn once again to the traditions of pre-industrial city building for guidance: not it must be said in nostalgia for a return to a mythical golden age, but to assist in the search for sustainable form. This country has a rich and fine-grained history of vernacular or regional architecture. The regional architecture of Britain is deeply embedded in the landscape and its underlying geology (Clifton-Taylor, 1972). The architectural landscape ranges from the timber and plaster façades of Chester, the red brick of Kent, the honey-coloured stone in the Cotswolds to the dour stone of Yorkshire (HRH, The Prince of Wales, 1989). It is not, however, the intention here to extol the aesthetic and appealing virtues of this intricate web of vernacular architecture, which can also be found in other European countries, but to understand why it developed in that way and to see if any of those conditions prevail in a world seeking a more sustainable future (see Figures 2.2 to 2.5).

Until the nineteenth century and the later stages of the industrial revolution, settlements were constructed largely from the building materials close to the site. Bath, for example, was constructed in the eighteenth century from Bathstone found in the quarries of Ralph Allen, one of the developers in that city. The city of York including its great Minster is built of local Yorkstone; while Edinburgh, like the rock that supports its castle, rises in grey granite from a Pre-Cambrian foundation. The reason for this use of local building material is not far to seek. At a time when travel was difficult and transportation costs high in relation to other costs it would seem reasonable to build with those materials close at hand. Within the limitations of local materials the latest style in architecture was freely and imagina-

tively interpreted. Special or non-local materials were sometimes used but, being scarce and therefore precious, they were kept for ornamental work (Moughtin *et al.*, 1995). Even in the nineteenth century the use of foreign, non-local materials was unusual. While brick became the common structural material used throughout this country, nevertheless local brickworks supplied local markets. Nottingham with its tradition of bright red, almost vermilion, hard pressed brick, or the ubiquitous use of the softer brown brick in London, are evidence of a regional variation and use of this common material. Clearly a green approach to the choice of building material for urban projects would be conditioned by a strong preference for those materials originating in the local region. This process of sustainable urban development dependent, in the first instance, on the use of local materials, would have to be tempered by other considerations such as the availability of suitable local materials and the balance of capital energy inputs from transportation as opposed to the energy content from manufacture. In a fully developed sustainable society, which may be a little way in the future, regional markets in building materials may result in a pattern of building resembling more closely the traditional patterns of regional vernacular architecture (Amourgis, 1991).

Materials such as stone, and to some extent brick, require energy in terms of labour to form, dress and to erect them. The energy expended on these procedures is entirely renewable and furthermore extends work and therefore remuneration to additional numbers in society. In so doing it fulfils one important aim of sustainable society which is to pursue more equitable policies:

A fundamental Green principle is that labour is a renewable source of energy. It follows that its substitution, especially in the form of craftsmanship, for high-energy expenditure on materials and manufacturing processes, is environmentally desirable. Another principle is that energy should be expended as closely as possible to its need. The original village or noble estate supplied its own blacksmith, farrier, dressmaker, hairdresser, carpenter and joiner, shoemaker, leech, herbalist, builder and so on, and a great deal of its own food. (Fox and Murrell, 1989)

While a return to the feudal system is not being advocated here the model for a sustainable building industry may be closer in organization and structure to the alternative or black building economies currently responsible for expansion of third world cities rather than the engineering industry which has been busy extending Britain's motorway system. Clearly the building industry of the future will not be engaged in the mass construction of pre-fabricated buildings, which as a structural system was a logical outcome to the thinking of the pioneers of the Modern Movement in architecture:

Mass-produced elements God forbid that there should be any question in the architect's mind of mass-produced houses; .... Module of height under ceiling, for example, that shall fix the lengths of all elements of the fabric: columns, beams, partition surfaces, the glass screen and a certain number of standards for doors, windows and so forth ... All these building elements come within the orbit of mass-production. They will even acquire, out of their factory origins, unsuspected qualities: exactness, safety, adaptability, even beauty. (Le Corbusier and de Pierrefeu, 1948)

Probably the most visible effects of the building industry on the environment are the spoil heaps and degraded landscapes which are the result of quarrying. The great slate quarry of Blaenau Ffestiniog in North Wales, the stone quarries of Derbyshire or the scars left after the extraction of building clay result from the needs of the rapacious building industry (see Figure 2.1). A major part of the building industry is the infrastructure necessary to construct, repair and remodel the country's road system. The questioning by the British government in 1994 of the need for additional roads is a welcome though belated acceptance that additional roads, far from

increasing access and reducing congestion, simply move the points of congestion and stimulate greater demand for car travel. This understanding of the relationship between the generation of traffic demand and road building programmes was being expressed as long ago as the 1960s (Jacobs, 1965). In addition to the destruction of the city and the damage to global atmosphere caused by excessive car use, the building of roads results in a voracious appetite for additional building materials. The need for road building materials in increasing quantities eats into hillsides leaving behind ever larger quarry faces in swathes across once fine landscapes. From this viewpoint alone a moratorium should be placed on all new road building programmes with the possible exception of small-scale local improvement schemes to facilitate traffic calming in town or city centres.

Because of the need to minimize carbon dioxide emissions it would be most appropriate to invest in new buildings with a long life and low energy use. Interesting examples of low energy use buildings

Figure 2.17 Queen's Building, School of Engineering and Manufacture, De Montfort University, Leicester

2.18

2.19

2.20

2.21

include Queens Building, School of Engineering and Manufacture, De Montfort University, Leicester and the NMB Bank Headquarters in Amsterdam (Figures 2.17 to 2.21). In parallel with this strategy existing building stock should be upgraded where possible in terms of the standard of thermal insulation. The implementation of both strategies would probably involve a 'one-off' investment in materials with a high embodied energy cost. This, however, would be mitigated by long-term savings in energy revenue, that is, in the savings of energy used during the building's life span. Since trees take up carbon dioxide from the atmosphere, then to some extent the capital energy content of the building could be defrayed by the planting of trees. By balancing the planting of trees, in sufficient numbers, with the

emission of carbon dioxide during the manufacture of materials for development, it would be possible in theory to develop a sustainable building industry. For example: 'A typical three-bedroom house has materials with a capital energy content equivalent to the generation of 20 tonnes of carbon dioxide and would need about 20 trees to offset this over a 40-year period' (Vale and Vale, 1993). A major contribution in the effort to move towards a more sustainable culture would be a strategy to: link the planning of new development with tree planting which would act as an environmental tax; to specify in the building regulations more stringent standards of insulation based on the Swedish or Danish experience; and to move towards a labour-intensive building industry dependent on regional materials.

BUILDING DESIGN

A number of factors, other than the materials from which it is made, determine the degree to which a building is green. The shade of the green label which can be assigned to a building reflects its sustainability over a long lifespan with low energy inputs and is dependent upon: the location of the building in relation to the means of access; the geometry of the building envelope; the relation of the building to its site; and the ways in which the users and builders relate to the building.

Access to buildings will be dealt with more thoroughly in Chapter 3 which examines transportation in the city. It is sufficient to point out here that the green building set in a park on the periphery of a city served only by roads used entirely by the private motor car is a contradiction in terms. Any energy savings made by the greening of the building would be lost over the building's lifetime through the expenditure of energy in maintaining the essential links with the users. The first requirement of the green building, however pale the shade of green, is its location – which should be in close proximity to the public transport system or sited within walking and cycling distance of important connected activities. Any other location is precluded by the need to reduce to a minimum transport energy costs, a factor which should be a prime consideration in the design process and in the development control exercise.

A building which can be used for many different purposes and which is easily adapted to serve many different activities during its lifetime has a robustness which eliminates or reduces the need for demolition and rebuilding to serve changing needs (Bentley *et al.*, 1985). Buildings are usually designed to meet the requirements of one particular owner or organization. This results in highly specialized buildings created by a designer for his or her clients. During this process some thought may be given to the current users but very little to the general public and none at all to future generations. A building designed in this way to accommodate special-ized activities is difficult to adapt to changing needs. Traditional robustness in design is exhibited by the Georgian or Regency terrace designed originally for middle or upper middle class families. In a number of cities fine eighteenth century terraces have been adapted for use as offices or multi-family occupation: in Abercrombie Square, Liverpool, for example, the terrace blocks on three sides have been converted for use by the university (Figure 2.22). The green approach to urban design supports and fosters architectural solutions which exhibit the robustness typical of the Georgian terrace, that is, building designs which because of their geometry and internal structural organization are capable of varied uses.

Flexibility in built form should be achieved without resort to the use of energy from non-renewable sources: preferably the building should be super-insulated, relying on passive solar heating, natural lighting and ventilation. Air-conditioning should, even in tropical climates, be reserved for specialist or essential use, in, for example, hospitals.

Figure 2.22 Abercrombie Square, Liverpool

The discipline of sustainability and flexibility poses complex problems and presents great challenges to the designer. Once again a return to an examination of some of the traditional forms developed in the past, both in the temperate climatic zones and in the tropical regions of the world, hold out the prospect of developing an innovative but essentially simply urban architecture.

The first limitation imposed by the strict regime of sustainability is a maximum building height normally of four storeys. At this height most activities, including residential, can be accommodated without resort to the use of a lift by the able-bodied. In some countries with a tropical climate, and even in some Mediterranean regions, four storeys may be too high for user comfort and a lower limit to building may be more appropriate. It may, however, be necessary to organize the structure so that those with special needs are catered for on the ground or first floors. The width of a building in temperate climates should be determined by the conditions necessary to achieve good natural lighting in all main rooms. Since the best-lit areas in the building are within four metres of the external walls the optimum width of the building is between nine and thirteen metres wide (Bentley *et al.*, 1985). A nine-metre wide building permits the planning of two well-lit rooms on either side of a corridor while a building greater than thirteen metres wide with deep floors has an excessive amount of badly lit space at its centre. A plan shape with nine to thirteen metre wide floors is capable of a number of different arrangements and so can accommodate different user requirements. A number of authors have suggested that the sustainable city should consist of mixed land uses (Vale and Vale, 1991; Owens, 1991). It has been suggested that the mix of activities should occur within the building envelope so that the city retains a vitality resulting from activity in its streets at all times of the day. Buildings designed for a combination of, for example, flats and offices is more likely to be successful if the width of the block is eight-ten metres: buildings

greater than this width are unsuitable for double aspect residential accommodation which is the most flexible housing type in the British climate, where it is important for sunlight to reach all the main rooms. With the double aspect home, most orientations are acceptable. The standard building block in the sustainable northern European city is one, therefore, which is nine to thirteen metres wide with a maximum height of four storeys high: it will have a traditional roof to protect it from the snow and rain while at the same time providing an opportunity to insulate the building adequately.

In the harsh conditions of the humid tropics conditions are such that good natural ventilation is important. These conditions impose certain requirements on the plan form of a building and its cross-section: buildings should ideally be one room wide with an access veranda along one elevation and openings in both long façades to ensure cross-ventilation, essential if air-conditioning is to be avoided. In contrast, the traditional building form in arid tropical regions is often deep with internal spaces lit and ventilated from secondary sources (Moughtin, 1985; Koenigsberger *et al.*, 1973).

A key element in the design of green or robust buildings which are capable of modification for different activities is the staircase and associated facilities. The staircase, landings and service ducts are usually grouped to serve a number of units on different floors. When a building changes use and is remodelled internally these shared facilities, since they serve the same function, remain unchanged. Because this element is the most expensive to change during any modification or refurbishment they have been referred to as the 'hard zone': 'Usually these spaces are hard', and '... must be positioned where they will not restrict the use of the remaining space' (Bentley *et al.*, 1985). According to Bentley *et al.* the optimum position for such hard zones is at intervals of ten to twenty metres apart. In this way a variety of spaces can be arranged including small single or double aspect office units and also larger floor areas of open office space. This particular spacing of staircase unit or 'hard zone' also permits the use of the building for residential purposes, for example in buildings which have hard zones ten metres apart it is possible to accommodate two-storey maisonettes of about fifty square metres. When the hard zones are twenty metres apart it is possible to accommodate single-floor flats of a similar floor area.

The building envelope, that is the external walls and roof together with the ground slab, is the part of the building where heat loss is registered. It is here, too, that the building has to be made weatherproof in other ways. A building which has the lowest ratio for the area of the envelope to the usable floor area not only costs less to build for any given building volume, assuming the same materials, but also uses less energy to construct and is more efficient in terms of energy use during its working lifetime. The sustainable building is one which uses least capital energy in its construction and during its occupation has minimum energy revenue requirements. These two qualities of the sustainable building may not be entirely congruent and a trade-off between factors may be necessary. The precise nature of the trade-off, however, does not change the relationship of both factors to the shape of the building: both the energy capital and revenue costs of the building are related to its geometry in a similar way. Both types of energy costs tend to increase as the ratio of the area of the building envelope to the usable floor area increases. The sustainable building is, therefore, one where its envelope is the smallest for a given usable floor area. The single-storey square plan has an advantage over the exaggerated rectangular plan shape but two, three and four storey buildings are more effective than both in terms of energy conservation.

The relationship of energy expenditure and building geometry has been considered so far for buildings standing in isolation as three-dimensional forms in space. In cities this is not always the case. It has been argued elsewhere that the city consists of spaces surrounded and formed by buildings

(Moughtin, 1992). In terms of energy conservation there seems much to commend this built form. By grouping small units together, the semi-detached house rather than two detached houses, or the terrace rather than semi-detached houses, it is possible to make savings in the area of external walling or building envelope. Furthermore if the plan shape of each unit is changed from a square to a rectangular one with a narrow building frontage then additional savings in the size of the external walling can be made: there is then a corresponding conservation of energy. By composing the individual units into three and four storey blocks of flats or maisonettes, maximum savings in external walling per unit can be achieved without the need to use lifts. This rather oversimplified argument presupposes that disadvantaged or special needs groups are allocated ground-floor accommodation.

Further energy conservation can be achieved by designing the building to work well within the conditions set by the local climate. The vernacular tradition has much to teach in the art of relating buildings to the site. The traditional dwelling in countries with colder climates is often sited just below the brow of the hill on a southward slope, protected by the hill which is often supplemented with a shelter belt of trees. The northern face of the building usually has only a few openings and if it is a farmhouse it may be protected by outhouses. The southern façade contains the main openings, maximizing the benefit of the limited sunshine. This common-sense approach to the siting of a building and its internal organization mitigates the worst effects of a cold winter climate and has valuable lessons for the greening of building design. It would appear from this model that the ideal orientation for a building in our climate is with its long axis running east–west. The northern façade should be fronted by accommodation not requiring good views or lighting and rooms where the highest levels of heating are not required, that is, this wall of the building should be flanked by accommodation that can form a barrier between the cold outside world and the main living rooms. The type of accommodation facing north would be circulation space, storage, toilets and, possibly, working kitchens. The rooms with a southern aspect would be the living rooms and bedrooms. Large windows are desirable in the southern face of the building not only to provide light but also passive solar heating.

Passive solar energy can: 'provide up to 20 per cent of the annual space heating energy required for a well insulated building' (Vale and Vale, 1993). As Robert and Brenda Vale point out in their paper, making use of solar energy has implications for the orientation of the building. For effective solar gain, window openings should be in walls with an orientation within 30 degrees east or west of south with a southern orientation being the optimum position. There are, however, problems with large south-facing windows in domestic buildings in this country where we give such great emphasis to privacy. It is usual for frontages, particularly in residential areas, to face other frontages. An arrangement where the front of one house overlooks a neighbour's backyard is generally unacceptable in our particular culture. A north–south orientation for

the long axis of terrace housing is more suited to British conditions. Using this orientation it is possible for the front of one house to face the front of the house opposite while both living rooms receive sunshine, one side the afternoon sun and the other side the morning sun. Large south windows designed to generate solar heating, if overlooked, will be unacceptable to the occupant and will simply be draped in net curtains to increase privacy. Unfortunately the use of curtains in this way defeats the purpose of the large window and its contribution to heating the home. In buildings not dominated by the need for privacy such as schools, universities and offices it may be possible to give greater priority to an orientation which maximizes the use of passive solar heating.

The conservatory, a common feature of many Victorian and Edwardian villas (Figures 2.23 and 2.24) is popular once again with home owners. It is a reasonably low cost and culturally acceptable method of passive solar heating for the home. It also forms a useful buffer between the external climate in winter and the interior of the building, increasing its comfort. The conservatory is most

Figures 2.23 and **2.24** The Orangery, Wollaton Hall, Nottingham

2.23

2.24

appropriately placed on the south, east or west walls. When placed on the north sunless façade the conservatory tends to be a drab uncomfortable place for sitting or resting. If not properly designed the conservatory, even when well sited, can be a source of heat loss in winter and can cause overheating in the summer. The conservatory should be adequately ventilated and the wall to which it is attached to the house should be well insulated, any windows in the wall being double glazed. Buildings designed specifically for use with a conservatory or sun space offer great scope to create comfortable spaces together with energy savings. In addition as a device the sun space or conservatory offers an opportunity for innovative design. The glass atrium and the more traditional street arcade are both features which, like the conservatory, modify the internal climate. They also enhance natural lighting within a building complex while being exciting visual additions to the urban realm (Figures 2.25 to 2.28).

It may appear from the previous paragraphs that the application of the principles of sustainable development will result in an urban form comprising a blanket of four-storey blocks arranged in parallel rows in order to maximize solar gain and achieve an optimum density. Each new addition to the city, however, is designed for a specific site. The existing patterns of development therefore condition the ways in which the principles of sustainability are applied. Additions to the city will be located along particular street lines and abut specific neighbouring properties. It is these existing conditions which set the parameters for new development and to which the discipline of energy conservation must be applied. Even on greenfield sites, which in a sustainable city would be avoided if possible, the urban designer is not presented with a *carte blanche*. The contours, special landscape features and local architectural form and detail cannot be ignored by the urban designer: they will stimulate the development of culturally acceptable solutions whereby the general principles of sustainable development can be applied for a site-specific purpose.

2.25

Figures 2.25 and **2.26** Leadenhall Market, London

2.26

Figure 2.27 Shopping
Arcade, Southport
Figure 2.28 Atrium,
London wall

2.27

2.28

CONCLUSION

Traditions of vernacular architecture have many
lessons for those seeking sustainable forms. There is
much to commend the common-sense approach to
energy conservation and environmental protection
practised by many builders in the past (see Figures
2.2 to 2.5). The first principle gleaned from a study
of past practice is a priority given to the conservation and reuse of buildings, infrastructure and
materials. The second principle is the use of local
regional building materials for construction work:

where possible it is preferable to use materials
requiring low inputs of energy in fabrication, transportation to the site and in the construction
process itself. Preference should be given to materials which can be sustainable when farmed or
extracted and to those which are labour-intensive
rather than energy-intensive in their extraction,
dressing and erection. The third principle is to
avoid materials which cause environmental damage
leaving behind unsightly spoil heaps, massive
quarries, or a denuded rain forest. The worst effects
of such damage when it occurs should be mitigated

and new buildings should be linked with tree-planting schemes in an effort to offset some of the effects of pollution caused by the manufacture of the building materials. The fourth principle is to relate the building to the local environment. In the cold European climate it is important: to insulate the building to high standards; to reduce the amount of external wall surface; to orientate the building towards the sun; to organize the interior of the building so that a buffer of storage rooms and other similar accommodation faces north; and to arrange for conservatories or sun spaces to be sited on the south, east or west façades. Buildings set into the hillside with part or all of the roof covered by earth and vegetation, while fitting into the landscape with little intrusion, also make great use of the insulating properties of the earth itself. There are a growing number of projects of this type, the Visitor Centre at Navan Fort, the ancient seat of the Ulster Kings, near Armagh being of particular interest. The centre fits snugly into the landscape leaving the great earth mounds of the fort to dominate the scene. (Figures 2.29 to 2.31). The fifth principle is to design buildings for flexibility so that a mix of uses can be accommodated under the same roof and so that floor plans are robust, in the sense that they can be adapted for different uses during the building's lifetime. Finally, buildings should be located on public transport routes and with close connections to other parts of the existing urban infrastructure. Where possible building should take the form of infill within existing development or on 'brown land', that is, on previously used land or wasteland. 'Greenfield' or new sites, particularly on the periphery of urban areas, should where possible be avoided and other options considered.

2.29

2.30

2.31

Figure 2.29 Navan Fort, Armagh. Ancient capital of Ulster

Figure 2.30 The Navan Visitor Centre: the building is buried within a grass-covered mound and is centrally lit with clerestory lighting

Figure 2.31 The Navan Visitor Centre

ENERGY AND TRANSPORT

3

INTRODUCTION

This chapter examines the relationship between transport, energy and pollution. The chapter begins with a critique of a transport policy based upon the idea of free and, if possible, the unimpeded movement of the car; investment priority being given to the road building programme. It then outlines the features of a sustainable transport system giving priority to walking, cycling and public transport. The chapter concludes with a discussion of the regional and local political and administrative structures necessary for achieving a sustainable transport system, emphasizing the need for public participation in the design, development and management of the system. This chapter is the background for chapters 4 and 5 which discuss urban form.

The eighteenth report of the Royal Commission on Environmental Pollution (1994) states: 'The unrelenting growth of transport has become possibly the greatest environmental threat facing the UK, and one of the greatest obstacles to achieving sustainable development.' Twenty years previously the Royal Commission in its fourth report (1974) had warned that it would be dangerously complacent to ignore the possible environmental damage caused by the increasing numbers of both motor vehicles and commercial flights. In 1974, therefore, it was: 'becoming increasingly apparent that it is not possible to cater for the unrestricted use of vehicles without engineering works on a scale that is socially unacceptable.' The Commission suggested: 'We may therefore expect that limitations on their use in some areas will be imposed in order to safeguard the local environment. This will lead to a reduction not only in their exhaust gases but also of their noise, which many regard as a worse problem.'

Eleven years before the Royal Commission's fourth report the Buchanan Report, *Traffic in Towns* (Buchanan, 1963) had set out clearly the problems for urban areas of the projected increase in traffic. Buchanan was also asked to examine the effect of traffic on the quality of the local environment, and in particular to study the problems of noise, fumes, smell, the effect of vibration on buildings, accidents and visual intrusion. It did not, however, include the wider remit of examining the effects of pollution on the climate, nor were the effects of energy constraints so apparent at the time. Buchanan's prognosis revealed the strong possibility that saturation in car ownership would be achieved by the year 2010. By saturation of car ownership was meant a car being available for anyone wishing to use it. According to this definition the total number of cars on the road by 2010 would be 37 million or half the then forecast population for 2010 of 74 million. Buchanan warned that there was nothing more dangerous than underestimating the demand for personalized transport and the effects it would have on the environment.

In the Buchanan Report the motor car was accepted as an inevitable fact of life. It was assumed that numbers of cars on the roads would increase and the use made of them would also increase: 'There are so many advantages in a fairly small, independent, self-powered and highly manoeuvrable means of getting about at ground level, for both people and goods, that it is unlikely we shall ever wish to abandon it.' He went on to add that the car may change in a number of ways but: '... for all practical purposes it will present most of the problems that are presented by the motor vehicle of today ... given its head the motor vehicle would wreck our towns within a decade ... the public can justifiably demand to be fully informed about the possibilities of adapting towns to motor traffic before there is any question of applying restrictive measures' (Buchanan, 1963). It is difficult to say with any certainty if Buchanan's blind acceptance of the growth in car ownership was born of a realism later proved in all essentials to be correct, or that the projections he and others in the field made simply became a self-fulfilling prophecy.

In the case study of Norwich, a city with a fine architectural heritage, Buchanan did point out the basic incompatibility between demand for unrestricted accessibility and the preservation of a good quality environment: '... the main principle is abundantly clear - if the environment is sacrosanct, and if no major reconstruction can be undertaken, then accessibility must be limited. Once this simple truth is recognised ... then planning can be started on a realistic basis. It becomes a matter of deciding what level of accessibility can be provided and how

it can be arranged, and then it is a question of public relations to ensure that the position is clearly understood.' In Leeds his study led him to conclude that: '.... there is no possibility whatsoever, in a town of this size and nature, of planning for the level of traffic induced by the unrestricted use of the motor car for the journey to work in condition of full car ownership.' It is his study of a part of London, Marylebone, which is sometimes used as the basis for criticism of the findings of the report on *Traffic in Towns*. The urban motorways which now devastate many towns are believed by some critics as originating in the ideas formulated in Buchanan's study. It was for Marylebone that he developed the concept of the environmental area, a district of about 4500 feet square. The environmental area, while not pedestrianized, was to be a high quality environment with restrictions placed on the moving vehicle and the pedestrian given priority. It was to be surrounded by high carrying-capacity roads interrupted infrequently by junctions so that traffic moved freely at speed. Buchanan calculated that an environmental area of this size would generate a maximum capacity of 12 200 cars per hour, which could be absorbed by the surrounding network of major roads. It was, however, this system which he found to be impractical for Leeds and totally unsuitable for a city such as Norwich. As Houghton-Evans (1975) quite rightly concludes: 'He had proved that, beyond a certain size, it was impossible to design for mainly "private" transport, and that for our larger cities at least, we had to continue to place considerable reliance upon a public service. In the practice of urban renewal, regrettably little understanding has been shown of the principles he was urging - in spite of much lip-service. Regrettably also, he misleadingly pursued his discovery concerning public transport in terms of still trying to please the motorist.'

The physical impossibility of meeting the demand for the unrestricted use of the motor car was being strongly argued by a number of scholars and activists in the 1960s and 1970s. The simple thesis being propounded was that the act of building new roads, far from solving the problem, actually generated additional traffic and also diverted the congestion to other parts of the road network, thus exacerbating conditions. Despite the influential book by Jane Jacobs (1965), *The Death and Life of Great American Cities*, the traffic engineering fraternity continued with expensive origin and destination surveys to feed into basically flawed computer models. Such models were then used to justify the demolition of valuable city infrastructure and more destructively to scatter the communities housed there. Instead of this attrition of the city by the motor car, Jacobs was advocating its strict control by making footpaths wider, slowing the traffic down, discouraging traffic intrusion in areas where it is not required. These suggestions, made nearly thirty nears before the traffic calming policies now being actively pursued in some cities in this country, are the forerunner of the *voonerf* in Holland (Figures 3.1 and 3.2).

There is a strong case for limiting accessibility of traffic in urban areas, on the grounds that the problem of mobility and movement within the city cannot be solved by building more roads at great cost, their non-acceptability in social terms and because such a procedure will not in the end solve the problem. The message, that creating more roads is not the solution to traffic problems in urban areas, is at last being accepted in the Department of Transport and the Department of the Environment in this country (Ghazi, 1995): this change of attitude also informs the public statements of some Ministers in the present government.

The case for a change in attitude to the problem of the movement of people and goods within and between urban areas has been strengthened by studies of pollution caused by, amongst other things, the use of fossil fuels for transport. The result of the pollution increase affects, as we have seen, the global climate. Local pollution caused by heavily used roads also affects the local environment, resulting in health hazards.

3.1

3.2

Figure 3.1 The voonerf, Amsterdam
Figure 3.2 Traffic calming, Letchworth

Official reports resulting from the report of the World Commission on Environment and Development in 1987 and the Earth Summit in 1992, together with the growing environmental movement, have outlined the problems associated with pollution caused by transport, while suggesting broad measures for dealing with it and with energy conservation. These measures include fiscal proposals for taxing the polluter, suggestions for encouraging the development of improved technologies, together with urban structuring which reduces the need for movement relying on greater use of public transport, cycling and walking for any necessary mobility. Blowers (1993) suggested that the following four principal types of mechanism are necessary to achieve a sustainable transport strategy:

1. Regulatory mechanisms aimed in particular at restricting pollution levels to prescribed limits.
2. Financial mechanisms through taxes and incentives, notably energy taxes, whereby each travel mode accounts for its true overall cost (including the environmental cost), thereby favouring modes which consume less energy and which produce less pollution.
3. Inducements to encourage research and development into more fuel-efficient vehicles and alternative transport technologies.
4. Planning - a greater emphasis on the integration of land use and transportation planning, key aims being to minimize travel distances, to encourage the use of modes other than the car and to improve accessibility to facilities.

It seems that the current received wisdom for those working the field of urban design and planning is a philosophy which advocates pursuing policies and plans which wean the general public from its love affair with the motor car. The Royal Commission on Environmental Pollution (1994) set out a list of eight objectives for achieving a sustainable transport policy. They are:

a) To ensure that an effective transport policy at all levels of government is integrated with land use policy and gives priority to minimising the need for transport and increasing the proportion of trips by environmentally less damaging modes.

b) To achieve standards of air quality that will prevent damage to human health and the environment.
c) To improve the quality of life, particularly in towns and cities, by reducing the dominance of cars and lorries and providing alternative means of access.
d) To increase the proportions of personal travel and freight transport by environmentally less damaging modes and to make the best use of existing infrastructure.
e) To halt the loss of land to transport infrastructure in areas of conservation, cultural, scenic or amenity value unless the use of land for that purpose has been shown to be the best practicable environmental option.
f) To reduce carbon dioxide emissions from transport.
g) To reduce substantially the demands which transport infrastructure and the vehicle industry place on non-renewable materials.
h) To reduce noise nuisance from transport.

Each objective is specified in detail using combinations of quantifiable standards, sets of principles and firm recommendations. This is, indeed, a formidable agenda which the Royal Commission deems necessary to avoid serious environmental damage, while preserving access for people needing to pursue their livelihoods and leisure activities. A sustainable future requires a fundamentally different approach to transport and planning policy and radical modification, perhaps even reversal, of recent trends. No longer should it be seen as inevitable that the car and its requirements will dominate city form in the future. It is a small step from here to the acceptance of the notion that a good public transport system is necessary for sustainable development and that its provision is a legitimate concern, perhaps the most important concern of city government in the twenty-first century. The urban designer working within a philosophical framework for sustainable development does not plan or design urban structure specifically for the free movement of the private motor car, with public transport taking low priority; nor does the urban designer manipulate public transport to conform with an unsympathetic urban form which has been designed for the needs of the motor car. The form of the city under the new imperative of ensuring sustainable transport should be designed for public transport, the bicycle and the pedestrian, with the motor car playing a subordinate role. The change in the perception of the role of private transport will, in the medium to longer term, induce a major cultural shift which will have a far-reaching effect on urban form.

RECAPITULATION: THE PROBLEM RESTATED

Quotations from the Report of the Royal Commission on Environmental Pollution (1994) makes the problems associated with the projected growth in traffic abundantly clear:

> Over two-fifths of the petroleum products used in the UK are used in road transport ... In all, surface transport causes 21 per cent of the carbon dioxide emissions produced by human activities in the UK, or about 24 per cent if emissions from refining and electricity generation for transport are included. Road transport accounts for 87 per cent of the emissions attributable to surface transport ... On the basis of the forecast growth in road traffic, carbon dioxide emissions from the transport sector will show further substantial growth over the next 25 years ... Significant environmental damage has been caused over recent years by the construction of transport infrastructure ... there is much concern about the effects the present trunk road programme would have in damaging the landscape, causing loss of habitats or species, and damaging historic buildings and archaeological features. Providing sufficient road capacity to carry the levels of traffic predicted in the government's 1989 forecasts would require a massive programme of road building and improvement, over and above the schemes already included in the trunk programme.

If past trends continue unchecked then passenger and freight transport by all modes will probably grow by about 20 per cent per decade over the next 25 years. According to the Royal Commission a sustainable transport policy cannot accommodate more than half that amount. It is this problem to which those working in the field of urban development must turn their attention in the immediate future.

SUSTAINABLE URBAN TRANSPORT

The process of developing the sustainable city of the future will involve a major cultural change which for many will mean a change in lifestyle, one no longer dependent upon the car. A feature of this necessary cultural change is a holistic perspective of the city region, its people and the technology that supports and sustains their social, economic, political and physical infrastructure. This new paradigm, or way of viewing the city as a series of overlapping and interconnected systems, if it is to be successful, will result in planning mechanisms which comprise sets of interrelated and mutually supportive policies. The paradigm for sustainable development is akin to the holistic or synoptic method of the Geddesian planner rather than the sectoral approach used in resource allocation or the limited solutions offered by road engineers to discretely defined traffic problems. For the purposes of this discussion the nature of sustainable urban transport will be analysed within the framework of the city and its region. However, it is clear that sustainable urban transport requires the support of a balanced combination of pricing measures to promote public transport, changes in governing institutions, advances in transport technology including recycling of materials, and new initiatives in the design and structuring of all future urban developments.

THE POLITICS OF SUSTAINABLE TRANSPORT

Equity, both inter- and intra-generational, together with local participation in decision-making, are two of the cornerstones of a green philosophy and the essential foundation for sustainable development. For example, the imposition of a tax on the use of petrol or a pricing structure for heavily used roads, if implemented in isolation, would be regressive, that is, it would place a heavier burden on the poorer sections of society and widen the levels of mobility between poor and rich. Such policies without the development of public transport would be contrary to the principles of sustainable development (Royal Commission on Environmental Pollution, 1994). Sustainable development is possible only when policies and their effects are understood by the community and when they are legitimized through popular acclaim: 'The problems of "economic development" without democratic participation have been made manifest time after time. Unless individuals are able to share both in decision-making and in the actual process of development, it is bound to fail' (Elkin *et al.*, 1991b). Only by empowering people is it possible to improve the environment. Successful planning, whether it is for housing or roads, begins with the people, their aspirations and perceived needs: it is a bottom up process. Macdonald (1989) suggests that: 'unless people can, in some way, create, manage, change or participate in activities that affect their lives, dissatisfaction, alienation and even illness are likely outcomes.' Movement towards sustainable development will revive the idea of community, public provision of basic services and also planned intervention to endure an equitable distribution of resources. This agenda, however, requires the political will and commitment to make radical changes to the way in which society is governed and organized: it would mean a shift in power from central government to the regions, cities and, above all else, to the local community (Moughtin, 1992).

A return to some of the ideas developed in the Skeffington Report, *People and Plans* (Department of the Environment,1969) provides a useful framework for the discussion of the role of public participation at the local level in planning for traffic. Some of the recommendations made by Skeffington have been acted upon in the years since his report was published. It is probably true to assert that the public are better informed about planning matters since Skeffington. It is now common practice to hold public meetings for the discussion of planning proposals and to mount planning exhibitions to inform the public about such proposals. There are, indeed, examples of residents engaging more actively in planning based upon games such as *Planning for Real* (Gibson, 1979) or *Do it yourself Planning* (Moughtin and Simpson, 1978). One radical idea in Skeffington, however, was not acted upon in any structured form: that is the concept of the community forum.

Skeffington's fourth main recommendation was:

> Local planning authorities should consider convening meetings in their area for the purpose of setting up community forums. These forums would provide local organisations with the opportunity to discuss collectively planning and other issues of importance to the area. Community forums might also have administrative functions, such as receiving and distributing information on planning matters and promoting the formation of neighbourhood groups. (Department of the Environment, 1969)

The report also recommended the appointment of community development officers with a remit to secure the involvement of those people who do not normally join organizations. Clearly Skeffington took 'people and planning' to include public participation in the preparation of proposals for dealing with traffic problems:

> We have noted that the Minister of Transport has asked certain authorities to prepare traffic plans for their towns and we understand that several have

been submitted. These plans, which involve short-term measures to manage traffic, will frequently have a considerable impact on people's lives, especially where the flow of traffic is re-routed. We think it would be anomalous if authorities did not provide opportunities for participation when plans of this kind are prepared and urge that they should do so on future occasions. (Department of the Environment, 1969)

People and Planning is a seminal work in defining the role of the public in the field of planning: 'Our immediate task was to suggest practical ways in which local planning authorities could best implement the Town and Country Planning Act, thus enabling people to contribute their ideas while plans are being prepared for the area in which they live.' Despite the many good features of the document, activists in the field of citizen participation tended to be disappointed in the report. The disappointment centred around the limitation imposed on the concept by Skeffington because of his acceptance of existing power structures dominated by professional planners and traffic engineers: 'There are limitations to this concept. One is that responsibility for preparing a plan is, and must remain, that of the local planning authority. Another is that the completion of plans - the setting into statutory form of proposals and decisions - is a task demanding the highest standards of professional skill, and must be undertaken by the professional staff of the local planning authority' (Department of the Environment, 1969). Some would say that participation has come to mean better publicity, informing the public, or the participation of groups working within an agenda determined by the professionals associated with any given project. This is particularly true of planning for traffic. The procedures governing enquiries into trunk road proposals are weighted very much against inputs and the ideas from residents or environmental groups. The Royal Commission on Environmental Pollution (1994) was quite clear on this point, making the recommendation that:

Trunk road schemes have been criticised for being imposed without regards to the needs of an area or the ensuing development pressures. If a system of trunk roads is retained, we recommend that all trunk road schemes be considered initially as an intrinsic part of local authority structure plans and integrated into the development control system. We also recommend that the rules of procedure governing enquiries into trunk road proposals and compulsory purchase orders be amended so as to permit government witnesses to answer questions about the merits of government policy and allow the inspector to take account of the interactions of the proposal with other government policies in his recommendation. (Royal Commission on Environmental Pollution, 1994)

Opposition to road proposals is further diluted by the exploitation of the NIMBY (not in my backyard) syndrome. Alternative routes for proposed road improvements, in theory, give choice to the general public and offer an opportunity for lay opinion to be voiced. In practice the strategy sets one community against another and environmentalist against community activist as each group tries to have the road located far from their own back door or away from the area of their personal environmental concern. Clearly, once the need to assuage the voracious appetite of the motor car, supported by the powerful roads lobby, is accepted, then the ever-increasing traffic projections, those self-fulfilling prophecies, lead inevitably to road improvements. The only issue then remaining to be resolved is where the blight is to be located. The employment of some form of environmental impact study assists in the location of a line for the road which is the least obnoxious for the majority in the area or for those groups having the greatest clout.

The 'divide and rule' strategy of the traffic engineer is strengthened by the adoption of a phased or piecemeal development of road improvements. Less contentious sections of the road are completed first. The completed improvements to one section of a road system have the effect of weakening the arguments of objectors to later more contentious proposals. It seems irrational to disturb the flow of traffic on the newly completed road because of congestion in other parts of the sub-standard system. The nature of the argument acts as a ratchet leading to a programme of never-ending road improvements.

The community forum may be an instrument for breaking this circular argument which leads to an expanding and unsustainable road programme. Certainly, the community forum based upon the idea of the elected Parish Council is a necessary structural component of an administrative system dedicated to effective public participation in the development of a sustainable transportation network in an urban area. The community forum, however, should not be called into being at the behest of a higher authority or indeed on the recommendation of those professionals pursuing development propos-als for such a body. The community forum should be established in its own right, legitimized by elections, served by a small secretariat and with powers and duties clearly defined. One specific duty should be the responsibility for the generation of proposals to deal with the movement of goods and people in its district.

POLITICAL STRUCTURES FOR SUSTAINABLE TRANSPORT

Sustainable development requires a sound political and administrative structure for its successful implementation. The pattern of authorities which may emerge from the current review of local government could include a number of relatively small authorities, some areas with two-tier struc-tures together with a number of larger unitary authorities. Such a patchwork of authorities may be all that is politically possible, but, most certainly, the new structure will not assist in achieving a balanced approach to transport

provision, nor will it foster the implementation of policies for sustainable development. It is suggested here that any proposals for the restruc-turing of local government boundaries should be orientated to the major aim of securing sustainable urban forms.

Definitions of sustainable development are built on a premise which recognizes the virtue and necessity of grass roots community activity in the development process. 'Think globally, act locally', is a phrase which is often used in any debate on sustainable development. Citizen participation in development and the political structures which sustain it is clearly an essential requirement of local and regional government in a sustainable world. It has already been suggested that the lowest level or tier of government should be the local community which occupies a clearly defined district or quarter of the city. It can, however, be argued that 'community' in the late twentieth century is not necessarily associated with a physi-cally identified place. Many associations, friendship patterns and communities of interest extend far beyond the confines of the local neighbourhood: they form a rich web of overlapping communities. It is not the intention here to dispute this explana-tion of community, nor is it the intention to suggest the need or desirability to change this particular aspect of urban culture. It is, however, asserted that people see the city partly in terms of named and clearly identifiable districts. The district, quarter or neighbourhood may not be essential for some social relationships, but it is, along with the main paths people use and centres they visit, an essential mental construct. The neigh-bourhood: '... is no longer the space within which people know each other because they live next door, but a space which is commonly defined and given a name, and within which people find it relatively easy to band together when things get dangerous' (Lynch, 1981). One such threat is the destruction of local environmental quality by proposals for road improvements.

A basic consideration in city design is the question of political control. Since citizen participation is a key concept in the pursuit of sustainable development the question arises as to the precise areas of management which might properly be placed under community control. Accepting the concept of subsidiarity, that is, taking appropriate decisions at the lowest practicable level or tier of government, raises two important questions. Which service provision should be delegated to the very local or community level of government and how much power should be vested in these authorities? The power of communities to say 'no' to all developments would lead to stagnation and not necessarily to sustainable development. The city government has been the main actor in the field of urban infrastructural development since the earliest civilizations. To some extent that power has been weakened during the last century. The importance of the city is being overshadowed by the growing might of the state. This has been in evidence particularly in Britain during the 1970s and 1980s, where policies seem designed to strip the powers from local government. The power to develop a sustainable infrastructure, including the transportation network, must be returned to the city.

In a world of sustainable development the city should be paramount in matters of transport planning. Nevertheless, there is an important role for the neighbourhood community council in this as in many other fields connected with development. There are four main features of the role of the community council in transport matters. They are: it should act as a political check or counter-balance to the higher centres of authority; it should act as a source of ideas about transport provision; it should act as a powerful lobby for improved local transport facilities; and it may develop into a provider or manager of local public or commercial transport services. Such facilities could include a taxi service, car pooling, or community bus service. The community council may also be involved in traffic management or environmental improvement schemes.

REGIONAL PLANNING AND SUSTAINABLE TRANSPORT

Clearly ideas about sustainable urban form are located both conceptually and theoretically within the field of regional planning. The main concern of regional planning is the development of a network of sustainable metropolitan areas, cities, towns and villages. It is also concerned with the development of the rural areas not only as places where people live and work but also as places which provide the urban population with food and areas for leisure. In addition the rural areas surrounding the towns and cities are important for maintaining the nation's biodiversity which also contributes to the well-being of the global ecological system.

Sustainable transport, the specific topic of this chapter, in addition to having a powerful influence on urban form and city design, is also a vital strategic element in the regional pattern of development:

> In principle, it is obvious that urban form will affect patterns of transport, which in turn will affect fuel consumption and emissions. By the same token, the viability and patronage of public transport facilities, and also consumption and emissions, will be affected by urban form. Such form may also affect rates of conversion of land from rural to urban uses, and by extension, the loss of habitats for flora and fauna. (Breheny and Rookwood, 1993)

The foundation for a sustainable urban transport system is the regional administrative and political structure which underpins the implementation of policy. This point, however, raises fundamental questions about regions and regionalism. There are divergent views about the nature of regions and the effectiveness or even the need for regional planning. It is appropriate to review again regional planning in the light of the debate about sustainable development. This is particularly true in Britain after a number of years of government which has eschewed all notions seeking an equitable distribution of resources throughout the country: political dogma has dismissed intervention in the market for the social objective of regional balance.

Before discussing regional structures for sustainable development some clear idea about the nature of regions is a fundamental requirement. Indeed, is there such a phenomenon as a region, or is it merely a mental construct (Glasson, 1978)? At one level any idea, method of classification or definition is a mental construct. Of great relevance for regional planning is the degree to which a region has homogeneity in both human and ecological terms. Relevant, too, is the degree to which the homogeneity is a sound basis for political and administrative purposes. Since the main purpose of such a polity is sustainable development, it is clear that the region should have meaning for the group of people who occupy the area within their boundary: the regional boundary should, therefore, be the mental construct of the region held by its constituent members.

There are two main methods of regional classification (Glasson, 1978). The first main type is the 'formal region', the other being the 'functional region'. The earliest definitions of the region were based mainly on the physical characteristics of the landscape, early geographers believing that the survival of man was dependent upon his adaptation to the environment. Later developments in the ideas about the definition of the formal region included an analysis of economic activities. Economic activities such as the types of industry or agriculture were used as criteria for regional classification. A classic amongst such systems of regional classification is the work of Dudley Stamp in Britain (Figure 3.3) (Stamp and Beaver, 1933).

Geographers such as Herbertson (1905), Unstead (1916, 1935) and Vidal de la Blanche (1931), using criteria such as topography, climate, vegetation and population, divide the world, continents and countries into natural regions. All such approaches have as a philosophical basis the idea of environmental determinism, the physical features of the planet and its climate determining, to some extent, the pattern of settlement and to some degree the

THE AGRICULTURAL REGIONS OF ENGLAND AND WALES.

LEGEND.

1 The Lake District or Cumbria.
2 The Pennines.
3 Wales and the Welsh Borders.
4 The Southwestern Peninsula.
5 Northumbria.
6 The Eastern Slopes of the Pennines.
7 The Plain of Lancastria.
8 The Vale of York.
9 The Midlands of England.
10 Northeast and East Yorkshire.
11 Lincolnshire.
12 The Scarplands and Clay Vales.
13 The Fenlands.
14 The Plain of Somerset.
15 The Chalklands of the Southeast.
16 East Anglia.
17 The London Basin.
18 The Hampshire Basin.
19 The Weald.

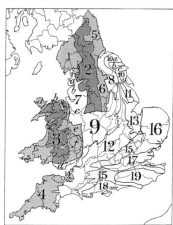

Figure 3.3 The agricultural regions of England and Wales (Stamp and Beaver, 1933)

functions of those settlements. The extent of man's occupation of the planet today, particularly in the economically advanced countries of the West, gives the impression that anything is possible. The limit to settlement, apparently, is not nature but man's will.

Opposing man and nature in this way is artificial - man and the natural world are one. The present climatic crisis, problems of pollution and the rate of finite resource depletion are a result of this schism which divides nature and man. This philosophy undervalues the natural environment and leads to its exploitation. The exploitation extends beyond the 'natural world' to include man; the poor and vulnerable occupying areas at risk from flooding and drought. It may be appropriate to give greater weight, in regional definition, to the physical environment and its ecology, and in particular to the role of the environment in sustaining the local population. Maintaining a more balanced relationship between a community and its local environment may be of great importance in the next century.

In contrast to the formal region which is defined in terms of homogeneity, the functional region is concerned with areas which display an interdependence or interrelationship of their parts. The functional region may consist of heterogenous components such as cities, towns and villages but which are functionally related. The relationship of the parts is usually measured in the form of flows, such as journey-to-work, shopping patterns and bus services. The analysis of the functional region is mainly concerned with the movement of people, goods and messages. As such the concept of the functional region is important for any discussion of transport planning. The founding father of planning in Britain, Patrick Geddes, was aware of the importance of the interdependence of components within the region. His diagram 'Place–Work–Folk' (Figure 3.4) and his phrase 'City Region' illustrate perfectly this understanding (Geddes, 1949). In Europe Christaller (1966) developed a central place theory based upon a hierarchical relationship between centres in southern Germany. This theory of Christaller is a seminal work in the development of ideas about the definition of the region (Figure 3.5).

Two tiers of regional administration, adopting features from both systems of geographical classification may prove necessary for a political structure which will give legitimacy to programmes for local sustainable development. The idea of the city region has been discussed by many authors since Geddes first coined the term. Howard's earlier concept of

ENVIRONMENT ACTS, THROUGH FUNCTION, UPON THE ORGANISM:
AND
THE ORGANISM ACTS, THROUGH FUNCTION, UPON THE ENVIRONMENT.

	E F O	
	O F E	
E PLACE Holland	F WORK makes	O FOLK the Dutch
O FOLK the Dutch	F WORK make	E PLACE Holland

3.4

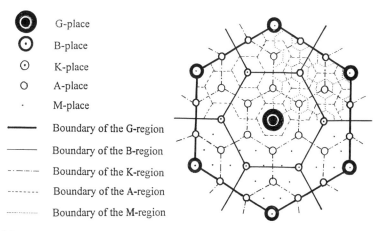

- ◉ G-place
- ⊙ B-place
- ⊙ K-place
- ○ A-place
- · M-place
- —— Boundary of the G-region
- —— Boundary of the B-region
- ·—·— Boundary of the K-region
- ------- Boundary of the A-region
- ········· Boundary of the M-region

3.5

the Garden City was in effect a proposal for a city region. It comprised clusters of cities linked to each other and to a central city by a strategic transport network. The basic idea was the development of a functional arrangement of settlements with clearly defined physical identity but with social and economic interdependence (Howard, 1964). It is ideas such as the city region which hold out a prospect for managing a sustainable city together with its transport network. This concept has been developed further by the Town and Country Planning Association. The term used by the Town

Figure 3.4 Geddes' diagram: Place–Work–Folk (Geddes, 1949)

Figure 3.5 Christaller hierarchy of settlements (Christaller, 1966)

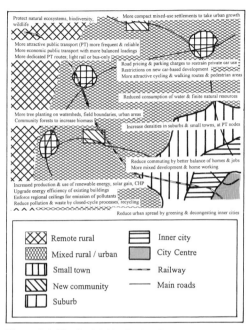

Protect natural ecosystems, biodiversity, wildlife

More compact mixed-use settlements to take urban growth

More attractive public transport (PT) more frequent & reliable
More economic public transport with more balanced loadings
More dedicated PT routes; light rail or bus-only

Road pricing & parking charges to restrain private car use
Restrictions on new car-based development
More attractive cycling & walking routes & pedestrian areas

Reduced consumption of water & finite natural resources

More tree planting on watersheds, field boundaries, urban areas
Community forests to increase biomass

Increase densities in suburbs & small towns, at PT nodes

Reduce commuting by better balance of homes & jobs
More mixed development & home working

Increased production & use of renewable energy, solar gain, CHP
Upgrade energy efficiency of existing buildings
Enforce regional ceilings for emission of pollutants
Reduce pollution & waste by closed-cycle processes, recycling

Reduce urban spread by greening & decongesting inner cities

Remote rural
Mixed rural / urban
Small town
New community
Suburb
Inner city
City Centre
Railway
Main roads

Figure 3.6 The Social City Region (Blowers, 1993)

and Country Planning Association is the Social City Region (Figure 3.6) (Breheny and Rookwood, 1993). If a country such as Britain is seeking sustainable development as a major goal, then the city region would be the chief unit of local government. It would be the main provider of local public services and it would be responsible for managing the environment including the rural hinterland. Naturally the city region would be the polity responsible for the management and development of the transport system. This would include achieving the balance between different modes of transport and the relationship between public and private provision. The management of transport at city region scale facilitates the implementation of continental innovations such as regional, annual and family ticketing of public transport, and the coordination of the timetable for different transport modes. These are

some of the features that make the use of public transport in some German cities a pleasure to use. Proposals such as these would, or course, involve a radical rethink of bus deregulation with greater emphasis being given to public service rather than private gain in the transport sector.

A debate on regional government often returns to the question of the correct size for a city region. The short answer to this question is, of course, that there is no one correct size for a city region. The idea of the city region has many similarities with the Hellenic city state. The literature on city size dates back to the fifth century BC when Plato proposed that a 'good city' should have a population of 5040 landowners or citizens. This number was to be maintained by emigration, that is, by the founding of colonies, and also through the laws of inheritance. Plato failed to explain why this particular number was ideal but, it being factorial 7 ($1 \times 2 \times 3 \times 4 \times 5 \times 6 \times 7$) it may have symbolic power (Plato, republished 1984). Aristotle was far more circumspect when discussing city size. He said: 'ten people would not make a city, and with a hundred thousand it is a city no longer.' His idea was that the city should be big enough and self-sufficient enough for its citizens to lead a good political life. It should, however, not be too big for citizens to lose personal touch with each other so that offices of state could be allocated according to merit and to men known to the citizens (Aristotle, republished 1981). The model for the city region, Hellenic Athens, may have had about 40 000 citizens with a total population, including slaves, of about 250 000. Many other city states of the time were, of course, much smaller than Athens.

The discussion about city size has changed considerably since the times of Plato and Aristotle. The political system in Athens at the time of Athenian dominance of the Aegean was a participatory democracy. All free citizens in Athens were involved in major decisions concerned with governing the state and also in the election of office bearers. Our system of government is quite different. It is a representative democracy, that is, the citizens elect representatives who in turn take decisions on behalf of the electorate (Pateman, 1970). This fundamental difference between the modern democratic system and that of Hellenic Athens, to some extent, reflects the greater complexity of governing the larger cities of today.

Writers and planners deliberating about ideal city size have tended to increase this size as the present century has developed. Howard, at the end of the last century, was suggesting satellite cities of 32 000 and a central or core city of 58 000 people. The planned sizes of new towns built after the Second World War were increased progressively from 50 000 to 250 000. While arguments about the ideal size of cities have occupied the minds of some scholars, cities, particularly in the developing world, have grown at a very rapid rate, so that cities having a multi-million population are now common.

Lynch (1981) sums up the position on city size concisely: 'Unfortunately, the evidence that there is a general optimum city size is weak indeed.' It is not the aim here to dispute this view, although the philosophy of sustainable development may add a new dimension to the discussion. The aim of these paragraphs is to discuss the nature of the political and administrative unit best able to manage the environment and to deliver sustainable development: subsumed within this general goal is an interest in the type of authority best able to organize transport. The city region appears to be the structure most appropriate for the delivery of sustained and sustainable development. The size of the city region to some extent is irrelevant. The flexible proposition suggested by Aristotle to determine city size may well be appropriate today for the city region: it should be big enough and self-sufficient enough for the citizens to lead an active political life. Aristotle's upper limit for the city of 100 000, however, would appear to be below the size recommended for a city region in a representative democracy (Senior, 1965). The smallest size for a city region in this country would be 100 000. More important than crude size

is the population's sense of belonging to the place and to a particular polity, so that meaning is derived from citizenship. The other important aspect of Aristotle's prescription for the 'good city' - face-to-face contact or the knowledge of fellow citizens - would be a feature of political life in the neighbourhoods or quarters through the work of the community councils.

Regionalism has many meanings (Glasson, 1978). It is used in this book to mean an intermediate level of government and administration between the city region and the state. The prime reason for this additional government structure is to make planning for sustainable development more effective by devolving power and decision-making closer to the population. Being larger in population terms than the city region, such provinces provide a stronger counterbalance to central authority. One key to effective regional management of environmental resources lies in legitimizing actions and decisions through the election of the governing body. Non-elected bodies and quangos such as Regional Economic Councils or Regional Advisory Commissions are no substitute for an elected regional government. Regional boards, commissions or councils, though capable of fine work, lack the political muscle to implement sustainable development and to coordinate, for example, the transport plans of the lower authorities within their regional boundaries.

Like the city region, it is difficult to determine an optimum size for a regional province. Cultural identity is more significant than size in determining boundaries. A new government elected in the last years of this decade will probably accept current pressures and create elected assemblies for Scotland and Northern Ireland. If a Labour government is elected there will probably be a similar assembly for Wales. The case for regional provincial assemblies for England seems more problematical, though it may be just as necessary for an effective national programme of sustainable development. The Fabian Society, for example, in 1905 advocated the formation of seven large-scale regions or provinces for England with each province containing several counties (Sanders, 1905).

Later Fawcett (1961) divided the country into twelve provinces. Fawcett's principles for the regional sub-division of the country may still be appropriate in the last decade of the century (Figure 3.7). He suggested that the regional boundaries should interfere as little as possible with the ordinary activities and movement of people. He thought that each province should have a definite capital city easily accessible from all parts of the province. Fawcett was quite circumspect about the size of the province, placing the lower limit at one million but harking back to Aristotle's definition of city size by suggesting that the province should contain a population sufficiently numerous to justify regional self-government. In terms of population size he added a further caveat recommending that no

province should be large enough to dominate the others. The growth of London and the south-east since Fawcett wrote would now make this principle difficult to implement. Two of Fawcett's principles which seem particularly appropriate for sustainable development are, firstly, his suggestion that regional boundaries should be drawn near watersheds not across valleys, and rarely along streams; and secondly that boundaries should pay regard to local patriotism and traditions. The first of these principles could be considerably strengthened for purposes of sustainability by the inclusion of ecological factors other than watershed boundaries, such as patterns of soil and vegetation.

The Second World War provided the impetus for government action on regional organization. An effective war effort required an effective administration for the country. Perhaps the threat of losing a war in the 1940s is a good parallel for the present situation in the 1990s and the environmental threat which hangs over the head of mankind like the 'sword of Damocles'. In the 1940s, Regional Commissioners were appointed to control the affairs of nine Civil Defence Regions. Ministries had representatives in the regional capitals to coordinate regional transport and other aspects of the regional economy in order to maximize efficiency for the war effort.

The development of regionalism in Britain since the war, with the exception of Scotland, is one of vacillation, confusion, compromise and neglect. The wartime regional framework was maintained by the Attlee Government as Standard Treasury Regions, their main purpose being to facilitate post-war reconstruction. Also in the 1940s and 1950s several Statutory Boards with their own regional boundaries were established. These Boards dealt with hospitals, railways, gas, electricity and coal: all were major components of the economic and social life of the country. After a period of stagnation in the 1950s there was a reawakening of regionalism in the early 1960s which culminated with the establishment of the Regional Economic Planning Regions under the

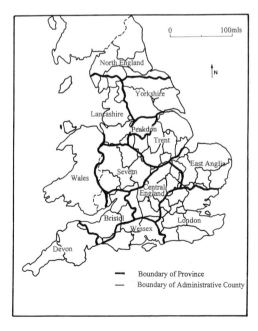

Figure 3.7 Fawcett's regional structure (Fawcett, 1961)

Labour administration in 1965. The new planning regions were similar in geographic structure to the original post-war Standard Regions with the exception of an enlarged south-east region and an integrated Yorkshire and Humberside (Figure 3.8). Under the Conservative Government from 1979 onwards regionalism, indeed local government itself, has been out of favour and has declined in influence. There has been a growing shift of power to the centre, that is, to the national government. The Conservative Government's attitude to regionalism was clearly illustrated in its dissolution of the Greater London Council at a time when its 'Fair Fares' policy was a first step towards an integrated and sustainable public transport system for the capital. Proposals, such as those of the Labour Party in late 1995, for reinvigorating civic leadership by devolving power to locally elected councils or possibly to locally elected mayors may revive the spirit which launched the local innovations in social provision for which the nineteenth century municipalities in this country are known. Poor relief, hospitals, clean water supplies, schools and subsidized housing were often, in the last century, the result of local initiatives. The same process and spirit are needed to serve the requirements of sustainable development centred upon civilized cities.

The privatization of water, gas and electricity, the break-up of the National Health Service, the deregulation of bus services together with the impending privatization of the railways all have great consequences for regional planning. Such delegation of power to the anarchy of the market or, at best, the tyranny of the board rooms is counter to ideas being formulated in the Economic Union and elsewhere about sustainable development: it will do little to achieve sustainable development with all that term implies for inter- and intra-generational equity. With the prospect of a change of administration in 1997 regionalism, decentralization and devolved power may once again be on the political agenda. Change in direction holds out the prospect and opportunity for Britain to organize the political

Figure 3.8 The Standard Region 1975 (Glasson, 1978)

and administrative structure of the country so that the result of development is more likely to be sustainable regions comprising cities, towns and villages maintaining a closer balance with the rural hinterland.

One important component of sustainable development is the effectiveness of public transport: how it is organized should be a key factor in any decision taken about structures and boundaries for provincial and regional government. Another key factor is public perception and affiliation. The sense of belonging to a place by the provisional and regional electorates is important for any successful devolution of power. There will probably be devolved assemblies for Scotland, Wales and Northern Ireland. In both Scotland and Wales there is a cultural cohesion which makes devolved government to assemblies a natural progression. Northern Ireland with its two traditions seems to have intractable problems for any devolution of power (Rose, 1971). Scotland over many years has been structured around regional administration of local services, which unfortunately will change with the present local authority structuring. A devolved assembly in Scotland may wish to examine this whole exercise again in the light of its own programme of sustainable development. An important question facing the incoming administration in Westminster will be to decide how far the former successful Scottish system of regional devolution can be applied to England and Wales. Alternatively, should local government in England, for example, be restructured around 30 to 35 smaller city regions as advocated by Senior (1965). This chapter has argued for a system of city regions having the responsibility for the provision of local authority services but located within 8 to 10 larger elected regional governments. The region is a flexible concept and its size and boundaries vary according to its purpose; therefore, any regional system of government adopted will have its anomalies. The two guiding principles for regional structures, the development of effective public transport and an electorate with a cultural commitment to the area, should be kept clearly to the fore in any future restructuring exercise.

The role for national government in the task of weaning the general public from the motor car and encouraging freight back onto rail and waterways has five main aspects. They are:

• to enact the legislation for sustainable development
• to provide financial incentives for the support of sustainable developments
• to encourage and support research into sustainable technologies including transport
• to provide planning and development guidance for regional and city authorities.

The role of the European Commission is:

• the coordination of legislation and practice of sustainable development throughout Europe
• the disbursement of grants to weaker regions
• the awarding of capital grants for public transport initiatives
• giving advice about sustainable development
• disseminating knowledge about good practice.

Neither the European Commission nor the national governments should fund road programmes except where it can be clearly shown to be in the interests of sustainable development or economic development in a particularly depressed region.

CONCLUSION

Transport, in addition to bringing benefits to society, also involves large costs. Some of these costs, such as pollution and noise, are incurred directly or indirectly by the users or by those passively affected by developments. Other costs are the result of environmental damage. Many of these costs, particularly from road building programmes and the resulting increase in traffic, have fallen on the community rather than the developers of the transport system or its users. The price signals, such as road construction costs and cost of petrol, given by the transport market, because they ignore environmental costs, mislead the users into believing that personal mobility is cheaper than it really is. The depressed costs have therefore resulted in transport decisions harmful to the community. Individual transport users and developers will continue to make similar decisions, that is, they will continue to make greater use of the roads than real costs would support, until national governments increase fuel pricing and/or introduce road pricing to an extent where the price of road use reflects the true environmental costs. Taxing measures of this nature should be preceded by proposals for improving public transport. Taxes gathered from road users should be earmarked for public transport initiatives. If taxing proposals are implemented before public transport improvements the effect would be felt by the poorer sections of the community, that is, those less able to pay extra taxes: such a tax in that case would be regressive and counter to the main thrust of sustainable development. The Royal Commission on Pollution (1994) believes that the government's commitment to a 5 per cent increase in fuel duty each year is not sufficient to encourage manufacturers to improve the technical efficiency of vehicles and recommends that: 'fuel duty be increased year by year so as to double the price of fuel relative to the price of other goods, by 2005.' If the Commission's targets in this area are to be met and not be regressive then the work on improving public transport in our cities is required urgently.

In addition to measures outlined above, and in parallel with them, the aim of planning policies and urban design solutions must be to reduce the need for movement. Past planning policies and the resulting urban forms have been based on the notion of unrestrained movement and maximum mobility of the individual in his or her private car. Planning and designing urban forms for the reduced need for mobility is a longer term solution to the problems facing society. It depends upon individuals gradually changing their lifestyle to one less dependent on the private car for mobility. The remaining chapters aim to outline urban forms and policies which conform to the philosophy of sustainable development: they are directed towards explaining the new design paradigm for city planning where urban design is viewed as a component of a holistic programme of policies covering all aspects of the culture of city life.

CITY METAPHOR

4

INTRODUCTION

A number of theoretical forms have been suggested for the sustainable city. All are based on the notion of reducing the need for movements by private car and a reduction in the transportation of goods by road. From continental European sources the compact high density city is advocated. At another extreme are proposals for low density decentralized urban areas. A third school of thought suggests urban form based on policies for 'decentralized concentration'. The fourth theoretical position develops the concept of the Sustainable City Region, extending the ideas of Howard and the Garden City Movement (Breheny and Rookwood, 1993; Elkin *et al.*, 1991a; Howard, 1965; Owens, 1991). Authors also differ in their preference for the type of detailed city structure for sustainable development. Such preferences include: linear forms, dispersed structures, centralized and polynucleated urban forms or some variation of the grid. Despite the many theories and the strength of views held by some of the advocates there is, at the moment, little hard evidence in terms of energy efficiency to support any of the structures unequivocally. It is not possible to state categorically that one particular

theoretical urban structure is more sustainable than another. In view of the inconclusive evidence this chapter will review the origins of the ideas for city form. In particular it will discuss the nature of the three main metaphors which have been used as a basis for understanding and coming to terms with the city. The theme of the chapter is symbolism and the city: it will form the basis for the analysis of specific city forms in Chapter 5.

THE FIRST CITIES

City formation is an act of human will. However obscure the reason, however ineffective the means and however tawdry the result, city development or reformation is a conscious act. The act of city foundation may be the decision of a great leader, the result of corporate action by a group or simply accretive development, the outcome of many individual spontaneous actions. Cities first emerged independently in six or seven places, and all after a preceding agricultural revolution. Toffler (1973) in *Future Shock* said that the changes in the society of today are so great that the only comparison in history is the period of change associated with the agricultural revolution which predates civilization. To support his argument Toffler quotes Marek, author of *Gods, Graves and Scholars*, as saying: 'We, in the twentieth century, are concluding an era of mankind five thousand years in length ... we are not as Spengler supposed, in the situation at the beginning of the Christian West, but in that of the year 3000 BC. We open our eyes like prehistoric man, we see a world totally new.' Today amidst great societal change, and with a command of a powerful technology, man is being forced to reassess the effect of unlimited development upon the environment. In the process of coming to terms with the limits of the environment the city is being reinvented in sustainable forms. The creation of the sustainable city is an act of will, a determination to confront the limitations imposed upon human settlement by the environment.

It may be possible to gain some insight into the problems of city design by examining the origin or birthplace of early cities. The birth of cities saw the simple and to a large extent egalitarian life of the village community replaced by a more complex social grouping. The new social grouping in the city exhibited: unequal ownership; a clearly distinguished power structure; warlike tendencies for defence and colonization; a monumental architecture; and a city structure which clearly expressed the highly stratified society. The city was also a vehicle for learning – it is associated with specialists not involved in farming, with the birth of science and writing. The city is also associated with naturalistic forms of art and with craft and distant trade. Wherever this complex heterogenous society developed spontaneously it followed a path which started with a settled society producing a surplus of food. Amongst the Hausa people of Nigeria there are folk tales about the coalescing of small villages to form larger towns (Moughtin, 1985). A reasonable explanation of city formation is based on the hypothesis that stateless societies, which define their solidarity by co-residence on a clearly delimited tract of land, contain in their cultural systems the germs from

which state organization can develop. Stateless societies of this type still exist in West Africa, though they have been absorbed into the large modern nation state. The important principles of political organization are co-residence on common territory and submission to the laws sanctioned by the spirit of the land. These ideas are close to the concept of sovereignty and a body of laws to which all comers are automatically subject. The first occupants of the defined territory have a closer and more intimate relationship with the land than late comers, which provides a potential differentiation between royal and non-royal lineages (Horton, 1971). The reasons for the initial growth of particular cities are lost in antiquity: a particularly effective shrine and its wise man may have attracted gifts or followers from far afield or a chief may have been able to unite disparate groups in a formal coalition for mutual safety or economic benefit.

Early cities functioned as warehouses for the food surplus, break points on trade routes, fortified centres for war or administrative centres for managing great public works such as irrigation schemes or the building of pyramids. Finally early cities were religious centres of importance. The early city is both a great centre of activity and a place of oppression and aggression. Its form and layout was carefully planned to express the power structure in society and to create a theatrical backdrop for religious ceremony. The form of the early city is, therefore, designed to reinforce and enhance the sense of awe and dependence of those subject to the state: at one level it is a device to assist the process of psychological control and domination. The city was, at the same time, a seat of learning and a place for the meeting of minds. As such it was a physical expression of pride in man's achievements, a shelter from both foe and the elements: it also promised hope for the future.

There are common structural and physical features in the layout of cities in most of the great early civilizations of Egypt, Mesopotamia, India, China and Mezoamerica. These common features included the use of the grid, the straight axial street, an orientation of the settlement or its main building to the path of the sun and, with the exception of the inaccessible reaches of the Nile, encircling fortifications (Figures 4.1 to 4.7). Teotihuacan in Mexico, at its most powerful in about AD 450, covered eight square miles and had a population of 200 000. It was laid out on either side of a great ceremonial way running along the valley floor for three miles. The processional route terminated in the north at the Pyramid of the Moon. The Citadel and the Great Compound, the administrative centre and commercial heart of the city, were located at the junction of the north-south processional route and the main east-west cross street. The houses of the nobility were on the main axial street together with the pyramid of the sun (Millon, 1973). The idealized city plan in Pharaonic Egypt is best illustrated by the cemetery at Gizeh where the tombs of the courtiers and high officials crowd close to the pyramid tombs of the Pharoahs. Being close to the Pharaoh in death was obviously as important as it was in life. The Egyptian city of the dead is laid out in a rectangular grid with the less influential members of society buried in graves on the outskirts of the cemetery (Fairman, 1949).

Orientation and relation to the environment was of paramount importance in the planning of the early city. The parts of the building were also organized to be in harmony with the forces of nature and the local environment. Chinese city planning emphasized the need to relate built form with the environment. The sensitive relationship of buildings and the landscape is epitomized by the Chinese city. In China over many centuries the ideal layout for the city was codified as sets of principles. In China the ideal city should be square, regular and oriented correctly: a strong emphasis is on enclosure with gates and approaches to the enclosed areas related to the cardinal directions and to the meaning given to those directions. In addition symmetrical compositions were used to maintain the balance between left and right (Wheatley, 1971).

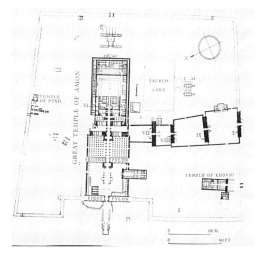

4.1

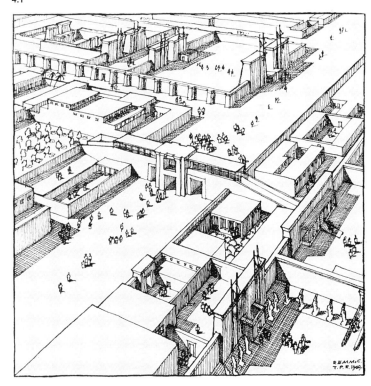

4.2

Figure 4.1 Plan of the Temple at Karnak in Egypt (Stevenson Smith, 1958)
Figure 4.2 Central Area, Amarna in Egypt (18th Dynasty) (Fairman, 1949)

4.3

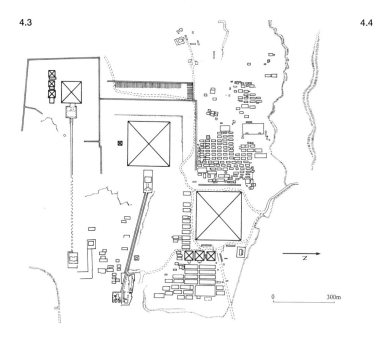

4.4

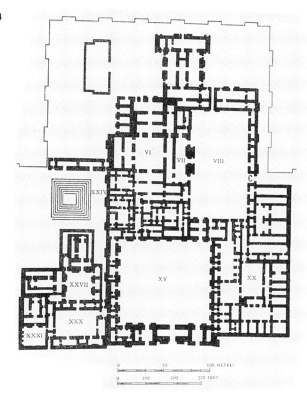

Figure 4.3 City of the Dead, Gizeh, Egypt (Stevenson Smith, 1958)
Figure 4.4 Plan of Sargon's Palace, Khorsabad (Frankfort, 1954)
Figure 4.5 Reconstruction of the Citadel, Khorsabad (Frankfort, 1954)

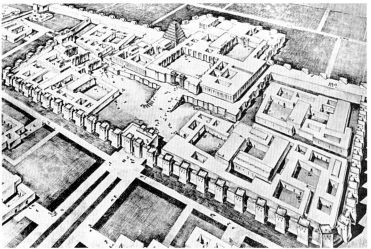

4.5

This complex relationship of physical city form and the environment has developed into an intricate geomancy for environmental layout. This ancient geomancy, *Feng Shui*, is still in current use in Asia; prominent business people in Hong Kong take advice from the local expert in Chinese geomancy for the layout of home and workplace (Lip, 1989).

There are records in Niger as late as 1945 of settlements being laid out according to pre-Islamic cosmology of the Hausa people (Nicolas, 1966). In traditional non-Muslim Hausa society the layout of fields, houses, granaries and towns are regulated by an ancient cosmology which also regulates numerous facets of daily life. Each important activity is the occasion for a preliminary ritual, more or less

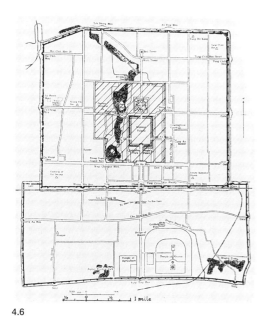

4.6

Figure 4.6 The Chinese city
(Boyd, 1962)

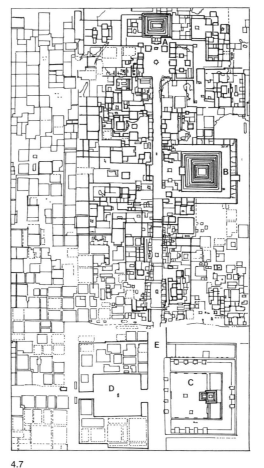

4.7

Figure 4.7 Plan of the
Central Area of Teotihuacan.
(From *Urbanization at
Teotihuacan*, Mexico,
University of Texas Press, ©
René Millon, 1973)

exclusive to the particular activity undertaken. An activity may only be undertaken in a limited and defined space protected from the malevolent spirits which inhabit the world. This space, when defined correctly and orientated within a precise schema, becomes the domain of favourable forces.

In Hausa mythology the eastern and southern cardinal points are masculine, the western and northern ones are feminine. In ritual these cardinal points become personified. By nature, everything is situated facing east. A person is born into this world facing east, enters home facing east and makes sacrifices facing east. A person is surrounded by four beings or groups of beings: male to the front and right; female to the left and to the rear. A man's strong sides, to the front and right, are male and his weak sides to his left and rear are female. The four major spaces surrounding a person are divided into two sexual components. Certain couplings of the spaces are permitted and others forbidden. The relationship between the cardinal points is experi-enced as a matrimonial alliance: the line linking north-east and south-west is a line of sexual exclusion; the axis joining north with south and east with west is the coupling or copulating axes. Space in

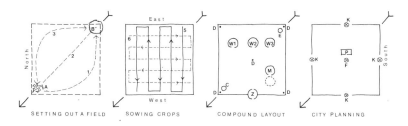

SETTING OUT A FIELD   SOWING CROPS   COMPOUND LAYOUT   CITY PLANNING

Figure 4.8 Hausa spatial structure

non-Muslim Hausa cosmology appears to be a field of convergent and divergent forces which maintain a delicate equilibrium. In setting out a field, a house, a market or a city, the Hausa, through geometrical ritual, try to maintain this delicate balance with the forces of the cosmos (Nicolas, 1966) (Figure 4.8).

Most Hausa fields are square or rectangular, the important axes being north-west/south-east. Crops are sown in a rectangular pattern. Where millet and sorghum are planted together in the same field, they are sown in rows at right angles to each other. Millet, because of the phallic shape of the seed, is thought to be a masculine crop, and is sown in an east-west direction; sorghum, a feminine plant, is sewn in a north-south direction. After such a marriage the millet and sorghum become fertile.

The traditional Hausa compound in Niger, unlike its Muslim counterpart in Nigeria, is laid out with its sides facing the cardinal points. In order to establish a new dwelling the head of the household buries five pots containing charms, one each at the cardinal points and one at the centre of the site. The whole site is surrounded by a boundary wall. Each male adult member of the family arranges his own hut in the compound, the entrance facing west so that entry to the hut is eastward. Houses of the spouses of each man are arranged in a line along a north-south axis: the first wife has the hut to the north and the most junior wife the one to the south. This physical arrangement reflects the social hierarchy of the wives: the first wife is the mistress of the house and is called the 'woman of the north'.

In 1945 when the French moved the cities of

Katsina and Gobir the local inhabitants insisted that the layout of the new towns follow their own planning principles. In both new capitals, the main rites consisted in anchoring the new city into the supernatural structure by placing offerings at the centres of sacred energy in the five nerve-centres of the traditional plan. Charms and talismans were buried at the four doors sited at the cardinal points and at the centre of the main axes where the ruler's palace is located (Moughtin, 1985; Nicolas, 1966).

In this enlightened age we dismiss magical models of the universe together with the gods which sustain the universe. We still, however, accept the psychological efficacy of some of the forms which control behaviour. These ideas still permeate Western city building. China and India have left to posterity the most highly developed heritage of cosmic city models. Nearer home, however, in Africa, Egypt and Etruscan Rome, similar traditions have been followed. These ancient traditions in the symbolic expression of power have been absorbed into Western civilization. For example, the ideal city of the Renaissance was in part a symbol of the mathematical order and unity of the universe. In contrast, Baroque city planning with its use of interconnected axes was used by Pope Sixtus V to stamp his and the Church's authority on Rome. As a device to symbolize power, the axial arrangement of streets became the model for other potentates and was used in Karlsruhe, Germany, by L'Enfant in Washington and by Hausmann in Paris (Figures 4.9 to 4.16). In Ireland the authority of Britain was stamped upon town form. For example, in Roscommon the axis of the long main street terminates in the Court House and the towering shape beyond of the jail where the state's ultimate sanction, execution, took place. The stone-built jail, still in good condition, has had several lives, being converted first into a Lunatic Asylum, then Tourist Office and now the home of boutiques - an example of the conservation and reuse of a building with a grim past (Figures 4.17 and 4.18).

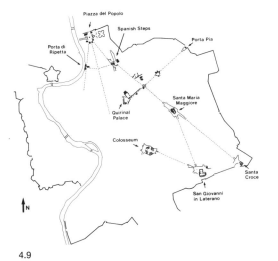

4.9

4.10

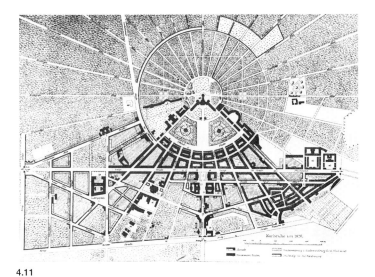

4.11

4.12

Figure 4.9 Rome and Sixtus V

Figure 4.10 Rome: termination of the vista at S. Maria Maggiore

Figure 4.11 Karlsruhe (Morris, 1972)

Figure 4.12 Plan of Washington DC (Lynch, 1981)

Figure 4.13 Washington. (a)
The Capitol; (b) the
Washington Monument
Figure 4.14 Paris:
transformation by Hausmann
Figure 4.15 Paris. (a)
Avenue de L'Opera; (b)
boulevard

4.13a

4.13b

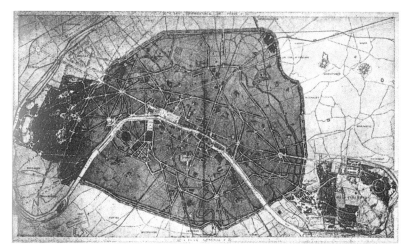

4.14

4.15a

4.15b

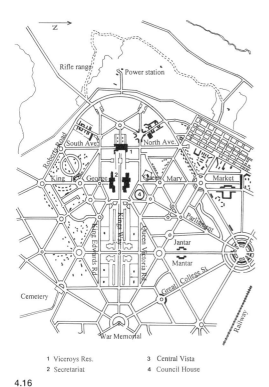

4.17

4.18

4.16

1 Viceroys Res.   3 Central Vista
2 Secretariat   4 Council House

These forbidding instruments of civic power did not end with Hausmann in Paris or even with Lutyens in New Delhi: they persist in the urban structuring of today. These ancient devices of control still maintain their psychological power. For example, a boundary wall or privet hedge with garden gate still encircles the Englishman's semi-detached castle, forbidding entry to unwelcome guests. Less urbanely the high income residential complex in the United States of America is surrounded by a strong protective wall and entered through a guarded gateway. The parade route is still important for British pageantry: the Queen on state occasions takes possession of her capital city, processing from Buckingham Palace to Parliament or

Figure 4.16 Plan of New Delhi
Figure 4.17 Roscommon, Ireland: The courthouse with jail beyond
Figure 4.18 Roscommon, Ireland: former jail

St Paul's Cathedral. The annual parade in Moscow of the Red Army together with its lethal firepower is a blatant exercise in control. In Northern Ireland during the 'marching season' in July the Orange Lodges with pipe band and fearful Lambeg drum reassert the Protestant right to city territory. Provocatively, the Orange march is always planned to invade or skirt sensitive Catholic areas: the route is festooned with arches and banners proclaiming the Protestant ascendency (Figure 4.19). The landmark is a symbol of possession: the possession of the land. The landmark of the modern city is the tall building, which dominates its surroundings. Business corporations have been competing to build the tallest skyscraper, following the example set by the powerful Medieval families in cities like San Gimignano (Figures 4.20 and 4.21). The sheer size and scale of some recent urban developments dominate and are meant to dominate the city and its citizens (Figure 4.22). Bilateral symmetry and elevation are key formal cues which are still used to emphasize position and power. The high table at College is an example in the use of physical cues to reinforce status. Staff and honoured guests sit elevated above the rest of the College while the

4.19

Figure 4.19 Protestant March, Belfast

Figure 4.20 San Gimignano

4.20b

4.20a

4.21

4.22

4.23a

4.23b

Dean, Director or Warden sits at the head of the table on the axis dominating the occasion.

The distribution of land uses, together with the condition and density of the buildings which give the land uses three-dimensional form, graphically illustrate the disparities in wealth and power of the groups occupying city space. Harvey (1973) documented this particular phenomenon, showing how spatial use in a city is organized to favour those with wealth while the powerless members of society are located in the least advantageous positions. In third world cities this fact of urban life is visibly apparent. The poor occupy areas euphemistically called spontaneous development, slums of temporary, make-shift housing without services or sanitation. The poorest of the poor are often consigned to unstable land, that is to areas liable to flash flooding and erosion (Figure 4.23).

How far should the sustainable city of the future jettison these anachronisms from the past? Or how far is it possible to do so? Sustainable development has for its philosophical and intellectual foundation three basic values: equity, citizen participation and

Figure 4.21 New York: roofscape
Figure 4.22 Romania, Palace of the People. (Photograph by Neil Leach)
Figure 4.23 Slums in Nairobi

good husbandry. The sustainable city is one that nurtures both man and the environment: its function as far as man is concerned is one of enabling. This process of enabling is predicated on the notion of democracy, some would suggest a highly participatory democracy. The city should give form to these basic values: a new symbolism is necessary to give expression to the new sustainable city structures. The sustainable city is not one that consigns the poor to cardboard box cultures, a homeless underclass occupying the space beneath the viaduct. The sustainable city does not emphasize private affluence and the policing technologies which maintain the relative peace in enclaves of privilege.

It would be unwise to reject all that originated with the birth of city life in ancient times. A fortunate result of many religious preoccupations, including Chinese geomancy, has often been a harmonious setting for urban development, a by-product of the great care taken with the siting of towns and buildings or the organization of landscapes. This heritage should not be lost in any restructuring of the principles of city planning and design. Many of the ideas originating from groups representing the richer hues of the green movement have overtones of a religious fervour. These more extreme green ideas extol the virtues of living within the laws of nature and attuned to the greater unity of the planet which is personified as an Earth Mother or all-encompassing being. Without going to these extremes it is clear that a respect for nature is something we can and must learn from the earlier periods of man's evolution. An important quality of the nurturing city would be the conservation and development of natural landscapes within its boundaries. Equally important would be the conservation of the building stock: the 'throwaway society' of Toffler has no place in the sustainable city. Conservation and a 'make-do-and-mend' process will inform urban development policies. The conservation movement, however, is more than simply being concerned with the conservation of energy: it represents a philosophy of life which relates people to their traditional roots, to those great urban traditions going back 5000 years.

The skyline of the sustainable city will probably be similar in form to the pre-twentieth century city, pierced only by the towers which remain as a memory of former state, municipal, commercial or religious power centres. Most new additions to the sustainable city will be limited in height to three or four storeys built in a regional architecture using regional materials and probably learning much from local traditions of building. The city spaces, its streets, squares and parks, will be pedestrian centred and designed for a walking pace: transport being predominantly public will thread its way carefully through the pedestrian and cycle dominated network of city pathways. This may sound utopian, and at one level it is, but this city form follows logically from the adoption of a philosophy which accepts sustainability as both necessary and desirable.

According to Lynch (1981) there are three main metaphors which attempt to explain city form. The magical metaphor for the earliest ceremonial centres of religious ritual attempted, as already discussed, to link the city to the cosmos and the environment. The other normative metaphors are the analogy of the machine and the analogy of the organism. The city, like the house, was seen by some modernist architects as 'a machine for living in'. In contrast many planners following Geddes (1949) and Mumford (1938, 1946a, 1961) described the city as organic in an extension of ecological analysis. These main normative theories have generated a series of model city structures, concepts such as: the central city; the star-shaped city; the linear city; the gridiron city; polynucleated cities; and the dispersed city. From these basic concepts of city form additional hybrid concepts have been developed such as the figure-of-eight structure used by Ling for Runcorn New Town (Figure 4.24).

The concept of the city as a machine is quite different from conceptualizing it as a microcosm of the universe, as a perfect unity modelled on the

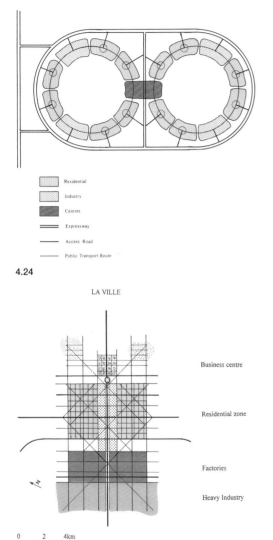

4.24

Residential

Industry

Centres

Expressway

Access Road

Public Transport Route

LA VILLE

Business centre

Residential zone

Factories

Heavy Industry

0   2   4km

4.25

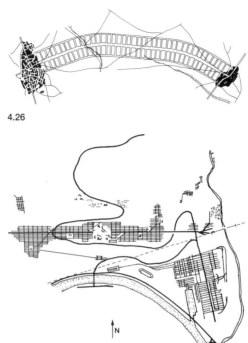

4.26

↑N

4.27

Figure 4.24 Runcorn, structure diagram
Figure 4.25 The radiant city (Le Corbusier, 1967). © FLC/ADAGP, Paris and DACS, London 1997
Figure 4.26 Linear city by Soria y Mata (Hugo-Brunt, 1972)
Figure 4.27 Cité Industrielle by Garnier (Wiebenson, undated)

position by movements such as Futurism and the writings of Le Corbusier (1946, 1947, 1967, 1971), particularly his project for the radiant city (Figure 4.25). Other landmarks in the development of this theme, the city as machine, are the linear suburbs for Madrid by Arturo Soria y Mata in 1894 and the *Cité Industrielle* by Tony Garnier (Figures 4.26 and 4.27). The linear suburbs of Soria y Mata ran between two major radials of the city and were intended to encircle the whole of Madrid. They were designed to provide cheap housing for the middle classes. The main feature of the proposal was a tree-lined boulevard along which ran a private street car. The street car connected the linear arrangement of house plots with transport routes to the city centre. Unlike the later suggestions of

universe. The idea of the city as a machine is not purely a twentieth century phenomenon - its roots lie much deeper. This century, however, the idea has been developed and elevated to a predominant

Figure 4.28 Building by Le Corbusier, Stuttgart
Figure 4.29 Drawing by Le Corbusier (Le Corbusier, 1967). © FLC/ADAGP, Paris and DACS, London 1997
Figure 4.30 Workers' village, Amarna, Egypt (Fairman, 1949)

Garnier the Madrid project was built and operated by the designer's family until the 1930s. Garnier's project for the *Cité Industrielle* was on a much greater scale. The city was to be served by a linear transport route with the land uses segregated and arranged in linear fashion along its length. Both linear urban projects, like the work of Le Corbusier, place great emphasis on the transport system. Le

Corbusier's designs were primarily concerned with the glorification of the motor car while Soria y Mata was developing ideas about mass transport.

The city when thought of as a machine is composed of small parts linked like the cogs in a wheel: all the parts have clear functions and separate motions. In its most expressive form it can have the clarity of a crystal or be a daring exhibition of rationality. In this form it is seen in the heroic or early modern work of Le Corbusier both in his architectural forms and monumental city planning projects (Figures 4.28 and 4.29). It can also appear coldly functional with undertones of social dominance and state control. Miliutin develops the machine theme to an extreme in his ideas for Sotsgorod (Miliutin, 1973). He uses the analogy of the power station or the assembly line for the city. Miliutin also pays great attention to transportation and, like Garnier, separates the city into autonomous parts or separate land uses.

The city as machine is as old as civilization itself. The machine is not only the complex assembly line made famous by Chaplin in *Hard Times*, it also predates the nineteenth century and the industrial

4.28a

4.28b

4.29

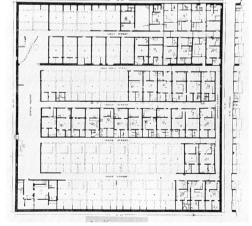

4.30

revolution. A machine can be as simple as a lever or a pulley or that great invention the wheel. The concept of the city as machine can be found in the plans for the workers' villages in Pharaonic Egypt (Figure 4.30). The concept is based on the use of the regular grid plan which is used for ease of development. All the parts are repeated in a regular pattern. The Greeks when establishing a colony also used a standard pattern of development in long narrow blocks, *per strigas* (Figure 4.31). It is an easy and quick method of development. It has often been used throughout history for colonial foundations or the planning of a new city. Another important example is the Roman military camp. The *cardo* and *decumanus*, the main streets of the camp, cross at right angles and connect the main gateways. The layout of the two main axes crossing at right angles was used by the Romans over large landscapes as a method of land sub-division (Figures 4.32 to 4.34). Similar forms of settlement also appear in Medieval Europe and in the later colonization of North and South America (Figures 4.35 to 4.36). The grid plan was also used in the plantation of Ulster. In Derry/Londonderry, the 'Diamond', a public square, is set at the crossing point of the two

Figure 4.31 Housing Layout Olynthus (Lynch, 1981)
Figure 4.32 Plan of the Roman Fort at Housesteads

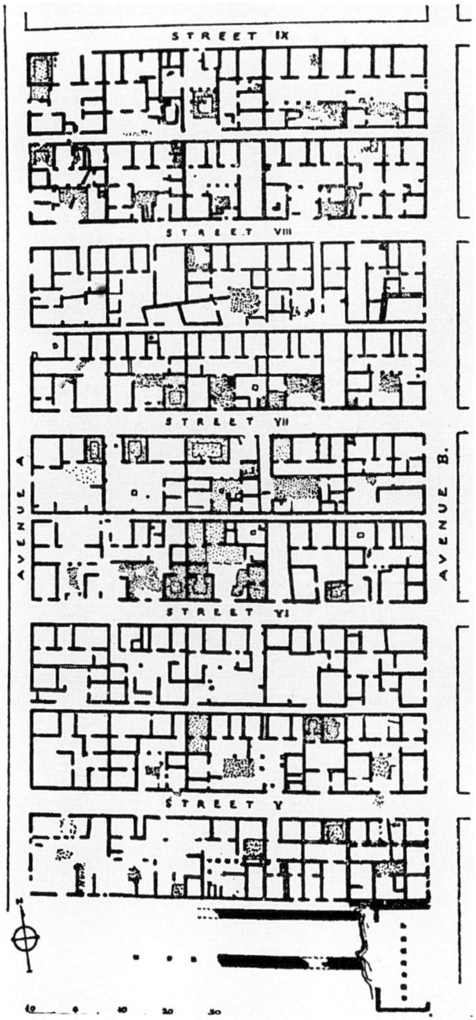

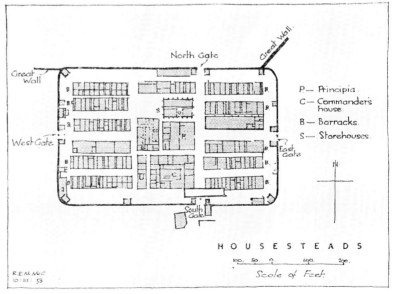

4.31

4.32

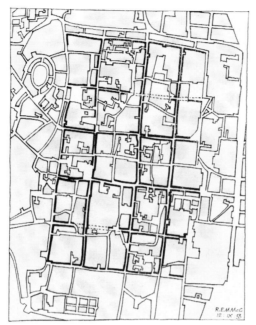

4.33

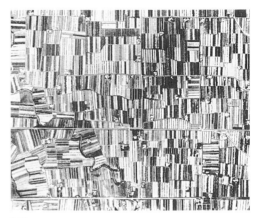

4.34

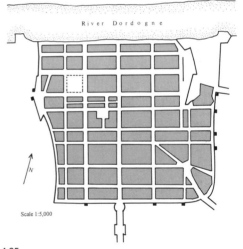

4.35

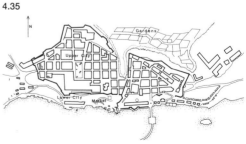

4.36

main routes which cross the town. In the conservation area within the walls of the old planned town, properties are being tastefully rehabilitated and given new uses to serve a tourist industry with great potential (Figures 4.37 to 4.39).

The machine aesthetic, if not explicitly stated by planners and city designers, still permeates much of the practice of city development. The philosophy of the machine aesthetic when applied to the city has many practical advantages. The city when viewed as a machine can be analysed in terms of its parts and therefore it can be structurally improved in sections. The methods employed in the practice of city development include: the techniques of the traffic engineer; the estate management and land assembly skills of the surveyor; and the technical codes devised, initially for public health purposes, by the sanitary engineer. This model of the city, in

4.37

4.39a

4.38

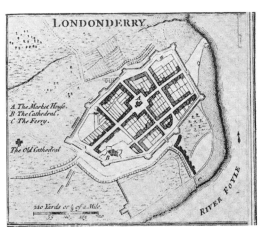

4.39b

Figure 4.37
Derry/Londonderry, Northern
Ireland
Figure 4.38
Derry/Londonderry, Northern
Ireland
Figure 4.39
Derry/Londonderry, The
Diamond (plan from
Camblin, 1951)

practice, results in the mechanical application of building codes and regulations, the enforcement of land use zoning and other planning standards, the uncritical use of mathematical modelling for the solution of transport problems and the advocacy of standardized solutions to building structures. The reasons for city development under the influence of the machine aesthetic, on the surface, appear to be ethically sound. The goals of development would include good access, choice, economic and technical efficiency, quality of life including good health, but above all else the package would emphasize freedom. As motives baldly stated, none could be challenged. Many of the motives which underpin the present mechanistic vision of the city, however, will require to be interpreted and redefined for a world governed by the quite different ethical notions of sustainable development with its emphasis on inter- and intra-generational equity. For example, freedom of the individual, while still important, will be qualified in the light of commitment to the community, to future generations and to the environment in general. Choice will have to be defined in terms of the limits imposed by the environment while access will be determined not by the ability of an individual to pay but be more closely related to the needs of the community. The machine model of the city emphasizes the parts rather than the whole, the individual as opposed to the community; it emphasizes the components of urban form rather than the city as a whole. It is for this main reason that the machine is not an appropriate metaphor for the sustainable city. The metaphor for the sustainable city must be holistic; so too must be the methodology for problem identification and the design concepts used to solve the urban problems.

The third metaphor for the city is the analogy of an organism - the city being seen as organic and composed of cells. According to this metaphor the city can grow, decline and die. This particular way of looking at the city is associated with developments in the biological sciences during the

eighteenth and nineteenth centuries. At one level it can be seen as a reaction to the worst features of the industrial revolution and the rapid growth of cities. It is probably this view of the city which has infused the thinking in many planning schools. In contrast, the dominant theme of architectural education has been the machine aesthetic. This, of course, is a great oversimplification but it is true to say that members of the planning profession have been educated in the mould of Howard, Geddes, Mumford and Olmstead with Sitte, Unwin and Perry giving architectural form to those ideas. Architects to some extent have been more influenced by the writings of Le Corbusier, and many of the other Masters of the Heroic Age of Modernism have also been captivated by the romance of the machine and high-tech solutions to urban problems. Architects also write about organic order, the order of nature as it applies to urban or civic design. A cursory examination of Frank Lloyd Wright's work in the early part of this century sets a pattern for an organic architecture which appears wedded to the landscape (Lloyd Wright, 1950) (Figures 4.40 and 4.41). This particular strand of architectural theory was later taken up by Alexander in *The Oregon Experiment* (1979): '... natural or organic order emerges when there is a perfect balance between the individual parts of the environment and the needs of the whole.' This third organic metaphor for the city is probably the analogy most in tune with the ethos of sustainable development.

The organic model of society may, in part, have its origins in religious communities such as the Moravians in Britain and Ireland or the Shakers in America. The search for a visual identity for a green approach to urban design may learn from the experience of settlements which were: '... designed and planned but were constructed to respect rather than over-ride the environment ... life in the community was uncomplicated and centred on the church. It was recognized that the community had to be fed and money had to be earned, but if the environment was to supply a

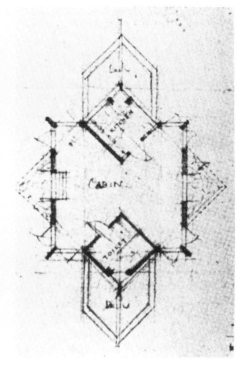

4.40

BARGE, "FALLEN LEAF"

4.41

Figure 4.40 House by Frank Lloyd Wright, plan (Lloyd Wright, 1957). © ARS, NY and DACS, London 1997
Figure 4.41 House by Frank Lloyd Wright, elevation. © ARS, NY and DACS, London 1997

living for the believers, then the environment had to be respected. The Shakers believed that their settlements should reclaim poor land and improve it as part of their realization of the construction of heaven in earth' (Vale and Vale, 1991). Gracehill, Antrim, Northern Ireland, like other Moravian settlements, centres on the chapel, burial ground, school and village green. Around the green cluster the family homes arranged along neat streets organized in a grid pattern. The architecture of Gracehill follows closely the local vernacular style. The buildings are simple, single and two-storey structures built from local materials. It is the idea of the community and the unified architecture giving form to that idea which is a powerful model for sustainable urban form (Figures 4.42 to 4.44).

The main principle of organic planning is the structuring of the city into communities each of which is a self-contained unit for many of the immediate necessities of life. Cooperation rather than competition is emphasized in the organic model for the city. Members of each community are interdependent within a unit of collaboration and mutual support. The healthy community is a mix of diverse individuals and groups tending towards some optimum or balance necessary for the smooth working of the community. Each member or group within the community has a particular role or function in society. In this idealized world of the organic city the community is organized in a hierarchy of units within which are sub-units which in turn are composed of smaller distinctive sub-sub-units.

4.42

4.43

4.44

Figures 4.42 to **4.44**
Gracehill, Antrim, N. Ireland

The early new towns in Britain after the Second World War followed this organic settlement model with parts structured like living cells. New towns such as Harlow by Gibberd are structured on a strict hierarchical basis. The city comprises four main districts each with its own district centre. Districts are sub-divided into neighbourhoods each with a neighbourhood centre. The neighbourhoods further divide into distinct housing areas which in turn sub-divide into housing clusters composed of the basic unit – the home of the nuclear family (Figures 4.45 to 4.47). McKei (1974) devised an interesting organic model for restructuring streets and neighbourhoods in inner city areas. McKei called his process Cellular Renewal, confirming a strong association with the organic model of city planning. His suggestion was to replace comprehensive redevelopment with a more sympathetic small-scale process of rehabilitation and regeneration. There was evidence at the time McKei was working to show that comprehensive redevelopment destroyed many vital communities in the process of renewing the physical infrastructure. Cellular Renewal depends on a survey of individual properties to determine the precise state of the physical structure and the nature of the social unit occupying that structure. Each unit or home was described as a cell. A soft cell, one ripe for immediate action, was one which was in poor condition and where the family was in great need of rehousing. A hard cell, one which could take low priority for redevelopment or rehabilitation, was seen as a property in reasonable condition

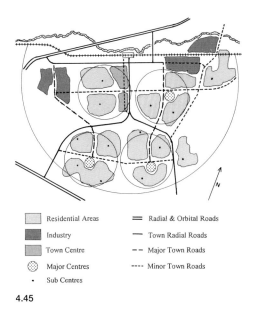

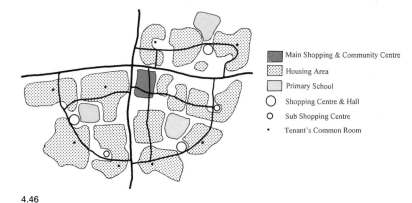

4.46

Main Shopping & Community Centre

Housing Area

Primary School

○ Shopping Centre & Hall

○ Sub Shopping Centre

• Tenant's Common Room

Residential Areas

Industry

Town Centre

Major Centres

Sub Centres

Radial & Orbital Roads

Town Radial Roads

Major Town Roads

Minor Town Roads

4.45

4.47

Figure 4.45 Harlow New Town, structure diagram (Gibberd, 1955)
Figure 4.46 Harlow, neighbourhood structure (Gibberd, 1955)
Figure 4.47 Harlow, housing cluster

and perhaps occupied by an elderly person who was unwilling to move. Such a property could be left until the occupant died or moved to sheltered accommodation. This organic concept of the neighbourhood proposed a slow renewal or rehabilitation of the properties in piecemeal fashion which did not disturb the community and which was in tune with the growth and decay of the families.

CONCLUSION

The organic city in general has an optimum size: the city is born and, like organisms, comes to maturity then persists if healthy. In the past cities have died, though, unlike organisms, have been resurrected on the same site. City health is maintained according to the organic model only as long as the balance of its components is maintained. Excess growth is managed by the propagation of new colonies. The

organic model for the city is most in tune with the concept of sustainable development when, in particular, it takes on the attributes of ecology. The analogy for the optimum stage in the development of the city is the ecological climax, that is, where there is a diversity in its components which maintains the balance between the energy inputs and outputs including recycling, waste reduction and pollution levels. According to this model of the city, decay is apparent in settlements when this delicate balance breaks down and excessive growth occurs or when self-healing ceases; the result can be likened to cancer or uncontrolled growth.

In developing a normative theory for the sustainable city the metaphor of the city as an organism has a clear advantage over both the concept of the eternal city of the gods, the microcosm of the universe and also the idea of the clockwork city of honest industry. The main contribution of organic theory is its holistic view of the city as a part of nature. The organic city is not set in an idealized but remote cosmos, nor is it limited to the pursuit of the technological control of the environment. Sustainable and organic city theory share the fundamental goal of conceptualizing settlement as a whole: the elements or parts of the city are not strictly separate but supportive. The organic city has the delight, diversity and subtlety of the natural world: indeed it is part of nature.

In both sustainable city theory and organic theory, process and form are one. While the process of city structuring results in the form, the form is apparent from the beginning: the pattern as Alexander *et al.* (1987) suggests is in the seed, at the point of origin. The growth of any acorn results in an oak tree and while each tree is composed of similar elements linked in specific ways, no two trees are identical. So too with the sustainable city, the pattern is established by the principles used for the design and linkage of the parts. The design of the parts and the nature of their linkages will form the content of later chapters. Certain forms, however, are associated with and act as symbols for the organic city, the most obvious being the green belt around cities and open landscaped areas within urban areas. Other forms associated with the organic city are buildings which appear to be grounded in the earth or to be a part of the environment through the use of traditional materials and local forms in harmony with the landscape. The urban structure of the organic city is non-geometrical: roads follow a curving path while spaces in the city are picturesque and in the manner of Sitte's ideal. In terms of the overall structure the pattern of the organic city has a distinct edge between town and country, a definite centre and clearly defined parts, districts or neighbourhoods. These symbols of the organic city appear to be useful concepts for the purpose of discussing the possible form of the sustainable city of the future. These concepts may form the basis from which to develop a design tradition for the sustainable city.

The organic metaphor has certain limitations. The city is not a tree (Alexander, 1965). Cities do not grow, reproduce and heal themselves: the agent for their change is man. Describing a city in terms of its heart, lungs or arteries does not help in the analysis of the problems of city centre decline, pollution and gridlock on city streets. Such terms for the parts of a city based on human and animal anatomy, however, may have value in suggesting ideas for problem solutions through analogy (de Bono, 1977; Gordon, 1961). For analytical purposes the most fruitful metaphor from nature is the ecosystem, that is, a stable arrangement of flora and fauna delicately balanced with other elements of the environment. The relationship or nature of the connection between the components of the ecosystem can be analysed and modelled. The effect, therefore, can be estimated of changes to any components in the system. McLaughlin (1969) and Chadwick (1966) and others in the 1960s were advocating this method for planning: the complex nature of the methods for the day-to-day practice of planning may have led to its too early dismissal. In aiming to develop sustainable cities it may be necessary to re-examine the technique of systems analysis to see if it could be used for a holistic presentation of urban problems. Systemic thinking is probably the conceptual framework which is essential for the analysis of urban processes of great complexity.

CITY FORM

5

INTRODUCTION

This chapter examines the relationship of urban form and sustainable development. In particular it outlines a typology of city forms. The three main archetypal urban forms discussed are: the linear city; the city set out in the form of a grid; and the highly centralized or inward looking city. The form of each archetypal plan may be modified by the prevailing metaphor: the city as a replica or model of the cosmos; the city as a machine; or finally the city as an organism. The grid layout, for example, has been used to express physically both the cosmic and the machine city metaphors (Lynch, 1981). More rarely, as in Gracehill, it has also been used to express the community needs of the settlement built according to the organic metaphor. The Chinese model city uses a grid to relate the city to a cosmic structure (Boyd, 1962; Wheatley, 1971; Wright, 1977). In Chinese culture the city is designed as a microcosm of the universe but complete in itself. The grid when used to give form to the city as a machine emphasizes the autonomous parts, each having a distinct function. Devices such as size, scale or the imposing axis are used to give emphasis to the dominance of the car or the world of business: they

are never used in this context to mirror the universe. This difference can be illustrated graphically by the contrast between a Roman encampment or the project for a contemporary city by Le Corbusier with the Mandala which sets out the Indian ideal pattern for city structure (see Figures 4.25, 4.32 and 5.1).

Ancient Indian city planning theory is based upon texts, *Silpasastras*, defining the methods of land sub-division which control the evil forces of chaos (Rowland, 1953; Dutt, 1925; Shukla, 1960). The Mandala adopted to give form to the city comprised a set of enclosing rings of development divided into squares, the most powerful point being the centre. Main movements, particularly processions through the enclosures, are clockwise following the apparent direction in which the sun moves in the northern hemisphere. Madurai (Figure 5.2), dating from the sixteenth and seventeenth centuries, follows the idealized pattern of the mandala. There are encircling streets, no radials as such and the use of a deformed but clear grid, while the most holy buildings occupy a central position.

The three main archetypal city forms have been converted into an array of hybrid types of city structures to serve different ends. The particular form of

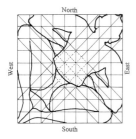

5.1

5.2

Figure 5.1 Indian Mandala
Figure 5.2 Madurai, India
(Lynch, 1981)
Figure 5.3 Medieval linear
settlement, Olney, Bucks
(Beresford, 1967)

a city may owe its shape to a number of factors such as imperatives of location, land values, or social structure. The choice of a structural concept for a new urban foundation may have been influenced by attitudes to: density; the form and distribution of central area functions; the predominant means of transport; the location of social infrastructure or places of work; and, more generally, ideas about ideal forms of lifestyle. Narrowing the range for use in sustainable development is a daunting task. Fortunately in Britain there are a number of new towns built after the Second World War which offer a wide range of urban structures available for close study (Osborn and Whittick, 1977).

LINEAR URBAN FORMS

Linear urban forms can be found in many unplanned developments of the Middle Ages (Beresford, 1967) (Figure 5.3). However, they are more usually a product of the industrial revolution. They are most

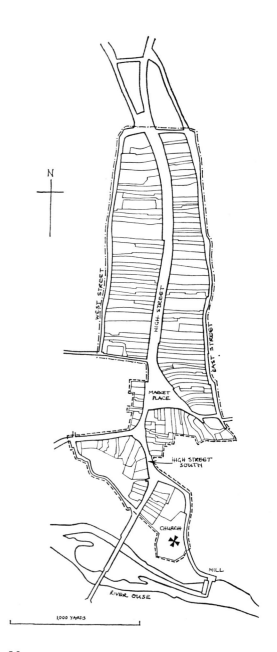

5.3

closely associated with the metaphor of the city as a machine. The main feature of the linear urban form is its ability to deal with the rapid and efficient mass movement of people and goods within and between cities. A further quality of the linear structure is its ability to deal, in theory, with infinite growth. Two early examples of linear urban forms are Ciudad Lineal by Soria y Mata for the suburbs of Madrid and Cité Industrielle by Tony Garnier (Figures 4.26 and 4.27). The linear suburb for Madrid has been discussed in the last chapter while the Cité Industrielle has been mentioned before. However, other features of this project are worthy of discussion in the light of sustainable urban form. The most important locational factor for Garnier's ideal city was to be an energy source (Wiebenson, undated). Garnier's prescient choice of energy source, hydro-electric power, foreshadows much of today's preoccupation with renewable energy. The form and layout of housing in the Cité Industrielle was to be governed by orientation. The design aim of the building form was to achieve good ventilation and high levels of sunlight into all homes. Both of these qualities are important considerations for the design of sustainable housing where the aim is to maximize solar gain and reduce the need for mechanical ventilation (Figures 5.4 and 5.5). Garnier's ideas about land use zoning was also a precursor of one of the important but perhaps less sensitive innovations of modern city planning.

Other manifestations of the modern movements in architecture and planning were developing in Russia early in this century. Early in post-revolution Russia the discipline of architecture was examined to see if it could serve the needs of the proletariat rather than the expensive taste of the aristocracy or wealthy bourgeoisie. Two main groups with conflicting ideas emerged: they were, the 'urbanists' and 'de-urbanists'. The urbanists were advocating high rise, high density development: 'a network of enormous communal houses with integrated collective services' (Houghton-Evans, 1975). The de-urbanists, in contrast, suggested communities of houses

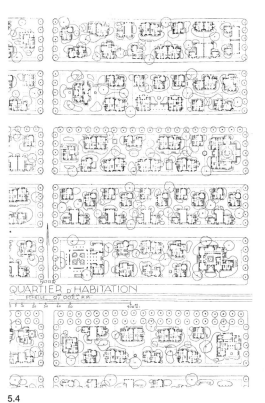

5.4

5.5

Figure 5.4 Cité Industrielle, residential quarter (Wiebenson, undated)
Figure 5.5 Cité Industrielle, housing (Wiebenson, undated)

Figures 5.6 and **5.7** The linear city of Miliutin (Kopp, 1970)

dispersed throughout the countryside. The aim of the de-urbanist was to end the distinction between town and country: 'The agricultural areas must become centres not only for producing but also for processing raw materials ... Rural housing ... is a prerequisite of production ... The transfer of manufacturing industry to the sources of raw materials, the integration of industry and agriculture, is likewise a new condition of residential planning and population distribution. But the new planning raises the problem of cheap housing built of local materials.' The view of the de-urbanist is holistic, the city is seen in its total environment: 'We must stop designing piecemeal and start to plan whole complexes, to organise the distribution of production and the territorial distribution of industry and housing over entire economic regions of the Soviet Union' (Kopp, 1970). Many fine thoughts are contained in the manifesto of the de-urbanists; some no doubt are in tune with the ideas being put forward in the name of sustainability. The developments in what was the Soviet Union did not, however, live up to the high sounding ideals of the 'de-urbanists'. The agenda of the urbanist was politically more acceptable, with state control and planning resulting in a dehumanized urban development. The planned exploitation of the environment to sustain the process of urbanization has also led to environmental degradation on a grand scale: a degradation which equals anything the free market of the West can achieve.

A significant contribution made by the de-urbanist was the development of the idea of the linear city. Muliutin in his writings and in his inter-war plan for Stalingrad used the linear concept as a flexible extensible form for the city and its region. According to de-urbanist theory, which Miliutin followed, populated areas were to be associated with a major road; dwellings were to be located in the countryside within easy reach of urban facilities dispersed in a ribbon about 300 metres wide and arranged on either side of the road. Each facility was planned to occur at different frequencies depending on the population required to support the service (Figure 5.6 and 5.7).

The linear city concept has occupied the minds of many urbanists since Miliutin. The Modern Architectural Research Group, who became known as MARS, were interested in applying the ideas of CIAM (*Congrès Internationeaux d'Architecture Moderne*) to conditions in Britain. They produced a master plan for the rebuilding of London after the destruction caused by the Second World War. It became known as the MARS Plan for London. The MARS group saw London as a deteriorating factory which was technically inefficient. MARS proposed a

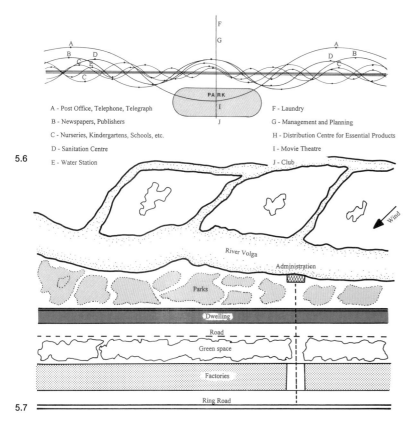

A - Post Office, Telephone, Telegraph
B - Newspapers, Publishers
C - Nurseries, Kindergartens, Schools, etc.
D - Sanitation Centre
E - Water Station
F - Laundry
G - Management and Planning
H - Distribution Centre for Essential Products
I - Movie Theatre
J - Club

5.6

5.7

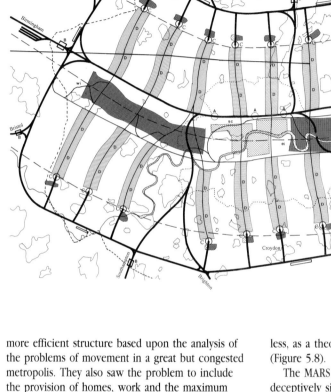

Residential districts
Commercial administration
Political administration
sc   Shopping Centres
cc   Cultural centre and park
wi   Western industries
ei   Eastern industries and Port of London
      Local industries, possibly combined
          with satellite towns
A - Main passenger station
B - Main goods station
C - Secondary goods station
D - Market halls

Figure 5.8 MARS plan
(Korn and Samuelly, 1942)

more efficient structure based upon the analysis of the problems of movement in a great but congested metropolis. They also saw the problem to include the provision of homes, work and the maximum possible number of amenities including adequate open space for the population. The approach was one of problem-solving, that is, discerning the salient characteristics of the problem, London, then devising: 'a master plan, a grid on which the town can be developed' (Korn and Samuelly, 1942). The plan was not based on a 'grid' in the conventional sense in which the word will be used later in the chapter. The MARS Plan for London was based on a series of linear forms arranged around the transport network. Each structural unit, though in practice constrained by existing development, was neverthe-

less, as a theoretical form, capable of expansion (Figure 5.8).

The MARS concept for the transport grid is deceptively simple. The reality, however, based on the rational movements of people and goods, led to the development of complex systems of interchange between great transport highways. An aim of the plan was to increase the importance of public transport: 'With an excellently organized public transport system, the number of people going to and from town in private cars will be few, being confined to certain professions. Other private cars would serve mainly for pleasure' (Korn and Samuelly, 1942). The group were also advocating the design of highways for use only by public transport. These bus-only highways would be without interruption by crossings and the service was to be strictly timed by schedule. Here in Britain in 1942 was the origin of the idea for an integrated public transport system of rail and bus. Furthermore, the urban form was designed to give equal importance to 'organized transport', or public vehicles, as to 'flexible transport', or the private car.

The MARS plan envisaged residential belts 1.5 miles wide by 8 miles long. The housing density was to be 55 persons per acre, which is the figure being quoted by some working in the field of sustainable development (Barton *et al.*, 1995). 'Green wedges' extending from the periphery of London to the city centre were to provide sites for recreation, health and education. All inhabitants would be living within walking distance of both borough centre and landscaped areas. The MARS group suggested the idea of landscape fingers connecting the countryside with the city centre, which may also prove to be a useful feature to be incorporated into a plan for the sustainable city of the future. The MARS Plan for London is a fine theoretical exploration of urban form. In practice, however, it was the ideas of Howard as interpreted by Abercrombie which were finally accepted as the basis for planning London and its region in the post-war period (Abercrombie, 1945).

A number of the second generation of new towns built after the Second World War in the 1960s were clearly based upon the linear city concept. Notable amongst these linear new town plans are: Redditch; the linear city for Central Lancs comprising Preston, Leyland and Chorley; Runcorn; and the first proposals for both Telford and the new city for North Bucks.

In his report on a regional study for Northamptonshire, Bedfordshire and Buckinghamshire, Hugh Wilson advocates a linear structure based upon a public transport spine linking all new development (Wilson *et al.*, 1965). Wilson also developed this idea for the new town of Redditch, for which he was commissioned in 1964. The basic structuring concept for Redditch is shown

in Figure 5.9. The fundamental feature of the plan is a road for public transport, unimpeded by other vehicles. Community facilities were to be placed on this public transport spine at the bus stops which were to act as the foci of the districts. The districts were to be of mixed use and to contain residential, industrial, recreational and other related land uses. All parts of the districts were planned to be within half a mile or 10 minutes walking distance of the district centre and its bus stop. These proposals in 1964 seem as fresh today as the time they were written: such proposals could appear in any proposals for sustainable development.

A regional study for mid-Lancashire included a proposal for a linear city incorporating Preston,

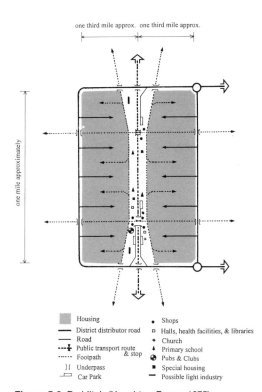

Figure 5.9 Redditch (Houghton-Evans, 1975)

Leyland and Chorley (Matthew, 1967). The three existing settlements were to be connected by a triple strand of routes, the central one being a 'community route' for use by public transport only. Both outer routes were to be roads for the motor car. The city region was planned for a population of 500 000 housed in Radburn style residential development on both sides of the public transport route (Figure 5.10).

Arthur Ling, who had worked on the MARS plan for London, was the first planner since Soria y Mata to implement a plan specifically designed for public transport. Runcorn in Cheshire was the extension of an existing settlement with a population of 30 000. It already had an industrial base and Ling planned to increase the population to 100 000, attracting additional employment outlets onto a strong local economic base. The population was arranged in a dispersed linear form: 'A linear arrangement of new residential communities, on either side of a spinal public transport route, has been evolved so that the majority of people will be within five minutes

walking distance, or 500 yards, of a route which is especially reserved for buses' (Ling, 1967). It was not possible to use a pure linear form for the town because of the existing development. Ling's solution to the problem was both simple and elegant: he turned the linear structure in on itself to form a figure-of-eight with the town centre in a focal position (Figure 4.24). The spine of the plan is the bus-only road which links all the neighbourhoods to each other and to the town centre. The expressways for private cars bound the urban area and have spur roads that enter each neighbourhood but do not traverse them to form direct connections. This is the only British new town which was designed primarily for public transport:

> In many post-war new towns and suburban extensions, the tendency has been to design the road layout for private vehicles and then route buses along the most appropriate roads. This has led in some instances to a minimum use of public transport which has made it uneconomical to provide socially convenient services. It is considered that the contribution of public transport to a new town is of such importance that it is essential to plan for it as an integral part of the town structure and not to provide it as an afterthought (Ling, 1967).

How appropriate these words sound today. Runcorn is a promising model for a sustainable city even though some of the early housing left much to be desired and was demolished (Figures 5.11 to 5.14).

Two other linear town proposals in Britain during the 1960s, though never implemented, carried forward the development of this concept in interesting ways. The first proposal for Dawley (later to become Telford) arranged the town centre functions in linear fashion along a town walkway. The town walkway was joined to form a loop. At the centre of the loop was the central town park. Encircling the doughnut-shaped town was open countryside. Each residential area, a section or portion of the doughnut, was linked to the town walkway, central park

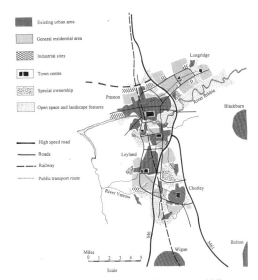

Figure 5.10 Central Lancashire (Matthew, 1967)

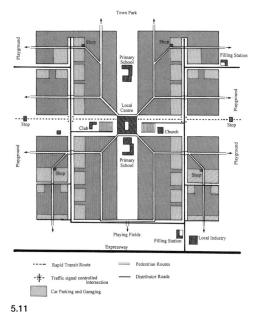

5.11

5.12

5.13

Figure 5.11 Runcorn, a
community (Ling, 1967)
Figure 5.12 Runcorn, town
centre
Figure 5.13 Runcorn,
busway

and open countryside by pedestrian paths (Figure
5.15). Vehicular access is quite independent of the
pedestrian routes and takes the form of a development of the Radburn system.

The first plan for Milton Keynes was also based
on a linear concept for urban structure. The original
proposal for Milton Keynes is far more interesting

for those concerned with sustainable development
than the 'drive-in-city' which was finally implemented. The County of Buckingham in 1959 was
seeking ways of dealing with the considerable
increase in population which was then forecast. The
County proposed to house the extra population in a
regional city of 250 000. The city plan at that time

5.14a

5.14b

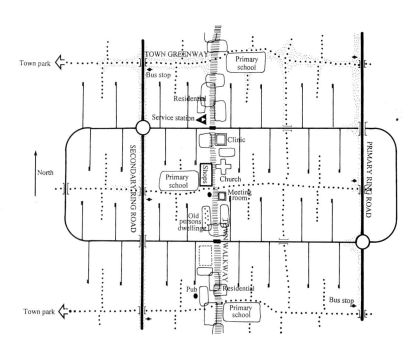

5.15

was to be based on a linear concept, the form being governed by public transport with development taking place at stopping places on that route. The public transport system suggested for the new city was to be a monorail. The community size was to be 5000 to 7000 and each such community was to be centred on a monorail station with a maximum walking distance of 7 minutes from the station to the housing. The overall density of the township was to be 50 persons to the acre. The housing was to comprise mainly patio houses of one or two storeys in height but with higher blocks near to the station (Houghton-Evans, 1975).

The first plan for Milton Keynes was to comprise four main circuits of linear groups of townships. The townships were to be connected by two inter-linked circuits of public transport joining home,

work and the central city. The central city was itself of linear form and capable in theory of expansion. The townships were also served by an independent road system giving Radburn type access to the housing (Figure 5.16). The monorail system was found to cost more than the infrastructure required for 100 per cent car usage. With monorail, however: 'the cost per passenger mile would be much less than travel by car, and a modest rate charge would allow the system to be paid for, operated and replaced after 60 years for much less than the alternative high capacity road system which would be needed' (Houghton-Evans, 1975). Taking account of the true environmental costs would without doubt tip the advantages further in the direction of the monorail in any debate where sustainable development is an important consideration.

Figure 5.14 Runcorn, early housing
Figure 5.15 Telford (Houghton-Evans, 1975)

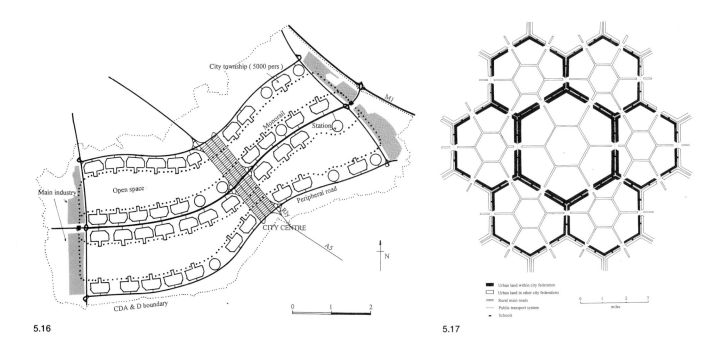

5.16

5.17

Figure 5.16 Monorail city
(Houghton-Evans, 1975)
Figure 5.17 Linear city
(March, 1974)
Figure 5.18 Fresnel's
square

The concept of the linear city has been developed into an idea for an urban structure stretching *ad infinitum* along transport and infrastructure corridors which cross regional and national borders (March, 1975). Central place activities would be located along these corridors in a manner similar to the one suggested by Miliutin. Unlike the proposals of Miliutin and the Soviet de-urbanists, the March proposals make a clear distinction between town and country. In this particular theoretical proposition every part of the city would be close to the countryside but it would still be possible to drive through country areas without seeing a town (Figure 5.17).

The starting point for March (1974) was 'to think line not blob'. The theory relied for its intellectual rigour upon the geometry of Fresnel's square (Figure 5.18). Each successive 'annular ring' of Fresnel's square diminishes in width from the middle but is exactly the same area as the central

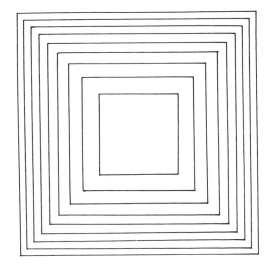

5.18

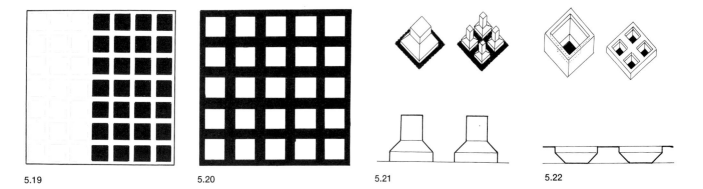

5.19   5.20   5.21   5.22

square, the 'blob'. If the rings are regarded as possible ways of arranging buildings or areas of urban development then each poses different problems of internal arrangement, servicing, lighting, heating and the use of external space. The greatest difference is between the central space, a pavilion of development, and the outer space, a courtyard type development (Figures 5.19 and 5.20). For example, imagine these two areas, the central square, the 'blob', and the area at the perimeter, the 'line', being developed with four-storey buildings. The outer 'line' of development would present fewer problems in terms of achieving reasonable levels of natural lighting and ventilation than the inner 'blob' of development. The pavilion type development on the inner square would require light wells of some description: in short it would require either buildings of greater height or an extension of the ground area to achieve the same building volume as the outermost line of development (Figure 5.21 and 5.22).

March (1974) points to the history of urban development to support his theory for the linear city. Development in the past has often been built along the route of a thoroughfare for reasons of economy (Figure 5.3). March in his theory did not, however, take into account the equally natural development of central places along transport routes. Such central places act as magnets attracting development to specific locations in ways Christaller discovered in Germany (Christaller, 1933 and 1966). This attraction of the central place distorts the pure form of linear development, creating real estate of high value. The result is the sort of blob of development March advises his readers to dismiss from their minds.

The arrangement of accommodation along the perimeter of a single plot has a long and well documented history. This form of plot development can be seen in, for example, the courtyard house of the classical world, and it is also a typical house form in some parts of Africa (Moughtin, 1985; Denyer, 1978) (Figure 5.23). This may prove to be a useful concept for the arrangement of accommodation on a well defined site and an appropriate form for the street block (Martin, 1974). The magnification of the concept for use on a regional, national and supra-national scale is to remove all meaning from the original idea; a linear city stretching from Birmingham through London across the Channel to Europe and along the Rhine belongs to the world of fantasy, if not to nightmare. Such suggestions do little justice to an elegant concept devised by Soria y Mata for the suburbs of Madrid. A limited use of linear forms for public transport corridors may prove to have a great potential in achieving local sustainable development.

Figure 5.19 Pavilion development (March, 1974)
Figure 5.20 Courtyard development (March, 1974)
Figure 5.21 Pavilion development (March, 1974)
Figure 5.22 Courtyard development (March, 1974)

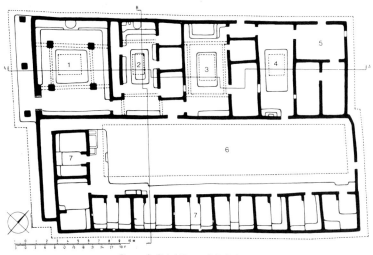

Figure 9 *Chief Uzana Edigi's house*

Key
1 Ogbe
2 Ikun-na-Aruerna
3 Ikun-na-Nogiukpo
4 Ikun-na-Aruiye
5 Enogie
6 Harem courtyard
7 Women's apartment –
   Ogua – Oderie

5.23a

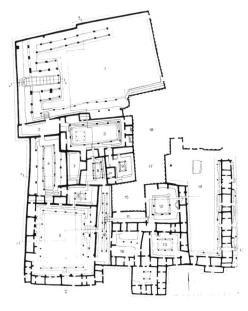

Yoruba
Afin Akure

5.23b

Figure 5.23 African
courtyard house. (a) Igbo;
(b) Yoruba (Dmochowski in
Moughtin, 1988)

THE GRID PLAN

The grid plan has been used in a number of ways to structure the city: it has also been used with all three normative city models. The grid, for example, was used at Teotihuacan to give form to a city as a religious symbol (Figure 4.7). It has also had wide use as a tool for land sub-division in colonial cities and new towns, where it is used to express the technical demands of a machine aesthetic. In contrast, Frank Lloyd Wright in Broadacres proposed a grid of high capacity roads extending over the regional landscape with each family occupying one acre of land on which to build an extensible do-it-yourself family home (Lloyd Wright, 1958). Lloyd Wright, in extolling the virtue of the nomad, the pioneer and wide open spaces while denigrating the old form of the city and 'pig piling' in high rise buildings, was expressing his ideals of back to nature and the organic city (Figure 5.24). The gridiron is a versatile method of city structuring which can be used to give form to quite different values.

The grid plan can take five main forms:

- the grid as a hierarchy of boxes, each nesting within one another
- the grid as a strict orthogonal geometrical figure, often called a 'gridiron plan', or checker-board pattern
- the directional grid
- the triangular grid
- an informal lacework of paths.

When associated with cosmic symbolism the grid is divided and sub-divided into boxes within boxes. The hierarchy of finer grids of nesting boxes found in Southeast Asian cities express in physical terms an equally hierarchical system of religious and civil power, each level of authority having its own appropriate location, colour and building materials. The enclosures, gateways and symmetrical approaches to each box were imbued with a magical protection which was reinforced by the ceremonies used both to found the city and to sustain its socio-political structures. The geometry and geomancy, the foundation for the structure of the grid used in many ancient cities, has little relevance for the sustainable city of the twenty-first century, except as an artifact of great historical and archaeological value. The search for a symbol of sustainable city form lies in other directions.

The grid becomes a 'gridiron pattern' when it is composed of standard square insulae similar to the standard structure used by the Romans for colonial settlements. In theory the gridiron plan permits the expansion of the settlement in all directions by the addition of further insulae at its perimeter. The use of the gridiron plan has proved to be a useful tool for the efficient sub-division and sale of development land. During the initial stages of urban development the insulae tend to be open with scattered properties. During later stages the frontages of the insulae are completed. Later still the back yard spaces are infilled with buildings. Before development pressures result in an expansion at the edge of the settlement the buildings in the old town are demolished: the central insulae are redeveloped, building heights throughout the older parts of town increasing. The traditional grid structure has proved in the past to be a most sustainable form surviving many centuries of development and redevelopment (Figure 4.33). For those advocating compact settlements as being the ideal model for sustainable urban form, the gridiron plan offers scope for further experiment. In its traditional form, however, the orthogonal grid appears to

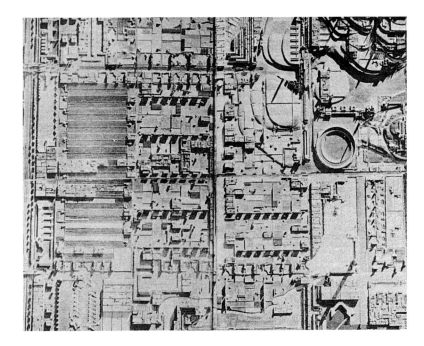

have limits of scale and may be of most use for settlements or parts of settlements which can be traversed by foot, that is, about a half mile square as in Gracehill, N. Ireland (Figures 4.42 to 4.44). Beyond this size the gridiron plan becomes visually dull and loses clarity; as Lynch would say, the form has a weak image.

A variation of the gridiron is the directional grid. The directional grid has some of the properties of linear structures: parallel roads in one direction are made more important which implies axial growth in two directions in a similar fashion to the linear city. A further variation is the triangular grid consisting of parallel road systems in three directions. The triangular grid adds flexibility of through movement. When combined with the orthogonal grid, as in L'Enfant's plan for Washington, it adds the possibility of easy diagonal movements (Figure 4.12). The triangular grid and other non-rectangular lattice structures based on it, such as the hexagonal grid,

Figure 5.24 Broadacres (Lloyd Wright, 1958). © ARS, NY and DACS, London 1997

Figure 5.25 Lacework grid
(Lynch, 1981)

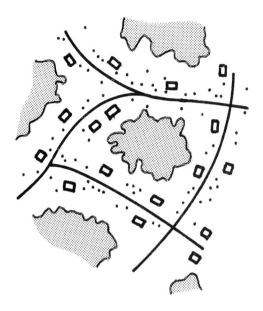

produce awkward road junctions and difficult building plots. One of the few practical uses of the triangular grid is the plan for New Delhi by Lutyens
(Irving, 1981) (Figure 4.16). Finally there is the
informal grid of streets, or lacework of paths, which
Alexander described in 1975 (Figure 5.25).
Alexander uses the term to identify a low-density
settlement in which the traffic routes are widely
spaced, and the insulae are occupied by large open
spaces consisting of farmland, intensive market
gardens, wooded areas and wild countryside. The
frontage onto the main roads is a linear strip of
housing and other urban uses. During this century,
particularly in its second half, the grid when it has
been used for urban development has not been the
rigid gridiron pattern but one of the more informal
variations of the concept.

In the 1960s there were a number of important
studies for new towns which gave priority to
planning for the free movement of the motor car.
These studies came to the conclusion that some
form of the grid best served the needs of the car. It
is not the conclusion of these studies which is
important for sustainable development, but the rational thought process which went into their construction. An exploration of sustainable urban forms
should use these studies as models of a design
process. They follow in single-minded pursuit of
clearly defined objectives, which in the case of
these studies is the overarching goal for personalized transport. For a study of sustainable urban form
the goal is to design structures predominantly for
the use of public transport supported by walking
and cycling, the private car taking low priority with
the limited exception of its use by those with
special needs. Despite many of the new town
studies of the 1960s dismissing the utility of the
neighbourhood they all, without fail, replaced it
with population groupings resident on a fixed piece
of land. Often the size of the grouping is based
upon the amount of road traffic the community
would generate and the best ways in which that
traffic can be absorbed into the main road system.
Sustainable development would start from a different premise in deciding a population size for a
district or quarter. Community groupings in a
sustainable settlement would be dependent more
upon the level of population required to support
public transport, political parameters and the catchment areas for schools and other social facilities.

Buchanan, in the early 1960s, used the orthogonal grid for his theoretical study of Marylebone in
Central London (Buchanan, 1963). Buchanan was
concerned to define the dimensions of his grid
according to the traffic the superblock or insulae
would generate. If the grid of bounding roads are
too widely spaced too much traffic is generated by
the land uses within the block for the roads to
carry and the internal roads within the insulae
would have to be designed as high capacity
primary routes. If, on the other hand, the distance
between the roads forming the main grid is too
small the number of junctions in the overall grid
would be too close and too many to facilitate free-
flowing traffic. Buchanan's calculations showed

that a grid 4500 ft square permitted the highest car generation, 12 200 cars per hour. This is the limitation or ceiling for traffic movement in an orthogonal grid. This limitation in the road system is caused mainly by the number of junctions, which ultimately determines the capacity of the system (Figure 5.26). It was Buchanan's study which influenced the further development of the grid in the British new towns of the late 1960s and 1970s. The orthogonal grid is a form of road system which is particularly suited to the free flow of traffic over a large urban area: 'Since access to a high-speed road must be limited to a few junctions, a system intended to distribute traffic over a wide area may quite logically be arranged as a gridiron, and this in contrast to the linear form, has been exploited ... by planners more concerned with achieving an even spread of traffic over a town

than with concentrating public transport along a limited number of routes' (Houghton-Evans, 1975).

The study for Washington new town in County Durham was yet another investigation into the most appropriate urban form for the 1960s (Llewellyn-Davies, 1966). Like the Buchanan investigation the planning of Washington placed great emphasis on freedom of movement for the motor car (Figures 5.27 to 5.30). The new towns of the 1960s were analysed as a functional part of a region: new towns in Britain were no longer seen as having a high degree of self-containment. The logic of a regional or metropolitan context for a new town was the design of an urban form which facilitates movement on a

Figure 5.26 Buchanan's grid for central London (Buchanan, 1963)
Figure 5.27 Washington New Town, half-mile square grid (Llewellyn-Davies, 1966)
Figure 5.28 Washington New Town, road hierarchy
Figure 5.29 Washington New Town, plan based on one mile square grid
Figure 5.30 Washington New Town, pedestrian pathways connecting village centres

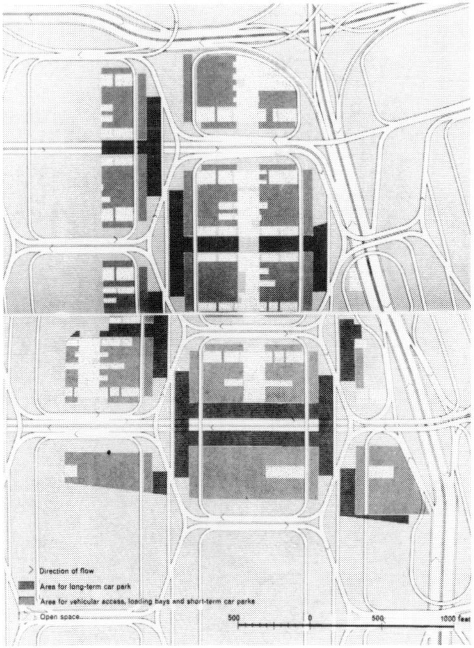

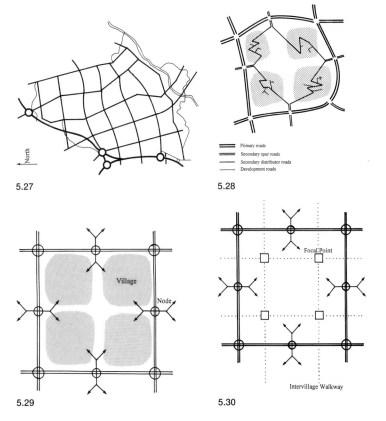

5.26
5.27
5.28
5.29
5.30

regional scale. A regional network of high capacity roads taking the form of a grid seemed to offer a solution for a dispersed pattern of daily movements. The appropriateness of the neighbourhood concept, which had been a guiding principle of the early post-war new town in Britain, was questioned. The new town was now conceived as a complex overlapping structure and was no longer seen as being composed of simple functional elements such as industrial zones, housing areas or town centre. Furthermore, the town was not envisaged as an object with an ultimate, finite or ideal size: a prime objective of the plan for Washington and other new towns of the same vintage was to accommodate growth and change.

Despite the rejection of the neighbourhood concept, the plan for Washington proposed a settlement pattern based on villages of 4500, that is, a village population which supports a primary school. The village, as in Runcorn, was a neighbourhood in all but name. A village of 4500 requires an area of a half mile square at normal densities with two-storey housing. The village, being easily traversed by the pedestrian, was an area of pedestrian priority with footpaths linking all parts of the village to the centre. Each village was bounded by a grid of primary roads which spread uniformly over the town. The local roads serving the villages joined the primary grid midway between the main junctions of the grid. The local roads themselves formed a secondary grid connecting the villages. The secondary grid is made unattractive as a short cut or rat run by linking the village centres to the primary grid diagonally and by taking a circuitous route.

The proposals were subjected to further traffic analysis which showed that junctions at quarter mile intervals severely disrupted traffic flow and that where the grid joined regional roads some sections of the system were more heavily loaded than others, defeating the objective of evenly dispersed traffic throughout the network. On the basis of these findings the scheme was revised in favour of roads at one mile centres, similar to the grid resulting

from Buchanan's findings. Within the square mile grid there were four villages each of 4500 people with a pedestrian system connecting all village centres to the town walkway (Figure 5.28). While the scale of the main grid was determined primarily by the needs of the private car, the secondary routes passing through the village centres were for the bus.

Buchanan returned to the study of the grid when he was commissioned to carry out the South Hampshire Study (Buchanan *et al.*, 1966). His proposals were for the growth and redevelopment of an already intensively developed urban region stretching from Southampton to Portsmouth. Buchanan started his study with an analysis of urban form (Figures 5.31 to 5.33). This part of the study is a landmark in the method of rational analysis associated with 'modernist planning' of the 1960s. Buchanan contrasts three basic urban forms: the radial-concentric, the orthogonal grid and the

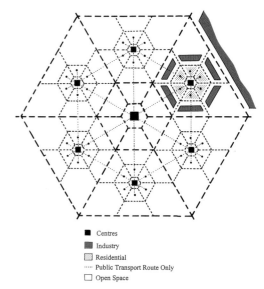

■ Centres
▨ Industry
▨ Residential
···· Public Transport Route Only
□ Open Space

Figure 5.31 South Hampshire Study, the centripetal structure (Buchanan *et al.*, 1966)

directional grid. He showed how each form could be adapted to serve both public and private transport needs at traffic levels thought inevitable at the time. Buchanan found that the radial-concentric form was less able to accommodate growth and change than either form of grid. He eventually argued for the directional grid which he believed combined the virtues of both the lattice and the line.

Buchanan followed the then standard procedure of grouping both facilities and routes in the form of a hierarchy. Corresponding to each step in the hierarchy of activities there is a type of link in the system of routes. For example, from home to school the link is a footpath; from local centre to district centre there is a minor road; from district centre to town centre the link is a larger distributor road. The hierarchy of roads extends from town to regional levels to national level. The hierarchy even embraces those roads of international importance. In this system there is a node placed where a lower order route intersects with a higher order route. When this hierarchical structure is combined with the 'directional grid' it leads to an arrangement similar to that shown in Figure 5.34. Routes in the lowest category are most closely spaced and run parallel to each other. These routes are crossed by routes in the next lowest category, again parallel to each other. They run at right angles to the lower order routes but at a much wider spacing. Routes in the next higher order are at right angles to those in the second order and at even wider spacing. These third order routes are parallel to the lowest order of route but with a number of routes in this lowest order between the pair of third order routes.

In his study Buchanan distinguished between local and long distance traffic movements, that is, between traffic which has a specific origin and destination within the system, and traffic which is moving longer distances to, from or through the system. Buchanan's solution to this problem was to designate alternate roads in each category for one of these purposes. The 'green' routes were designed

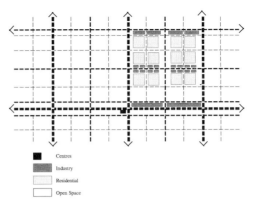

5.32

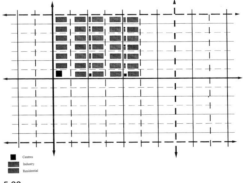

5.33

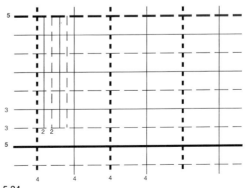

5.34

Figure 5.32 South Hampshire Study, a grid with different categories of route
Figure 5.33 South Hampshire Study, the directional grid
Figure 5.34 South Hampshire Study, illustrating the hierarchy of routes

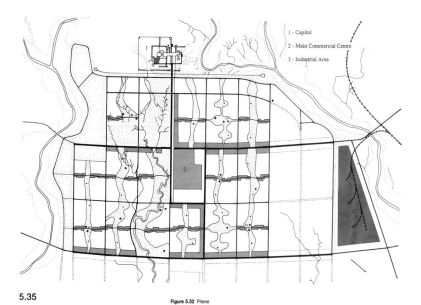

1 - Capitol

2 - Main Commercial Centre

3 - Industrial Area

5.35

Figure 5.52 Priene

for through or random traffic while the 'red' routes which alternated with them were designed for local traffic. Consequently the green routes had no frontage development while on the red routes are concentrated those activities which require access. This idea for alternating the functions of roads within a grid was earlier suggested by Le Corbusier for Chandigarh (Figure 5.35). The development plan for Chandigarh was divided into superblocks surrounded by major roads. Each superblock was further divided by minor streets alternating with 'greenways' for pedestrians and cyclists (Houghton-Evans, 1975). Designating streets in a grid plan for different functions has a long history. In the Hellenistic city of Priene the main east-west streets in the grid are wide and relatively flat, capable of easy use by wheeled vehicles and horse traffic. The north-south streets in contrast were built at right angles to the contours and in places they are simply a staircase (Figure 5.36). In Roman colonial foundations based on the gridiron plan the *Cardo* and *Decumanus* which cross at right angles are wider and connect the main regional routes to the centre of the settlement (Figure 4.32).

Buchanan completed the study by demonstrating how the directional grid could be applied to South Hampshire (Figure 5.37). He was concerned to design a structure which was capable of responding

Figure 5.35 Chandigarh
(Futagawa, 1974)

Figure 5.36 Priene

Figure 5.37 South
Hampshire Study (Buchanan
et al., 1966)

5.36

0   300m
Scale

A   Acropolis
B   Theatre
C   Agora
D   Gymnasium and Stadium

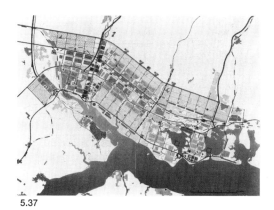

5.37

to different rates of growth. The directional grid which resulted from the study was designed to accommodate increasing levels of both car ownership and personal mobility. The linear grid could be described as a hybrid urban structure combining the strict geometry of the orthogonal grid with the adaptability for growth, a property associated with the linear plan:

> The structure is not fixed or static in size. This was a basic factor in our whole approach to the study of the growth of urban structure, that it should be a structure capable of growth in the future and should never be seen as a complete unit ... It does not result in a fixed static plan of development, but suggests a framework on, and within which, changing trends and strategies of growth towards different goals are possible. (Buchanan *et al.*, 1966).

The 1960s was a time when urban growth seemed natural and without end. It was not until the oil crisis of the 1970s that the strictures of the Club of Rome and the Environmental movement began to be heard. In contrast to the 1960s, plans in the last decade of the century are no longer predicated on unlimited growth. More emphasis is now given to a process of consolidation, conservation and the regeneration of existing centres. Many of the concerns which occupied the minds of planners like Buchanan in the 1960s seem now to be quite inappropriate and almost a lesson in what not to do.

Earlier in the chapter the first proposal for Milton Keynes was discussed. When the proposal for a new city in North Buckinghamshire was confirmed by the government in 1967 Llewellyn-Davies and Partners, the planners of Washington, were appointed as consultants to prepare the plan (Llewellyn-Davies, 1970). It is regrettable, in hindsight, that the County Council's architects were not permitted to proceed with their ideas for the Monorail City. Many innovative and green planning ideas were lost for thirty years because of that decision. The monorail system would have provided

the opportunity of creating, along its route, a series of ring mains, which is an economical way of distributing essential city services. There was also an idea for placing a power station at the centre of the city, circulating both power and district heating using the ring mains. Indeed, there was a proposal for heat and power to be supplied from the same plant which would also burn the city waste to recover the heat energy from it. Ideas like these, only now being resurrected, were current in the 1960s.

The final plan for Milton Keynes consists of:

> a grid of primary roads of approximately one kilometre squares. Within these squares are residential areas, called environmental areas, of about 250 to 300 acres (100 to 120 ha) each for about 5000 people. Estate roads branch from the grid to serve the residential areas, while a system of pedestrian routes traverse the whole city crossing the primary roads roughly in the middle of the sides of the squares and at the corners by over or underpasses. At the former points are the "activity centres" with major bus stops, and a concentration of residential facilities like shops, first schools, pubs, places of worship and other requirements. There will be about 60 of these centres with different groupings at each ... the residential areas are not planned as inward looking neighbourhoods, as in the first generation of new towns, but rather as outward looking to a transport route that links rapidly with other parts of the city. Following the principle of giving the maximum possible freedom of choice to future residents, the plan aims to give scope for the free use of the car unrestrained by congestion while at the same time providing a high quality public transport system from the beginning, not only for those who need it but also for those who might choose to use it instead of private transport (Osborn and Whittick, 1977).

Figure 5.38 shows the structure of the city which resulted from the extensive investigation of urban form carried out by the consultants with the assistance of an array of academic helpers. Essentially the planners were attempting to fulfil a set of high-minded goals (Llewellyn-Davies *et al.*, 1970):

Central Milton Keynes
Residential
Industry
Centres
Local centres
Education
Open Space
Lakes
Health
Public utilities

Roads
A5 Relief Road
Railways

Figure 5.38 Milton Keynes
(Llewellyn-Davies, 1970)

1. Opportunity and freedom of choice
2. Easy movement and access, and good communications
3. Balance and variety
4. An attractive city
5. Public awareness and participation
6. Efficient and imaginative use of resources.

In hindsight it is easy to be critical of a particular approach to the planning of any city, including Milton Keynes. Nevertheless it is useful to examine the plan in relation to the current debate about sustainable development to see if the Milton Keynes experiment has anything to offer planners of today. The consultants concluded that: 'only those plans offering potential for low concentration of work places and low residential densities were likely to

meet the goals' (Houghton-Evans, 1975). Such a conclusion limits the effectiveness of public transport and places an undue emphasis on mobility based on private transport. It also increases the use of land and urban infrastructure costs. Both of these effects result from the choice of urban form and run counter to the principles of sustainable development. The plan for Milton Keynes was criticized at the time by the National Farmers' Union and the National Union of Agricultural Workers. They claimed that the site was one of the most important grain growing areas in the country and with improved drainage they thought it could be an area of exceptionally high production. Despite current policy to take land out of agricultural production it would appear questionable, taking a long-term perspective, to use good quality agricultural land, or land capable of becoming so, for urban development at wasteful densities.

The North Bucks Association was formed by the residents to oppose the proposal for the new city. The Association represented the parish councils in the area. Amongst its objections was the need for a national physical planning policy for Britain before a decision should be taken to increase the population of Buckinghamshire. The association argued that it was necessary to secure a more evenly balanced distribution of population throughout the country: it was advocating development proposals which would relocate or retain population in less densely populated areas where space, water supply and sewage disposal presented less serious problems. Such a policy, it was argued, would relieve the pressures in the south of the country in places like Buckinghamshire (Osborn and Whittick, 1977). These points are those which would probably be made in an argument prepared today by those working in the field of sustainable development. The dismissal of these arguments prepared by a resident's group throws into question the vigour with which Objective 5 of the consultants' brief, 'participation', was being pursued. Participation, of course, is a key concept in the process of sustainable development.

It seems that on balance the first proposal for Milton Keynes by the County Council's architects is more imaginative in its proposed use of resources and more innovative and 'green' in terms of urban structure than the proposal which was eventually developed.

Public transport is seen by many as the key to developing sustainable cities. It seems, therefore, that the grid plan, in the way it was developed in the 1960s as a means of accommodating the motor car, is inappropriate for fulfilling the goals of sustainable development. There is a fundamental relationship between urban form and the transportation system which services the city. Buchanan, Ling, Llewellyn-Davies and the many others working on urban planning in Britain since the Second World War were fully aware of the close connection between transport and city form: an analysis of this relationship is given great prominence in, for example, the reports on new towns (some of which have been discussed earlier in this chapter). The different views on public as opposed to private transport to a large extent account for the different urban structures of Milton Keynes and Runcorn. The planning for sustainable development requires the application of a new paradigm for urban transport and consequently a new form. There are four main planning principles for sustainable urban transport. The first principle is that urban structure should reduce the need to travel. The second principle is that urban form should promote and encourage walking and cycling. The third principle is that urban form should be designed to give priority to public as opposed to private transport. The fourth principle seeks to develop an urban structure which encourages the movement of more goods by rail and water and discourages movement of goods by road.

Applying planning principles for sustainable transport results in a grid which is very different from the linear grid developed for the South Hampshire Study or the kilometre square of Milton Keynes. The grid designed to meet the requirements of sustain-able development would not result in a protected environmental area surrounded by major roads carrying fast-moving traffic. The sustainable grid would have at its centre the community facilities and activities which sustain the daily needs of the community. The spatial limits of the community and the extent of the local grid would be determined by a reasonable walking distance of about 1000 metres from the centre to the boundary of the community. At gross densities of 30 to 50 persons per hectare the community would be between 12 000 and 20 000. Unless densities are increased beyond those of the British new towns these figures appear to be the maximum size for a sustainable new settlement.

The most appropriate form of grid for a sustainable settlement would more closely resemble a Roman colonial town or that of Gracehill than the plan for Milton Keynes. Both main streets of the Roman Colonial town cross at right angles and a centre is formed at the crossing point. The two main streets are part of public transport routes connecting with other communities in the region. It is possible for the four quadrants of the settlement to be sub-divided by an orthogonal grid. The scale and dimensions of the grid would not be determined by the needs of the motor car but rather by the land sub-division requirements for housing, which is the predominant land use in the settlement. All roads in the settlement would be multi-functional, carrying public transport vehicles, private cars, bicycles and pedestrians, all moving at a maximum speed of 15 miles per hour, a speed which incidentally is faster than most traffic moves through cities at the moment. At the periphery of the settlement would be located the open space for recreation use and land for intensive market gardening. At the town portals would be sited break of bulk warehouses for goods destined for the town, delivery goods within the town being by small delivery vehicles.

It may be possible to design a grid form of land sub-division which would satisfy the functional requirements of sustainable development. The result-

Figure 5.39 Islamic city
(Lynch, 1981)
Figure 5.40 Ghadaia,
Algeria

ing settlement or extension to a settlement may incorporate some of the features outlined in previous paragraphs. It is not, however, altogether clear if such a settlement form would express in clear and unambiguous terms the values which would characterize a community practising the culture of sustainable development. The grid plan, unless similar to the loose low density lattice advocated by Alexander, appears too mechanistic and antithetical to the organic, natural or ecological ethos with which the philosophy of sustainable development is imbued.

THE CENTRALIZED CITY

The third main archetypal urban form is the centralized or inward looking city. The medieval city of the Islamic world is the centralized city in its most extreme and introverted form. The Islamic city is contained within a wall controlled by gateways (Figure 5.39). The neighbourhoods within the city are also closed and intensely private. Residential clusters occupied by families with close blood ties are approached along narrow culs-de-sac. Before entering the private world of the extended family, strangers negotiate tight dogleg passageways beneath accommodation bridging the street to form a gateway to the residential quarter (Figure 5.40). The house itself may contain locks or barriers between semi-public space, semi-private space before the intensely private and secluded area of the marital family home is reached (Figure 5.41). Except for space around the Friday Mosque, the Palace and the Market, open space within the traditional Islamic city is confined to small streets bordered by shops and commercial premises. These busy bustling streets contrast sharply with the quiet seclusion of the residential courtyards. Each ward of the traditional Islamic city is occupied by a distinct group practising the same trade such as weaving, pottery or building. At the heart of the ward is a local mosque and the ward chief's home. Within the

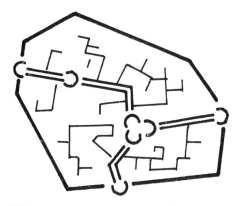

5.39

5.40

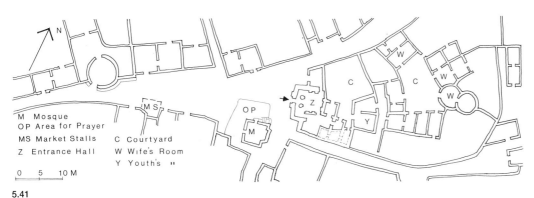

5.41

M Mosque
OP Area for Prayer
MS Market Stalls   C Courtyard
Z Entrance Hall   W Wife's Room
             Y Youth's "

0   5   10 M

Figure 5.41 House of the
Chief Builder in Zaria,
Nigeria
Figure 5.42 Rothenburg
Figure 5.43 Rothenburg

ward people of different incomes live as close neighbours, though the city is often segregated into wards for different ethnic groups (Moughtin, 1985).

The medieval European city, while not exhibiting the same preoccupation with privacy, has many features in common with its Islamic counterpart: it, too, is surrounded by a wall controlled by massive gateways (Platt, 1976) (Figures 5.42 and 5.43). The gateways closed at night for the economic control and protection of the city market; for most of the time this was a more important function for the gateway than defence against the marauding foe. The medieval city with its central market and clearly defined boundary appears to have its public space carved from the solid block of building forming the settlement. The streets and squares are three-dimensional spaces linked in the informal manner much admired by Camillo Sitte (1901). The picturesque structure of the city lends itself to Cullen's townscape analysis with its emphasis on serial vision as the means of capturing, in sketches, the organic or natural feeling and appearance of the spatial composition (Cullen, 1961). The city appears to be the product of nature, growing in agglutinative fashion apparently without the artifice of man. This city form is probably the inspiration of those 'green planners' who advocate dense three- and four-storey developments of limited extent.

5.42

5.43a

5.43b

Figure 5.44 Sforzinda
Figure 5.45 Palmanova
Figure 5.46 Owen's village
of cooperation (Houghton-
Evans, 1975)

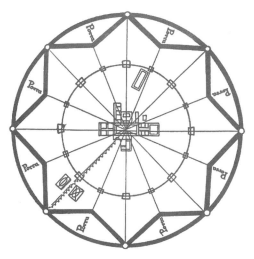

5.44

5.45

The concept of the centralized city has probably had the most influence on the development, in Europe, of ideas about ideal city form. In Renaissance Italy, Sforzinda, a model town by Filarete, is a centralized city: the plan of the city is an eight-point star made of two intersecting quadrangles set within a circle (Figure 5.44). Palmanova, planned possibly by Vicenzo Scamozzi, a sixteenth century Italian theorist, was built in 1593 to defend the frontiers of Venetian territory (Figure 5.45). It too followed Renaissance radial symmetry, being influenced strongly by the writings of Vitruvius and his follower Alberti: it played an influential role in the general quest for the perfect form (Rosenau, 1974). In Britain the work of Owen, though employing a rectangular plan for his villages, envisaged the development of centralized and enclosed settlements: these villages of industrial cooperation, though discrete in themselves, were planned as a regional solution to the social and economic problems of the early nineteenth century (Figure 5.46). Victoria, the model town of James Silk Buckingham, which appeared in his book, *National Evils and Practical Remedies*, was also a centralized concept. The town comprised squares of terraced houses and gardens alternating with squares of other land uses: the best houses were near the centre while at the boundary of the town it was planned to have a covered arcade for workshops. Outside the town were to be located the large factories,

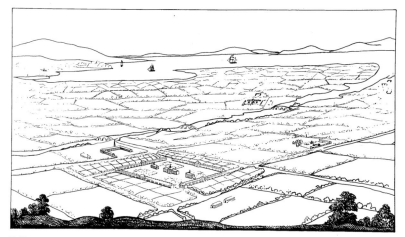

5.46

abattoirs, cattle market, public cemetery and hospital. Also outside the town were to be large sites reserved for suburban villas (Figure 5.47)

Titus Salt put into effect many of the theoretical ideas of earlier reformers such as Buckingham and Owen. He built a small town, Saltaire, four miles from Bradford, for 5000 people to house the workforce for his mill (Figure 5.48). The building of Saltaire has been dealt with elsewhere (Moughtin, 1992). For the purpose of this book on sustainable development, however, a number of ideas are important. Saltaire was planned as a centralized, self-contained town: it was located on the banks of the River Aire, the Leeds-Liverpool canal and on the main railway line connecting Scotland to the Midlands. At the time, these were the important means of mass transport for goods and/or people. The town itself was built at quite high densities, having 37 houses to the acre (80 approximately to the hectare). It occupied an area about one kilometre square so that all parts of the town were reached easily on foot. The town is built in the form of a grid plan with one main street on which

were located the community facilities, the church, school, shops, municipal hall and factory. In addition, and although surrounded at the time by countryside, the town had its own public garden and allotments. Saltaire, despite being built in the form of a rigid grid, falls neatly into the category of the highly centralized inward-looking urban structure: it also exhibits many features expected from a sustainable settlement.

Howard's 'Garden City' is very much in the mould of the centralized city. At the core of this ideal city are the public buildings set in a central park (Figures 5.49 to 5.51). Encircling this park is the 'Crystal Palace', a glazed shopping arcade. Then

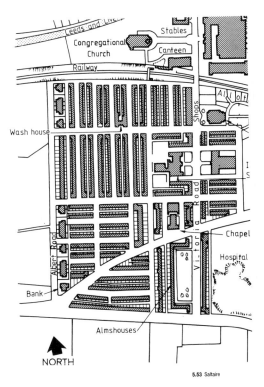

5.53 Saltaire

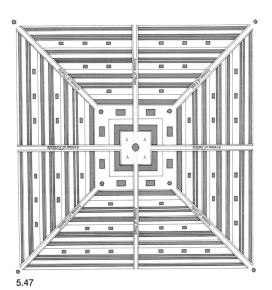

5.47

5.48

Figure 5.47 Victoria

Figure 5.48 Saltaire

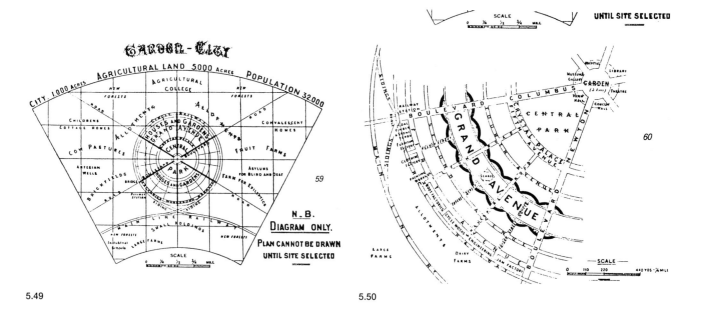

5.49

5.50

Figures 5.49 to 5.51
Garden City (Howard, 1965)

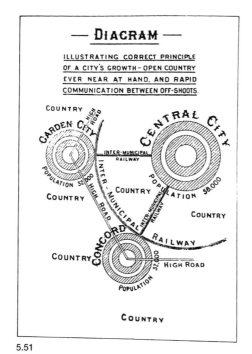

5.51

follow residential rings, the fifth such ring being for higher socio-economic groups and comprising: 'very excellently built houses, each standing in its own ample grounds.' Third Avenue, called Grand Avenue, interrupts the rings of housing: it is a linear park which completely encircles the town and contains the schools. Between First Avenue, which is the outermost ring of housing, and the circular railway are the town factories. The town sits in a large tract of agricultural land owned by the municipality, being kept free of urban development by the self-interest of the city population.

Garden Cities of Tomorrow, first published in 1898 by Howard, contains a wealth of ideas for urban development, many of which have been incorporated in new town developments in Britain and elsewhere in the world (Howard, 1965). Some of these ideas of Howard may prove useful to those seeking structures for sustainable urban form. For example, the notion that the town should be maintained at a size which facilitates pedestrian movements is central to the aim of reducing the use of non-renewable energy. Howard was quite clear that his blueprint for the garden city was a set of diagrams and not a town plan; nevertheless, in those diagrams he showed the distance between the railway station and the town centre to be about one kilometre or a ten-minute walk, the time taken to cross from one side of the town to the other being about a twenty- to thirty-minute walk. Furthermore, connections between towns for both people and goods is by rail, the rapid transport of his day. Both of these qualities of Howard's urban structure are fundamental requirements of sustainable development.

Howard's blueprint for the 'Garden City' reduces the need for movement in a number of ways. Schools are located at the nucleus of residential wards. Each ward was large enough to be a complete segment of the town, that is, containing a cross-section of its population. In embryo this is the idea of the self-contained neighbourhood or suburb, self-sufficient in daily needs. In size the segment is based upon the convenient walking distance from home to school of about 500 metres. This is a principle which should be paramount for any form of civilized planning, but most especially for sustainable development where the aim is to reduce to a minimum the need for movement. In addition, Howard's proposals reduce the need for the movement of agricultural produce. The city, being surrounded by agricultural land, is capable of sustaining many of the needs of the town in terms of food supply and in turn absorbing some of the waste products of the town.

Howard, following on from Owen, sited workplaces on the outskirts of the settlement. Instead of the town being considered a single productive unit such as Owen's or Salt's mill town, the 'Garden City' was designed as an industrial town with many firms grouped in an industrial zone. This concept has permeated planning practice in many countries during this century. In some cases this practice of zoning has been used with disastrous results. Large industrial and commercial zones in cities have died by night while desolate single-use

housing areas of social deprivation have blighted whole sections of the city. The problems associated with rigid zoning have led to suggestions for a return to a mix of land uses in towns. It is argued that a policy of mixed land use, if implemented, would lead to an urban structure in which the need for many to travel from home to work, for example, would be reduced. There may be much to commend this relaxed attitude to zoning, but large-scale industrial or productive units depending on bulk deliveries may still require locations with close proximity to intercity or regional transport networks, be they road or rail.

The core of Howard's financial proposals was the acquisition of land, on behalf of the municipality, at agricultural prices. The ownership of the land was to be vested in the municipality and 'betterment' in the value of the land caused by the development of urban infrastructure was to accrue to the community. The local community therefore had control of land in the green belt and could determine the nature and extent of urban growth. Using the increased value of the land the financial scheme was designed to meet interest charges on the original debt and to clear that debt in 30 years. The financial plans included the idea of a combination of municipal and private finance. Public buildings, roads and infrastructure were to be financed by the municipality, all other development being undertaken by private enterprise.

A key to sustainable development is the ownership and therefore control of land for the benefit of the community and its long-term survival. The eighteenth century land owners in London, using leasehold control, developed some fine residential property. In Bath, the Woods, father and son, through their clever control and manipulation of the development process, have left to the nation one of the great works of civic design. Howard extended this system of land banking to develop a whole town. In this case, however, the process was to be used not for the benefit of a single landowner or developer but for the benefit of the whole municipal

5.52a

5.52b

Figure 5.52 Reston, USA
Figure 5.53 Reston, USA

investment in infrastructure accrue to neighbouring landowners through unearned betterment in the value of their land (Figures 5.52 and 5.53).

Since the Second World War attempts in Britain have been made, without great success, to national-ize land or control betterment. It may, however, be time once again to consider the public ownership and control of land for the present and future needs of local communities. If so, then a system based on the local control of land in the Howard tradition may prove more successful than the rigid national-ization of land itself or even of a national system for taxing betterment values.

Many of Howard's ideas were put into practice at Letchworth and Welwyn. Later those ideas were to influence the planning of the first group of new towns built in Britain after the Second World War. Basically Howard's concept for the garden city was a means of controlling the growth of cities through the building of a series of new towns physically separated from each other and from the parent city. The garden cities were to be self-contained for many needs. Nevertheless, Howard considered the urban areas so formed to be integrated socially and econom-ically: the towns while physically separate were to be connected by an efficient transport network. Despite the social and economic integration the garden cities were physically separate, centralized and inward looking in their urban structure.

community. In the USA during the 1960s similar experiments of town building were carried out by private enterprise. Companies, in great secret, tried to amass land for town development at deflated prices. Where insufficient land for the full develop-ment was not acquired in the initial stages of the project, as in Reston, the benefits from the original

5.53a

5.53a

In 1945 the Reith Committee was appointed to:

consider the general questions of the establishment, development, organization and administration that will arise in the promotion of New Towns in furtherance of a policy of planned decentralization from congested areas; and in accordance therewith to suggest guiding principles on which such Towns should be established and developed as self-contained and balanced communities for work and living.

Purchase of the land for the New Towns was to be by public authorities. The population of each town was initially to be 30 000 to 50 000 closely approximating Howard's own suggestions. Each Town was to be surrounded by a green belt which was to be used for agriculture and smallholdings for the production of food for the local market. The brief developed for the New Towns was comprehensive and detailed. It included recommendations for a balance of income groups in the town, a mixture of those groups in each neighbourhood and a broad base of industries.

Cumbernauld is the British new town which, by its form, most closely expresses the concept of the centralized urban structure (Wilson, 1958). The planners of Cumbernauld were concerned to correct the deficiencies, as they saw it, of the neighbourhood concept. The planned neighbourhood was thought to encourage people to look inward on their local area rather than visualizing the town as a whole. It also, so the argument ran, attempted to regulate social life into a fixed pattern of local communities. A compact town clustered round a single centre was proposed as the solution to these problems associated with neighbourhood planning (Figures 5.54 to 5.56). The town of Cumbernauld was conceived as a hilltop settlement standing in the landscape with the clear profile of Italian cities like Montepulciano or San Gimignano. For such a hilltop town both the gridiron and linear forms of road pattern were considered to be inappropriate. A radial pattern was therefore proposed which had

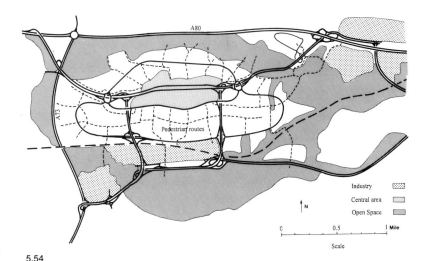

5.54

5.55

5.56

Figure 5.54 Cumbernauld (Houghton-Evans, 1975)
Figure 5.55 Cumbernauld, town centre
Figure 5.56 Cumbernauld, town centre

two ring roads, an inner one around the centre and an outer loop which gave access to the Radburn style housing areas.

In May 1959 the plan was revised after a detailed traffic analysis revealed potential problems (Wilson, 1959). The main changes to the plan were in the design of roads and the standards to which they were to be built. For example, the land required for roads almost doubled in price. The much increased road size and the traffic volumes for which they were planned in 1959 required intensive landscaping, using heavy tree planting to screen the housing areas. Although the planned population remained at 70 000 a report of 1962 included plans for 14 'grade separated' junctions. This was at a time when such junctions were highly unusual in Britain.

Another unusual feature of Cumbernauld is the elongated multilevel centre which sits along the ridge of the hilltop and around which the rest of the town sits uncomfortably. Pedestrians and vehicular traffic are arranged on different levels. The town centre is dirty, windswept and totally without architectural character. The centre is three-quarters of a mile from all housing areas and within easy walking distance from them: it has, however, none of the charm of the medieval Italian hill village on which it is modelled. The centre of Cumbernauld is the kind of place to which most would walk because of necessity and not for pleasure. Cumbernauld, with its tight centralized plan form, may exhibit some features of a sustainable settlement but it does also offer a salutary warning. The design of a settlement to meet the functional goals of sustainable development alone is not sufficient: aesthetic considerations are important if people's higher level needs are to be fulfilled. The centralized urban form, despite the obvious failings of Cumbernauld, appears to be a most useful model for new sustainable town developments of limited extent. The size of the development from centre to periphery should be about half a mile to 1000 metres. In a town of this size the centre can be reached by foot in 10 minutes from any part of the development. An appropriate form

for the development is one which expresses the organic metaphor applying the principles of visual composition found in many of the delightful European medieval towns. These ideas of organic layout have recently been interpreted by Leon Krier in his master plan for Poundbury, Dorchester in Dorset and also by Demitri Porphyrios and Associates in their master plan for Cavo Salomonti in Crete (Figures 5.57 and 5.58). The plan for Cavo Salomonti: 'draws on the experience of traditional towns which enhance rather than spoil the landscape ... The traditional urban fabric ... allows for buildings of two and three storeys with small gardens and courts that are closed off from the adjoining streets by two metre walls. The basic elements of the design have been the urban block, the street, the square and the public buildings' (Architectural Design, 1993).

A more complicated centralized city is the star shape (Figure 5.59). Blumenfeld in his paper 'Theory of City Form: Past and Present' has a thorough description of this model of city form (Blumenfeld, 1949). The star shape has been the basis for a number of city plans including Copenhagen, the classic development of this idea (Figure 5.60). According to the advocates of this theoretical approach to urban planning the star is the best form for any city of moderate to large size. The star city has a single dominant centre which should be high density and comprise a mix of land uses. From this centre a number of major transport routes radiate. Along these main radial routes would run the mass transit systems and the major highways. At intervals along the transport corridors would be located sub-centres around which would cluster other intensive uses and to which residential quarters would focus. Green wedges originating in the open countryside penetrate the urban areas between the transport corridors.

There are concentric traffic routes at intervals along the diameter of the star. These concentric rings link the fingers or radials. Where the radials and concentric rings intersect are located the main

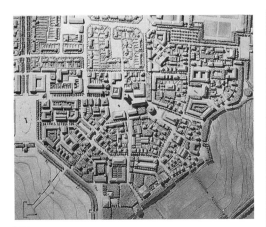

5.57a

5.57b

5.57c

5.58a

5.58b

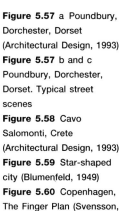

Figure 5.57 a Poundbury, Dorchester, Dorset (Architectural Design, 1993)
Figure 5.57 b and c Poundbury, Dorchester, Dorset. Typical street scenes
Figure 5.58 Cavo Salomonti, Crete (Architectural Design, 1993)
Figure 5.59 Star-shaped city (Blumenfeld, 1949)
Figure 5.60 Copenhagen, The Finger Plan (Svensson, 1981)

5.59

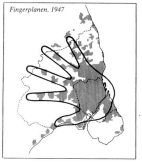

5.60

sub-centres. Along the length of the concentric rings development is not permitted to interrupt the green wedge. It is this last point which is the weakness of the star theory. Unless the planning control mechanism is particularly effective the pressure on the frontage of the ring routes results in the infill of the areas between the radials close to the centre of the star. The further the concentric rings are from the centre of the star the more important they become in connecting the distant radials. As the system expands the outer reaches of the star revert to an open network of roads (Lynch, 1981). The designation of some of the concentric rings as a rapid public transit link following the ideas of Soria y Mata converts the star into a form which may be useful in attempting to solve, in a more sustainable way, the movement of people in existing large urban areas.

A further model for urban structuring which is difficult to classify is based on the notion that landscape should be the chief consideration. It can be argued that, at one level, consideration of landscape form should influence all development. The location of Cumbernauld, for example, is

determined to some extent by the topography, the town structure being used to strengthen and reinforce the form of the ridge on which the town centre sits. The star pattern for city development places as much importance on the landscape as it does on transportation; the green wedges which alternate with the corridors or fingers of development have equal priority in forming the shape of the city. This argument, however, misses the point that landscaping can be used as the factor which unifies the whole urban form: it then becomes the dominant element in the urban composition. The role of landscape as the unifying element in the siting of building groups has been discussed elsewhere (Moughtin, 1992). This notion can be developed further so that landscape is elevated to the position of the predominant factor in the generation of urban form.

Respect for the landscape is deep-rooted in the British psyche. Amongst this country's greatest achievements are the landscape gardens of the eighteenth century, the high point of this achievement being the work of Capability Brown (Stroud, 1950) (Figure 5.61). The development of Howard's garden city ideas at Letchworth and Welwyn introduced the idea of landscaping as a feature unifying large areas of a town. In other countries the landscaping of suburbia has proved highly successful. This is particularly true of the USA where the freshness and boldness of suburbs such as Olmstead's Riverside near Chicago and Roland Park, Baltimore set new standards for landscaped residential areas. It was, however, Unwin with his pamphlet 'Nothing to be Gained by Overcrowding' who first analysed the effects of housing density and related it to development costs (Unwin, 1967). It was this analysis which was the intellectual rationale for the garden suburb: 'Unwin ... showed that by cutting down on the number of needless streets and devoting the areas so dedicated to internal gardens, he could provide almost the same number of houses, each with more usable garden land, and with more gracious surroundings, at the same price'

Figure 5.61 Landscape by Capability Brown (Stroud, 1950)

(Mumford, 1961). Unwin and Parker with their designs for Hampstead Garden Suburb set the pattern for most city housing in Britain until the Second World War (Unwin, 1909). It is probably true to say that most housing development in British cities owes more to Unwin and Parker than to Le Corbusier and the pioneers of modern design.

Harlow, designed by Frederick Gibberd, is the British new town which resembles most closely an urban structure where landscape is the dominant factor in determining its form. The plan for Harlow was published in 1947 and construction began in 1949. The master plan was designed originally for 60 000 people but was later increased first to 80 000 then to 90 000. The town was planned to be self-contained and balanced (Gibberd, 1955). Its primary purpose was to take overspill population from north-east London. Harlow is located 30 miles from London just south of the River Stort and west of the old village of Harlow. It is in a rural landscape and occupies over 6000 acres. The urban form of the settlement follows a strictly hierarchical structure; for example, shopping is arranged in a series starting from the lowest level of shopping, the corner shop, extending through the intermediate levels of shopping, the neighbourhood and the district shopping centres, to the highest level in the hierarchy, town centre shopping. Roads and housing follow similar hierarchical structures.

The dominance of landscape as a form determinant is best appreciated from Gibberd's own words:

> The main railway and river run in a valley along the north boundary, beyond which are the Hertfordshire hills. There is another valley running east-west across the site, and this flows out on the west side to link up with the main valley on the north ... The plan form has been evolved from the existing landscape pattern, and from the desire to obtain sharp contrast between urban and natural areas ... The housing groups are on the high ground, clear of the main traffic connections, with natural features, such as woods and valleys, forming barriers between them ... The valleys and hills on

the north of the river are left in their natural state, and a park is projected from them into the heart of the town. The agricultural land on the east of the town, and that on the west, are both projected into the area to bring rural life into immediate contact with the urban one. The two wedges are linked up by the central valley which is left in its natural state. Links to the countryside, on both north and south, are formed by green wedges designed to embrace natural features, such as valleys, woods and brooks (Gibberd, 1955).

It is clear from Gibberd's description of Harlow that his major preoccupation was to design a development in harmony with the existing landscape structure (Figures 5.62 to 5.64). Some of the architecture, particularly in the city centre is depressing, but the landscape scheme is expansive.

Implementing policies for sustainable development does not simply mean the sensitive location of urban development in relation to landscape features such as hills, valleys, streams and woodland. Of equal importance is respect for the ecological function of the landscape. Even a cursory reading of material by landscape architects such as Colvin (1948) shows that an understanding and an appreciation of ecology is central to the discipline of landscape architecture. Apart from the advocacy of an organic approach to design by some professionals in the field of city planning and urban design the

Figure 5.62 Harlow

5.63

5.64

main actors dealing with urban development have been reticent in adopting ecology as a fundamental concern for development strategies. Even those professing a concern for an organic approach to city planning appear to be supporting a particular design philosophy rather than a method built round an ecological strategy for the city. The organic school of design in the Sitte tradition or as later redefined by Alexander *et al.* (1987) is primarily concerned with the arrangement of buildings, streets and squares: such urban design elements should be formed in an informal or accretive fashion rather than the rigid, formal axial compositions associated with Baroque and later Beaux Arts urban structuring. Sitte, however, is a little ambivalent towards trees in cities: his main concern is for the judicious placing of trees for visual effect, trees grouped at the edges of public squares not in the middle, trees associated with water, while for him the *allée* was an abomination. Sitte spends some time reviewing the scientific literature of his day which analysed the effect of vegetation on the atmosphere and came to the conclusion that: 'The whole matter of vegetation as presumably beneficial to physical well-being can then be ruled out. There remains only the psychological factor, rooted in the imagination' (Sitte, 1901). Sitte distinguished two types of greenery: *decorative greenery* and *sanitary greenery*.

Decorative greenery was for use in cities while *sanitary greenery*: 'should not be found amidst the dust and noise of streets, but rather in the sheltered interior of large blocks of buildings, surrounded on all sides. Only when large in area can it afford to be open to the street, as in the suburbs. These extensions to cities, relatively untouched by traffic and with their uninterrupted expanse of trees, are certainly examples of *sanitary greenery*' (Sitte 1965). These particular views of Sitte on the use, almost the reluctant use, and location of natural landscape elements in the city would not be appropriate and of little relevance for sustainable development.

Leicester, the first Environment City in Britain, has adopted an innovative approach to landscape planning for the city. Leicester was one of the first district councils to adopt a city-wide ecology strategy based on a detailed habitat survey. The Leicester Ecology Strategy aims to develop a network of greenways and natural habitats. The strategy considers the full range of open space in the city including: formal open space; private gardens; agricultural land; land left to nature such as woodlands and wetlands; the natural network of canals, rivers, hedgerows, ditches, road verges and railway lines; and finally the land outside the city. The size and continuity of habitats are important factors in maintaining the ecological value of a city's landscape provisions. Establishing a green network is therefore important to secure biodiversity and a sustainable local ecology. According to the ecological strategy devised by Leicester:

> Protecting areas of highest ecological value should be seen as the minimum requirement for conserving nature in Leicester. Whilst other open land may presently be of lesser ecological value, it does nevertheless provide habitats for wild plants and animals and contributes to the quality of the City environment. It is the aim of the Ecology Strategy to encourage a greater abundance and diversity of wildlife and provide more opportunities to enjoy and benefit from natural landscapes. This will involve the protection of a network of open spaces and linear habitats. In order to achieve the aims of the Ecology Strategy the Council has devised a set of policy statements. Policy E2 is particularly important for achieving the aims of the green strategy: 'The City Council will define, and take appropriate steps to protect, a "green network" of wedges and other vegetated areas and features, so as to conserve an integrated system of wildlife habitats and will resist development on these sites' (Leicester City Council, 1989).

This is a pattern being followed in other cities and could form the basic structure of the sustainable city of the future.

CONCLUSION

This chapter has explored the three main archetypal urban forms. Each main form, the linear city, the gridiron plan and the highly centralized or inward-looking city, may have a role to play in achieving sustainable development. Very much will depend on the circumstances in which each form is used. A public transport strategy and an ecological strategy are probably the two most important factors in determining urban form. The star shaped plan, a derivative of the centralized and linear plan forms may have advantages for the city of moderate size. In this urban form fingers of development radiate from a dominant centre along public transport corridors. Alternating with these corridors of development are wedges of open space linking the centre with the open countryside. For smaller settlements of 10 000 to 20 000 people the highly centralized urban form seems most appropriate. Such settlements, to be effective, should be of a size determined by comfortable walking distances between activities in the settlement.

Most of the urban architecture which exists in the cities of today will be here for at least a further 60 years. Many parts of the cities will probably last for much longer, particularly if conservation is given priority over development as sustainable development theory would suggest. It therefore appears that a priority for the immediate future is making existing cities more sustainable, that is, discovering ways in which the great suburban belts of development which encircle Western cities can be made less energy-intensive in terms of mobility while maintaining a good quality of life for those living there. This aspect of city design will form the theme for the last chapter in this book. It will explore the practical steps which can be implemented immediately which will make existing cities more sustainable. The next two chapters will, however, be examining two other aspects of urban form, the design of the district or neighbourhood and the street block. Both subjects are necessary for an understanding of the scope of sustainable urban design and for determining an immediate practical response to the problems of our, at present, unsustainable cities.

THE CITY QUARTER

6

INTRODUCTION

Fundamental to sustainable development is active public participation in decisions which affect the environment. Popular involvement in the planning and management of the environment is most effective at the local level of the quarter, district or neighbourhood. It is at this scale of planning where the local resident has most knowledge and expertise (Moughtin, 1992). The resident of the neighbourhood has first-hand experience of problems faced by the family friends and neighbours. There is, therefore, a need to support, develop and institutionalize this local participation by creating formal political structures which empower the citizen. The development of local political structures which have the power to influence decisions which affect the local environment is the route to fulfilling the ideals of Local Agenda 21 and sustainability both locally and globally. This chapter seeks to explore the form the city quarter should take to fulfil this political role in the sustainable city.

It has been suggested that the city quarter is the main component of urban design (Gosling and Maitland, 1984). It has also been argued that clearly defined city quarters about 1.5 kilometres (1 mile)

across will be a major preoccupation of urban designers in the present decade and for the early part of the next century (Moughtin, 1992). The scale of development this century, but particularly since the Second World War, has increased significantly both in the public and private sectors. It is now possible to consider the city quarter as a single design problem undertaken by one developer or group of collaborating developers working with a single design team. Urban Development Corporations involved with inner city regeneration are involved with major components of the city such as the Isle of Dogs in London or the once great docks of Liverpool. While there seems broad agreement that the quarter is a legitimate subject for study by the urban designer, there is some doubt about its size and nature. This chapter will therefore explore the historical origins of the quarter, some reasons given for structuring the city in quarters, the various definitions of the quarter, particularly in terms of its size and its structure, and finally the chapter will end with examples of city quarters developed this century and an analysis of the qualities required of a quarter in a sustainable city.

The Roman city was divided into four quarters by its two main streets, the *cardo* and *decumanus*, which crossed at right angles. Evidence of this quartering of the city is to be seen in many cities of Roman foundation, such as Lucca, which are still important urban centres today (Figure 4.33). Alberti refers to many ancient authorities, including Plutarch and Solon to whom he attributes the notion of dividing the city into areas for different groups. For example, according to Alberti: 'Curtius writes that Babylon was divided into a number of separate quarters...' and 'Romulus separated knights and patricians from plebeians; and Numa divided the plebeians according to their respective employ-ments' (Alberti, republished 1955, Book 4 Ch 5 and Book 4 Ch 1). Alberti also quotes Plato as proposing the division of the city into 12 parts: '... allotting to each its particular temples and chapels' (Alberti, republished 1955, Book 7 Ch 1).

The classical tradition which divides the city into quarters was probably based upon the observation of the natural or unplanned cities of the Ancient World. Cities which appear to develop without the conscious intervention of man are organized into clearly defined neighbourhoods or quarters. The traditional cities of the Hausa people of Nigeria, for example, are still organized in wards (Moughtin, 1985). Each ward is associated with one of the great medieval gateways and is occupied by a group which practises a common trade. Other wards outside the walls of the old cities of the Hausa are occupied by other ethnic or tribal groups. Closer to home, cities in Britain still have a jewellery quarter or lace market. In Nottingham, like other British cities, there are areas which are named, have clear boundaries and to which people belong. In Nottingham, Lenton, Basford, Forest Fields, the Park and others are quarters or neighbourhoods to which people relate either as residents or outsiders. Even to the outsider these areas are major structuring elements by which the city is understood. Such patterns of quarters, districts or neighbourhoods are common to most if not all cities and is the basis of perceptive structuring which renders the city intelli-gible to its citizens (Lynch, 1960).

The city in the pre-motor car age developed naturally in the form of a cluster of quarters. The quarter as a major structuring element of the city is not so characteristic of the modern motorized city: 'The motor car, indeed, not only promotes the dissolution of the city: it virtually demands it. It demands space, and its use is facilitated by disper-sal. A city designed for its uninhibited use would be spacious indeed' (Houghton-Evans, 1975). The city encircled by suburbia is now the common urban form of the developed world. Furthermore, there is widening physical separation of socio-economic groups in the modern city, a process which tends to accelerate with increasing affluence. This separation of different interest groups, though present in the pre-industrial city, was never as endemic as it would now appear to be in the city of the twentieth century. When socio-economic pressures stimulate, as they are now doing, this dispersed pattern of development there is: '... the tendency to seek simplified design structures, which is often abetted by development convenience' (Gosling and Maitland, 1984). The result of these tendencies is a coarse-grained city that is a city where: '... extensive areas of one thing are separated from extensive areas of another thing' (Lynch, 1981). The motives, however, which produce a coarse-grained city with extensive areas of single land uses, unsafe centres that die at night and large socially homogeneous housing estates, are powerful. These powerful motives include the preference for living near similar people with similar interests and the group-ing of commercial activities which maximize the locational advantages of a dispersed network of roads. Constraints imposed on the poor by their unequal access to the housing market exacerbates the situation. The forces which are inhibiting the structuring of cities to form fine-grained quarters are real and powerful. Since this is certainly the case, why should the city designer be seeking an alterna-tive city of the future built on an outdated idea from the distant past? More importantly, even if an alternative to the present situation is desirable, is such an alternative future for the city anything other than a utopian dream?

The movement towards sustainable development, environmental protection and the reduction of pollution engenders an entirely new perspective for the city planning professions. The reorientation of planning and design priorities will inevitably lead to a reshaping of the city which, of necessity, will be dependent upon energy-efficient means of transport. While the car-orientated city demands space and the use of personalized vehicles is facilitated by dispersal, the efficiency of public transport supported by walking and cycling is promoted by concentration: 'Just as we have seen that the automobile and the bus pull the town in contrary directions so do they require totally different primary networks' (Houghton-Evans, 1975). The bus, in the same way as any other form of public transport, requires for its efficient and economic running a high density city where a large pool of prospective passengers live within easy walking distance of the routes: the car is more effective in a city which is dispersed with a widely spaced network of major roads. The sustainable city will give priority to the mixed street rather than the motorway and travelling through a centre rather than bypassing it. The thought process for the design of the sustainable city is the antithesis of that for the now defunct procedures used to facilitate the car. The new design paradigm requires a return to first principles and an examination of features of the traditional city which may, in an adapted form, be useful for greening the city. The quarter is one such component of the traditional city which deserves closer study.

The quarter, district and neighbourhood are terms with different meanings for different authors. In some cases the terms have been used interchangeably. Jacobs classifies neighbourhoods into three broad types: 'Looking at city neighbourhoods as organs of self-government, I can see evidence that only three kinds of neighbourhoods are useful: (1) the city as a whole; (2) Street Neighbourhoods; and (3) districts of large, sub-city size, composed

of one hundred thousand people and more in the case of the largest cities' (Jacobs, 1965). Furthermore, Jacobs identifies the causes of the failure of neighbourhood planning as ultimately failures of localized self-government. Lynch also recognizes the importance of a political function for the neighbourhood or district: his size for the political unit is considerably smaller than the hundred thousand suggested by Jacobs: 'It is in governmental units of 20 000–40 000 people that ordinary citizens can be active in politics if they wish, feel connected to an identifiable political community, and sense some control over public affairs ...' (Lynch, 1981). In Chapter 4 it was suggested that the local government of the regions should be strengthened, but it is also necessary to strengthen small self-governing towns and districts within the urban region so dissolving the scale of the big city into a finer political grain, and giving legitimacy to active public participation, to decisions about environmental quality.

The arguments about the size of the district, quarter, and neighbourhood like those about the region are inconclusive. We have seen, in Chapter 3, Plato suggested a figure of 5040 householders or citizens as the population necessary for political decision-making (Plato, republished 1975). Aristotle was more circumspect. He was concerned that a political unit should be big enough for its citizens to be able to live a full life but not so big that citizens lose personal touch with each other. For Aristotle face-to-face contact was important so that questions of justice could be decided with the full knowledge of those involved and so that offices could be distributed according to merit (Aristotle, republished 1981). The models for both Plato and Aristotle were Athens with 40 000 citizens and the other Greek cities having 10 000 citizens or less. If figures of this magnitude are thought desirable for the lowest level of government and also for the size of the quarter or district then the physical dimensions of the districts at Harlow designed by Gibberd give an approximation of this component of the sustainable city of the future. The districts in Harlow comprise four neighbourhoods of between 4000-7000 people so that the districts were approximately 18 000-22 000 people. There is probably no ideal size for the quarter or district, particularly in existing cities. It is important that the district or coalitions of districts can act as a check to the power of the city. The other chief function is the development of city structures which enable citizens to participate fully in both the administration of some city services and in decisions about the future of the city. As Alberti quite rightly stressed: '... the city itself ought to be laid out differently for a tyrant, from what they are for those who enjoy and protect government as if it were a magistery voluntarily put into their hands' (Alberti, republished 1955). If Alberti's statement is accepted then it follows that the city structure for a more participatory democracy will probably be different from one structured for representative democracy which stresses centralized power in the state and in the city.

One of the formative ideas of the first new towns in Britain during the 1940s and early 1950s was the neighbourhood concept. Overlaying this concept was the notion of forming a 'community'. The cooperative spirit which was prevalent after the end of the Second World War led to a belief that this community spirit could infuse the new planning system with life. The neighbourhoods in the new towns and the local authority housing estates in the suburbs were to be modelled on the old inner city working class communities of cooperation. Middle class families, doctors, dentists and teachers, were to live as neighbours with the families of the labourer, mechanic and factory worker and to provide the community leadership. As Gosling points out, one group of planners were concerned that: 'The apparent impossibility of making any technical decision about the city without thereby implying a corresponding social structure has persuaded many designers of the primacy of the social programme. Urban design is seen essentially

as the attempt to find the appropriate form to sustain this programme or perhaps more actively, to reinforce or even induce it' (Gosling and Maitland, 1984). To some extent the view of planning as social engineering prevailed, or was thought to prevail, into the 1950s. There was, however, another and more mainstream view of the neighbourhood which was held by planners. This idea of the neighbourhood is much more practical and is concerned primarily with the physical distribution of social facilities in relation to population thresholds: 'The neighbourhood is essentially a spontaneous grouping, and it cannot be created by the planner. All he can do is to make provision for the necessary physical needs, by designing an area which gives the inhabitants the sense of living in one place distinct from all other places, and in which social equipment, like schools and playing fields, are conveniently placed' (Gibberd, 1955). Gibberd in this passage stresses the spontaneous nature of community formation and suggests that the physical structure merely permits its development. It is not the pub, the corner shop or the chapel which created the British working class community but the strong family ties and the interdependence of the group in the face of financial crisis constantly present with the poor. It has long been recognized that 'community' is not necessarily a product of place. The 'community of interest' may draw members from the city, region or it may have a network of international contacts. The individual may, indeed, belong to several communities, including a local residents' group, a University fraternity and membership of an international professional association (Webber, 1964).

'The legible city, that is, the city easily visualized in the "mind's eye" has, according to Lynch, a clearly defined, easily recognized and distinctive perceptual structure' (Moughtin et al., 1995). Lynch suggested that five components - the path, the node, the edge, the landmark and the district - were the key to urban legibility (Lynch, 1960). To some extent the perception and understanding of the urban environment is personal, but groups within a culture share sets of images. It is this shared image which is the concern of urban design. A clearly structured city in terms of Lynch's five components, it is argued, will strengthen the common features of the city image shared by its citizens. Such a city will possess the quality which Lynch described as 'imageability' or the ability to stimulate a strong visual image in the eye and mind of the viewer (Lynch, 1960).

Norberg-Schulz has views on city structure which are similar to those of Lynch: 'Places, paths and domains are the basic schemata of orientation, that is, the constituent elements of existential space ... Paths divide man's environment into areas which are more or less well known. We will call such qualitatively defined areas as domains' He is not as clear in his distinction between place and domain as Lynch is between node and district: 'But the distinction place and domain is useful, as our environmental image obviously comprises areas to which we do not belong and which do not function as goals. The domain can therefore be defined as a relatively unstructured "ground" on which places and paths appear as more pronounced figures' (Norberg-Schulz, 1971). It appears that for Norberg-Schulz the place is somewhat smaller than the domain and possibly more like Lynch's node: 'Nodes are points, the strategic spots in a city into which an observer can enter, and which are the intensive foci to and from which he is travelling' (Lynch, 1960). It is Lynch's description of the district, however, which is most useful for this discussion of the quarter: 'Districts are the medium-to-large sections of the city, conceived of as having two-dimensional extent, which the observer mentally enters "inside of", and which are recognizable as having some common identifying character' (Lynch, 1960). It is this definition of the district by Lynch which will be used here as the description of the city quarter: while there is no standard size for a quarter it is larger than the neighbourhood, and has a population of about 20 000 to 100 000.

THE QUARTER AND ITS FORM

Modern theories about the form of the quarter, district or neighbourhood can be traced to Howard and his architects Raymond Unwin and Barry Parker in this country and to Henry Wright, Clarence Stein and Clarence Perry in the USA. Howard sited schools at the nucleus of wards. The wards were to be complete segments of the town. Here in this suggestion for structuring the city into segments is, in embryo, the idea of the city quarter which later developed into the neighbourhood concept (Howard, 1965). Residential communities in the USA such as Roland Green in Baltimore, though attractively landscaped, nevertheless comprised magnificent detached villas facing onto roads carrying through traffic. By the early 1920s in the USA traffic was already posing problems. A town planning movement developed in the USA which was influenced by the Garden City movement in Britain was attempting to come to terms with the motor car. Stein and Wright were elaborating the ideas of Unwin and Parker for the 'superblock' and applying them to American conditions. The buildings in the superblock were not arranged along through traffic routes. The homes were located around a central landscaped park, the whole superblock being planned as a large single unit, as in Chatham village, Pittsburgh (Figure 6.1). The superblock was surrounded by roads carrying through traffic while the homes were accessed by culs-de-sac (Figure 6.2). The design concept was demonstrated on a large scale in Radburn, New Jersey. The idea was to create a series of superblocks, each around a green but with the greens connected by pedestrian pathways. This pedestrian system of paths led to schools, shopping centres and other community facilities (Figure 6.3). At no point did the car interfere with or endanger the pedestrian. An essential feature of the Radburn principle was the organization of the town into clearly defined neighbourhoods. This idea was fully explained by Clarence

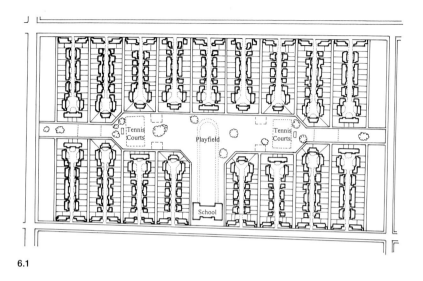

6.1

Perry, the theoretician of the North American offshoot of the Garden City movement, in his book *The Neighbourhood Unit* (Perry, 1929).

The Abercrombie Plan for London embraced the idea of the neighbourhood which had been fully developed by Perry (Abercrombie, 1945). It was upon this idea of the neighbourhood that a new concept of urban form was elaborated. The city was conceived as a multiplicity of basic cells or modules each independently viable for some services and connected to the whole urban area by an efficient transport system. The city can grow by the addition of cells or modules, each one being to some degree self-sufficient and having its own integrity. A number of architects were also making a similar point: 'In all great epochs of history the existence of standards - that is the conscious adoption of type forms - has been the criterion of

Figure 6.1 The Superblock
Figure 6.2 Greenbelt, Maryland (Lynch, 1981)
Figure 6.3 Radburn (Houghton-Evans, 1975)

6.2

6.3

a polite and well-ordered society; for it is a commonplace that repetition of the same things for the same purposes exercises a settling and civilising influence on men's minds ... The uniformity of the cells whose multiplication by street forms and still larger units of the city therefore calls for formal expression' (Gropius, 1935).

In *Homes for the People*, there is a summary of the principles of neighbourhood planning as they were envisaged for London and the early British new towns:

> A neighbourhood is formed naturally from the daily occupations of people, the distance it is convenient for a housewife to walk to do her daily shopping and, particularly, the distance it is convenient for a child to walk to school. He should not have a long walk and he should not have to cross a main traffic road. The planning of a neighbourhood unit starts from that. In the proposals of the County of London Plan the Neighbourhood unit is the area that can be served by one elementary school and it works out at from 6000 to 10 000 inhabitants. Grouped centrally near the school are the local shopping centre and such community buildings as a clinic, or a communal restaurant. There is no through traffic in the neighbourhood unit: it skirts it, along one of the main roads (Boyd *et al.*, 1945).

Harlow, designed by Gibberd, is one of the early new towns in Britain which employed the neighbourhood as a structuring concept for urban form. Gibberd in a number of places outlines his prescription for a well designed neighbourhood. The following quotations outline some of his views on this topic:

> The first aesthetic problem in the design of the neighbourhood is how to give the area its own physical identity, how in fact to make it a place with its own character distinct from that of other places ... The size of any particular neighbourhood is limited by the need to have all the social services ... within easy walking distance of any home ... The population generally taken by English planners is

from five to twelve thousand people, because between those numbers it is possible to provide the majority of communal facilities which help to bring people together and engender a community spirit (Gibberd, 1955).

The important design requirements of the neighbourhood as proposed in the early British new towns are: a physical extent determined by a ten to fifteen minute walking distance from the furthest home to the school at the centre; a population which supports a junior school and a number of community facilities including a local shopping centre; a clearly defined boundary employing landscape to reinforce that boundary where possible; an architectural treatment which distinguishes it from other adjacent neighbourhoods; a definite centre; and the elimination of through traffic by arranging the major roads at the periphery of the neighbourhood.

THE NEIGHBOURHOOD AND ITS CRITICS

A high point of new town planning is the report on the plan for Hook (Bennett *et al.*, 1961). The study for a further new town for London, which was never implemented, returned to first principles in an attempt to discover the critical parameters in the design of an urban centre for 100 000 people. The neighbourhood was not supported by the study group and was not used to structure the new town. The neighbourhood was faulted for a number of reasons: it was thought to be over-simplified, not representing the richness of the real world of social interactions; it was also thought to lead to a dispersed urban form and that it did not lend itself to effective public transport. The last two criticisms relate more to the way in which the neighbourhood concept had been implemented with large swathes of landscape between them than with the concept itself. As for the first criticism, the neighbourhood was not conceived as a device to replace the natural

6.4

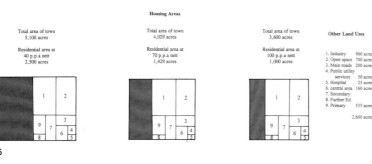

Housing Areas

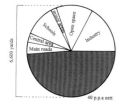

6.5

6.6

process involved in the development of communities but as a method for structuring the physical form of cities.

The plan for Hook, while aiming at urbanity, also aimed to accommodate the motor car. Further aims included maintaining a contrast between town and country and the promotion of a balanced community. The plan allowed for one car per household plus visitors' cars at the rate of a half car per household. The accommodation of the motor car was to be achieved in such a way that the pedestrian took precedence. The town form evolved for Hook in itself is of great interest to the student of planning and urban design, but it is the calculation of the spatial needs of the town which is an important consideration for those interested in sustainable development (Figures 6.4 to 6.6). The total area of the town was calculated in two main parts. The non-residential use was considered to be a fixed amount which for 100 000 people was calculated as 2600 acres. The residential area ranged from 3600 acres at a density of 100 persons per acre to 5100 acres at 40 persons per acre. Figure 6.5 shows how a decision about residential density can influence the area of the town development and distances travelled on foot in the settlement. It also influences traffic within the town – the higher the density the more effective the public transport system. The authors of the Hook report therefore argued for the highest possible density compatible with the house and private garden, which they noted was the type of home most British people wanted.

Figure 6.6 is a diagram which was added almost as an afterthought. It showed the various land takes as pie charts. This demonstrates that the same considerations of density when applied to a circular form do not affect the distances travelled from the perimeter in quite such a dramatic way as it does in an elongated rectangle. For the extremes of density used in the calculations of the 'land take', the radius of the circle increased from about two kilometres to three kilometres.

The criticisms of the neighbourhood have been directed mainly at the concept when it has been overlaid, mistakenly, with meanings of community. The neighbourhood concept when used as a physical structuring device is a most useful tool for relating population and facilities. Further confusion arises when the neighbourhood concept is used for structuring space at quite different scales. The term neighbourhood can be used to describe: a few streets with a population of about 500 to 600 inhabitants; the catchment area of a primary school having a population of 4000 to 5000; or the district or quarter with a political function and a population of 20 000 to 100 000. Alexander, for example, advocates the desirability of small neighbourhoods. According to Alexander, people need to belong to an identifiable spatial unit which should be no more than 300 metres across, with about 400 to 500 inhabitants: 'Available evidence suggests, first, that the neighbourhoods which people identify with have extremely small populations; second, that they are small in area; and third, that a major road through a neighbourhood destroys it.' In coming to a decision about the correct population for the neighbourhood, Alexander took as his standard the size of group which can coordinate itself to reach decisions about its community self-interest and the ability to bring pressure to bear on city authorities: 'Anthropological evidence suggests that a human group cannot coordinate itself to reach such decisions if its population is above 1500, and many people set the figure as low as 500' (Alexander et al., 1977).

The neighbourhood as used in the context of new town planning in Britain has already been discussed: its population is somewhere between 4000 and 10 000. These figures are based on the population which can be served by a primary school located within easy walking distance of every home. The school forms the nucleus of a centre for the neighbourhood: 'Grouped centrally near are the local shopping centre and such community buildings as a clinic...' (Boyd et al., 1945). It is for this spatial unit, and not Alexander's smaller unit, that the term neighbourhood will be reserved in this text. As Gibberd and others have declared, it is important for the neighbourhood to have its own architectural character and to be a discrete visual unit. Boundaries between neighbourhoods reinforce the integrity of the neighbourhood. In Harlow and other British new towns of that time landscape was the feature which established the boundary between neighbourhoods. While this is an effective visual method of separating neighbourhoods, it does tend to increase the distances between the different activities in the urban area and also weakens connections between adjacent neighbourhoods. In existing towns and cities large areas of open space between neighbourhoods is most unusual. Other edges for neighbourhoods include: main traffic routes; canals and other waterways; or an abrupt change in architectural style. It is unusual to find an edge between neighbourhoods as 'hard' as the 'Peace Line' running between the Shankill and the Falls in Belfast (Figure 6.7). Alexander, while supporting the notion of the need for an edge to define spatial units, believes that such features should be 'fleshy' rather than 'hard': 'There is the need for a certain ambiguity at the edge and provision for connection' (Alexander et al., 1977). The spatial unit of this dimension, that is, a neighbourhood covering an area one mile in diameter and served by public transport, would seem appropriate for the sustainable city of the future.

The third spatial unit for which the term neighbourhood has sometimes been used is the large district of a city, which will be referred to in this book from now as the quarter: it is a unit of between 20 000 and 100 000 people. This, according to Lynch and Jacobs, should be the main governmental unit within and below the level of the city council. (Jacobs, 1965; Lynch, 1981). Most writers since Jacobs would probably agree with her comments upon the vitality of cities and their quarters: 'This ubiquitous principle is the need of cities for a most intricate and close-grained diversity

Figure 6.7 Peace Line,
Belfast. (Photographs by Pat
Braniff)

6.7a

6.7b

6.7c

of uses that give each other constant mutual
support, both economically and socially' (Jacobs,
1965). Gosling, for example, quoting Jacobs,
proposes four conditions for a successful district:

'the need for mixed primary uses ... the need for
small blocks ... the need for aged buildings ... and
the need for concentration' (Gosling and Maitland,
1984). Leon Krier makes a similar point, stressing
the need to transform: '... housing zones (dormitory
cities) into complex parts of the city, into cities
within the city, into quarters which integrate all the
functions of urban life' (Krier, 1978).

From the argument developed so far it would
seem that there are two possible structures for city
sub-division into sustainable quarters. The first is a
city quarter of 20 000 to 100 000 people with a
major centre and sub-centres around which are
organized neighbourhoods of 5000 to 10 000
people. The second arrangement is a quarter of
about 20 000 people with one centre but sub-
divided into small neighbourhoods of 500 people.
These model structures may be applicable for the
planning of a new town or a large suburban extension to an existing city; however, such developments may not be the norm in the future. For the
foreseeable future Western cities will remain much
as they are today. The changes will be marginal: in
the early twenty-first century most city people in
the West will live in a suburbia already built and
inhabited. All cities have parts which are referred to
as districts, enclaves, sectors, quarters or precincts.
They are sometimes discrete areas having dominant
or all-pervasive characteristics. Not all cities,
however, can be neatly sectioned in this way: 'The
most prominent enclave may dissipate visually at its
periphery. Most urban enclaves lack outstandingly
prominent characteristics. Further, complexity in an
urban enclave should not be mistaken for confusion.
Urban complexity - the intense intermixture of
complementary activities - is one of the major
reasons for cities and the spice of urban life'
(Spreiregen, 1965). Cities are complex social,
economic and visual structures; nevertheless, the
users of cities simplify the physical structure so that
they are able to comprehend its form and therefore
react to it. It is the designer's task to assist in the
creation of cities and parts of cities with a strong

clear image. A strong image in part is due to a firm outline or edge to component parts (Lynch, 1960).

THE CITY QUARTER AND NEIGHBOURHOOD IN PRACTICE

AMSTERDAM SOUTH: BERLAGE

Amsterdam has a continuous tradition of town planning unbroken since 1900. During the late nineteenth and early twentieth centuries Amsterdam was growing rapidly. For example, the city grew by 50 per cent in the first two decades of this century. To accommodate this growth there has been almost uninterrupted building activity for most of this century. Town building in Amsterdam is particularly interesting during the early decades of the century when several new quarters were added to the city. These extensions were enhanced by a number of imaginative architects who were members of a group which became known as the 'Amsterdam School'. In addition to Amsterdam South, which is the subject of more detailed analysis other city extensions were built during this high point of urban design in Amsterdam: examples include a number of attractive garden villages built in Amsterdam North and Amsterdam East (Ons Amsterdam, 1973).

In London the wonderful squares and crescents of the eighteenth century were built for the gentry and the wealthy upper middle classes (Figures 6.8 and 6.9). The boulevards of Hausmann in Paris were for the middle class while the poor crowded into slum-like properties between the boulevards. The building in Amsterdam at the beginning of this century, in contrast, was mainly for the lower middle class and the working population. Giedion explains the development process which achieved this social programme in this way:

> Cooperatively organized building societies received building credits on very easy terms from the state, the credits being guaranteed by the community.

6.8

6.9

Figure 6.8 Bedford Square, London
Figure 6.9 Bedford Square, London

Thus the whole tendency of the act (the 1901 Housing Act) was to make the city a decisive influence upon all building activity. At the same time the city made intensive (though not always successful) efforts to constitute itself a great land-owner and to acquire the land for its housing settlements before speculation forced up prices. And, like the nobles who were landlords in London, the city of Amsterdam leased the ground instead of selling it (Giedion, 1954).

Another innovative feature of the Housing Act of 1901, in Holland, forced local authorities to determine extension plans for growth (Public Works Department, Amsterdam, 1975). As part of this programme of urban extension the well documented plan for South Amsterdam was submitted in 1917 to the Town Council by the architect Berlage. The style of the plan and the power of its design approach set new standards in the planning of the city quarter. It may be true to say as a plan for a quarter it has not been equalled since. The planning was complemented by an architectural process which succeeded in building whole districts which were both homogeneous in design but also met the needs of the community. Developers before receiving permission to build submitted designs to a 'Commission for Beauty'. This commission insisted upon uniform street façades. The discipline of the commission encouraged a fine urban architecture to develop, de Klerk and the other architects of the Amsterdam School responding to the challenge with flair and imagination (Figures 6.10 to 6.12).

6.10

6.11a

6.12a

6.11b

6.12b

Figure 6.10 Amsterdam South, statue of Berlage
Figure 6.11 Amsterdam South
Figure 6.12 Amsterdam South

6.13

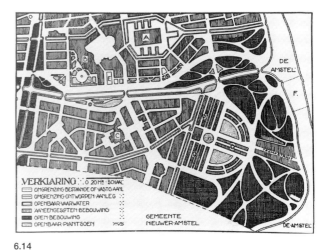

6.14

Berlage drew up his first plan for Amsterdam South in 1902 at the time the Stock Exchange building, Amsterdam, his finest work, was nearing completion (Figure 6.13). This first plan has streets of sweeping ovals reminiscent of French garden designs in Hausmann's public parks for Paris in the mid-nineteenth century (Figures 6.14 and 6.15). The first plan is both romantic in character and organic in the shapes used to structure the quarter. The plan may also have been influenced by Sitte's strictures against the use of the forced axis and artificial gridiron system of streets. Berlage was faced with the problem of giving identity to a large area of high density housing. The essentially low density garden city concept, even if Berlage had been aware of it, was not therefore appropriate for his purpose. Berlage relied upon the urban heritage derived directly from the Renaissance. Every neighbourhood within the quarter was to be dominated by an important public building. The neighbourhoods were therefore to cluster round a market, a theatre or college which was to give the neighbourhood its particular character. The quarter was structured to a human scale easily perceived and understood by its residents.

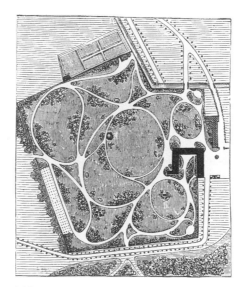

6.15

Figure 6.13 The Stock Exchange, Amsterdam
Figure 6.14 Berlage's first plan for Amsterdam South
(Giedion, 1954)
Figure 6.15 French nineteenth-century garden
(Giedion, 1954)

6.16

Figure 6.16 Berlage's second plan for Amsterdam South (Public Works Department, Amsterdam, 1975)
Figure 6.17 Bijlmermeer (Public Works Department, Amsterdam, 1975)
Figure 6.18 Bijlmermeer (Public Works Department, Amsterdam, 1975)

The second scheme for Amsterdam South by Berlage was made in 1915. The plan this time provided a framework of streets only (Figure 6.16). The most prominent feature of the scheme is the junction of three streets to form a 'Y' which is approached from the Amstel River. The streets are wide and airy with tasteful landscaping: behind the trees which line the roads are the continuous four-storey façades typical of the expressionist architecture of the Amsterdam School. Between the roads are street blocks of four-storey development surrounding in places spacious lawns with shrubberies. Though not as innovative as his first scheme of 1902, the parts of his adopted plan which were completed are civilized and urbane. Giedion, the apologist for the modern movement in architecture, is rather dismissive of Berlage's efforts: 'The example (Amsterdam South) may serve to show that in 1900 even the most progressive minds were affected by a tendency toward an artificial monumentality – an artificial or pseudo monumentality because it was used to hide the uncertainty and perplexity with which the organization of a town was approached, even when carte blanche had been

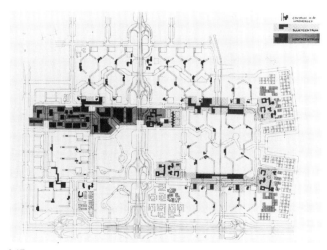

6.17

6.18

given to the planner' (Giedion, 1954). Where quarters followed the precepts of the modern movement in architecture as at Bijlmermeer in Amsterdam, built in the late 1960s and early 1970s they compare unfavourably with the delightful work of Berlage and his expressionist architectural collaborators (Figures 6.17 to 6.18).

VIENNA: OTTO WAGNER

Otto Wagner (1841-1918) prepared a planning scheme for a quarter in Vienna in 1910. Like his contemporary, Berlage, he did not pursue a garden city approach to planning the quarter, preferring the traditional urban form of the continental city which has as its basic module the street block of four, five or six storeys with central light well. Wagner's layout is rigidly formal, a dull rectangular grid with long axial streets (Figure 6.19). While Wagner's approach to urban design is pedantically formal he was among the first to see that the needs of the inhabitants of a city should govern its planning: 'Wagner's chief interest was the creation of a healthful environment for the man of ordinary means. He was one of the earliest to recognize that a great city embraces many different types of people, each type requiring a different kind of dwelling. He saw too that the residential needs of the average city-dweller changed with his circumstances' (Giedion, 1954). It is the insights into the needs of people which is Wagner's main contribution to city planning and urban design. Wagner's work on the Vienna subway led him to an interest in movement at different levels with different modes of transport. His drawings of combinations of railroads, streets and bridges presage the complex transport interchanges of the modern city or the multilevel town centres such as Runcorn or Cumbernauld (Figure 6.20).

DOXIADIS AND ISLAMABAD

One of the many ideas contained in *Ekistics* is the notion that settlements like growing organisms are composed of cells:

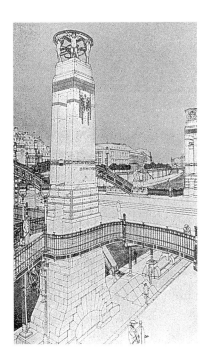

Figure 6.19 Wagner's plan for a District Centre, Vienna (Giedion, 1941)
Figure 6.20 Drawing by Wagner (Giedion, 1941)

A study of growing organisms in Nature will show that in most of them the cells remain the same size regardless of the growth of the organism. The cells are the same whether a person is old or young, or whether a tree is at the beginning or prime of its life. Here we can draw an important conclusion: the search for ideal solutions has to be geared towards static cells and the dynamic growth of the organism (Doxiadis, 1968).

Growth and transformation of settlements according to this theory should be cellular. If the village is regarded as a basic cell then its growth should be by the addition of another cell or village and not the expansion of its nucleus or centre together with the expansion of its periphery. To save the village from the destruction caused by development pressures leading to its growth and transformation, the roads must be realigned to retain the village intact as a cell. The new functions caused by development pressures should then be transferred to a new centre to form the nucleus of the next cell.

According to Doxiadis the smallest human community is about 2000 families with 500 and 3000 families being the lower and upper limits, respectively, for this unit. In Islamabad Doxiadis attempted to arrange communities of this size, the basic cells of urban structure, into larger districts within the city. In doing this he was concerned to combine the cells according to two scales: the human scale based on walking, and the non-human scale mainly associated with fast-moving vehicles. In Islamabad the basic cell or community is about one kilometre square and it is not traversed by major roads. Four such cells combine to form a larger community or district surrounded by major highways (Figures 6.21 and 6.22). 'Here (in Islamabad) we see how the non-human scale of the major transportation and communication networks

6.22a

6.22b

Figure 6.21 The Sector, Islamabad (Doxiadis, 1968)
Figure 6.22 Islamabad

6.21

that pass between the sectors with dimensions of 1800 metres (5094 feet), are gradually yielding to minor communications networks entering the sectors without crossing them and in a way not attracting through-traffic, thus defining three or four human communities within each sector' (Doxiadis, 1968). Such districts may reach a population of 40 000 to 50 000 people, though Doxiadis suggests that the grouping of communities and their size should be proportional to the size of the settlement.

HARLOW AND THE QUARTER

The new town of Harlow which has already been discussed earlier in the chapter is divided into four quarters or districts. As mentioned earlier, landscape and topography are the key features in the location of the main town quarters, dividing one quarter from the next. Each quarter, which has a major centre, was designed to have a population of approximately 20 000 people. The quarter comprises a cluster of neighbourhoods which focus on a major centre of 50 shops, church, health centre, branch library and hall. One of the four quarters has for its focus the town centre itself.

Mark Hall, the quarter to the north-east of Harlow is divided into three neighbourhoods separated from each other by main roads and landscaping. The neighbourhoods focus on the district centre at the crossing of the main roads serving the quarter. Each neighbourhood was designed to have its own primary schools located at its centre which was also to contain 4-6 shops, a hall and a public house. Each neighbourhood is further divided into distinct housing units of 150 to 400 dwellings centred on a local play space and tenants' common room: 'There are thus four stages of community groupings in the town: the housing unit and its play space and common room; the neighbourhood with its primary school, shopping centres and hall; the neighbourhood cluster with its large shopping and community group; and the Town Centre' (Gibberd, 1955).

The housing units are linked to the centres and to the main roads by a system of spine or loop roads that run through each neighbourhood. Separate cycle and pedestrian routes were designed to link the neighbourhoods in Mark Hall with the industrial estates, town centre and the other districts of the city. Though the form of Mark Hall is quite different from the grid used by Doxiadis in Islamabad, Gibberd, the planner of Harlow, also uses the term organic to describe his design for the town: 'The resulting pattern is an organic system in which the roads increase in scale the farther they are from the heart of the housing groups' (Gibberd, 1955). The term organic, when used by Doxiadis, Gibberd and other architects and planners can result in a wide variety of forms. In the case of Harlow, the organic analogy refers to the concept of a hierarchy of facilities, centres and roads rather like the branching of a tree; it also refers to the grouping of cellular units to form larger components of the city. The arrangement of the local centre and primary school within walking distance of all homes in the catchment area is a feature of the Harlow plan which should be common practice in the planning of the sustainable city of the future. More contentious, for sustainable development, is the low gross density in Harlow. This feature of the quarter increases distances between its different parts. The writings in sustainable development suggest a higher density regime within the quarter and major landscaping elements arranged around its edge. Such an urban solution, however, may not accommodate the British suburban lifestyle and in the case of Harlow would limit the effectiveness of the landscaping, one of this new town's most attractive features (Figures 6.23 to 6.26).

CLIFTON ESTATE IN NOTTINGHAM

New towns were not the only post Second World War urban developments in Britain. Around most major cities in the country large urban extensions were built by the local authorities. These estates were built for those unable to secure a mortgage or those with a preference for renting a home. Estates like Croxteth and Kirby in Liverpool were built in

Figures 6.23 to **6.26**
Harlow, housing and
landscape

6.23

6.24

6.25

6.26

the 1950s and 1960s throughout the country. Clifton in Nottingham is one such quarter. It was built beyond the River Trent to the south of the city. The new development, consisting mainly of two-storey terraced and semi-detached housing is the bulk of the quarter. It is separated from the old village of Clifton by the A453, a trunk road carrying heavy traffic, which divides this residential quarter. The old village of Clifton sits on a ridge overlooking an attractive stretch of the Trent valley. Adjacent to the old village of Clifton, and on the same side of the trunk road, is a large part of the new Nottingham Trent University campus comprising teaching, administrative and residential accommodation. This quarter of the city has a population

of approximately 27 000 people and is surrounded by the city green belt, the Trent valley, schools and other landscaped areas. Clifton is in effect a town on the edge of a city having its own main centre and subsidiary centres of local shops, pubs and community halls. The road pattern is not as highly structured as those in the new towns of the time. Most roads tend to be multipurpose with little evidence of planning for the pedestrian. The main local employment in Clifton is in the shops, schools and university. There is strong community activity; for example, the proposals by the Highways Agency for the widening of the trunk road and its placing in a cutting for part of its length is being strongly resisted by some groups of local residents. The

6.27

6.28

6.29

6.30

Figures 6.27 and **6.28**
Clifton village
Figures 6.29 and **6.30**
Post-war housing, Clifton

local resident groups, using their political muscle, persuaded the Nottingham City Council and the local MP to support them and object to the proposals at the public enquiry to be held in 1996. The community's suggestion for the building of a bypass and the development of public transport connections with the city seem more appropriate for sustainable development than the environmentally destructive scheme proposed by the Highways Agency (Figures 6.27 to 6.30). Existing city quarters such as Clifton would gain added political influence if their views were represented by an elected community council, rather than by ad hoc groupings of community activists. It would be the role of the community council to define the local planning agenda, to seek to improve environmental quality and to defend the area against any forces which may threaten an erosion of its cherished environmental stock.

PROJECT FOR A CITY QUARTER IN SHANGHAI: RICHARD ROGERS

Richard Rogers, in his Reith Lectures, after discussing the principles of sustainable development and their application to architecture, planning and urban design, went on to describe a project for a sustainable city quarter. Although this project in Shanghai may never be realized it is an interesting attempt to respond to the new and demanding environmental programme of city development.

In 1991 Richard Rogers was invited by the Shanghai authorities to prepare a strategic framework for a new district for the city. The Shanghai authorities were proposing a district of international offices employing 500 000 workers for the one kilometre square site. The district was to be planned taking the car as its focus, which meant massive roads to cater for rush-hour traffic. It also involved a multilevel pedestrian system of bridges and underpasses and, of course, massive car parking provision. Satisfying the demands of the car left only one-third of the site for buildings, each building being isolated by highways: 'the result would be a district of stand-alone individual skyscrapers surrounded by acres of cars: socially and environmentally unsuitable in every aspect of its design' (Rogers, 1995a). This is the Isle of Dogs in London's Docklands, but on a much larger scale and the perfect model for the unsustainable city quarter.

In contrast, Rogers approach was to: 'create not a financial ghetto separated from the life of the city but a vibrant, mixed commercial and residential quarter ...' The broader mix of activities and a greater emphasis on public transport reduced the area for roads by 60 per cent: 'Air pollution was dramatically reduced and we were able to transform single use roads into multi-purpose public space - vastly expanding the network of pedestrian-biased streets, cycle paths, market places, avenues and making possible a substantial central park. The overall aim was to locate the community's every day needs including public transport within comfortable walking distance and away from through traffic' (Rogers, 1995a). The quarter was further sub-divided into neighbourhoods, each to be given a different character and all within 10 to 15 minutes walk of important activity points. The buildings were designed to form streets and squares read internally as enclosed spaces while the profile as seen from outside was 'crowned by a series of towers'. Rogers' programme for the quarter as he described in his Reith Lectures sets the urban design strategy for the sustainable quarter.

QUARTIER DE LA VILLETTE: LEON KRIER

'A city can only be reconstructed in the form of *Urban Quarters*. A large or a small city can only be recognized as a large or a small number of urban quarters; as a federation of autonomous quarters. Each quarter must have its own centre, periphery and limit. Each quarter must be a city within a city. The *Quarter* must integrate all daily functions of urban life ... within a territory dimensioned on the basis of the comfort of a walking man; not exceeding 35 hectares in surface and 15 000 inhabitants ... The streets and squares must present a familiar character. Their dimensions and proportions must be those of the best and most beautiful pre-industrial cities' (Krier, 1984). Krier has attempted to interpret, in a number of projects, this design brief for a city quarter. It is proposed here to examine one such attempt, at Quartier de la Villette in Paris and to permit his fine drawings to speak for themselves accompanied only by a limited commentary. Krier's project for la Villette has as a theme a central park, a continuation of a recreation area which stretches along the banks of the Ourcq canal. At right angles to this canal is a grand boulevard one kilometre long and comprising two avenues 50 metres apart. The space formed by the avenues is occupied by large buildings having metropolitan functions such as hotels, cultural centre or town hall. In addition to these major buildings there are also major city spaces on the boulevard and spanning the space between the avenues. In the smaller neighbourhoods which are orientated towards the boulevard, there are subsidiary centres with social facilities grouped round small intimate public squares (Figures 6.31 to 6.33).

LAGUNA WEST, CALIFORNIA: CALTHORPE AND ASSOCIATES

In the USA, Calthorpe and Associates are experimenting with urban forms which are sustainable in the North American context. A useful concept developed for this purpose is the TOD or Transit-Orientated Development: 'A Transit-Orientated

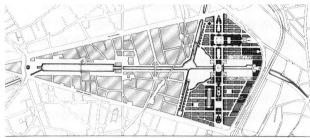

THE AREA OF LA VILLETTE BETWEEN AVENUE DE FLANDRE AND AVENUE JEAN JAURES

6.31

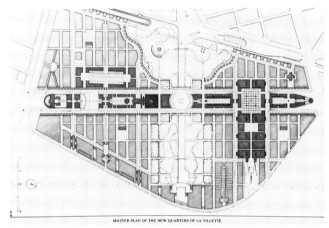

MASTER PLAN OF THE NEW QUARTERS OF LA VILLETTE

6.32

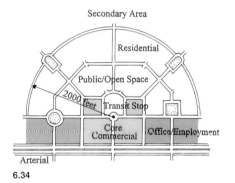

THE AREA BETWEEN THE BUTTES DE CHAUMONT AND MONTMARTRE

6.33

Secondary Area

Residential

Public/Open Space

2000 feet

Transit Stop

Core Commercial

Office/Employment

Arterial

6.34

Development (TOD) is a mixed-use community within an average 2000-foot walking distance of a transit stop and core commercial area. TOD's mix residential, retail, office, open space, and public uses in a walkable environment, making it convenient for residents and employees to travel by transit, bicycle, foot, or car' (Calthorpe, 1993). Developments of this type can be located throughout the city region on undeveloped sites in urbanizing areas, sites with the potential for redevelopment or reuse, and in new urban growth areas. They should, however, be located on or near an existing or a planned public transport route, preferably on a local feeder bus line within about three miles or a

10 minutes travel time to the main public transport route. The ideal size of the TOD is based on a comfortable walking distance to the public transport stop and in order to maximize the use of the land within that distance of public transport Calthorpe suggests moderate to high residential densities (Figure 6.34).

Laguna West, an 800 acre site in Sacramento California, was the first real test for the idea of the TOD. The town is planned to have a population of 10 000 people and is designed with tree-lined comfortable streets, parks and a 65 acre lake. There are five neighbourhoods totalling 2300 homes focused on the lake, community park and town

Figures 6.31 to **6.33** La Villette by Krier

Figure 6.34 The concept of the TOD (Calthorpe, 1993)

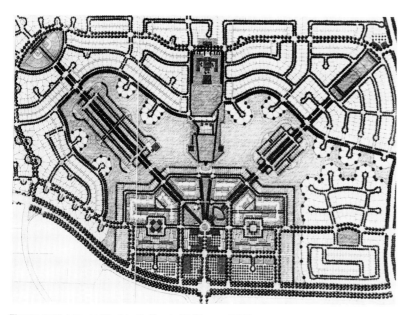

Figure 6.35 Laguna West in California (Calthorpe, 1993)

centre. In the town centre there are an additional 1000 homes at higher densities, together with shops and offices. The mix of housing types and costs are much broader than other developments: they range from large individually designed villas on large plots, through typical suburban family homes, small bungalows, terraced townhouses, apartments and flats. In the first 18 months 200 homes had been built, and the lake, village green and town hall were completed. In addition a major employer, Apple Computer Company, requiring 450 000 square foot of space had been attracted to the town. In many ways this project and the theory which supports it parallels ideas current in Europe. The needs of the car are not altogether ignored though other public means of transport are given priority in the arrangement of town activities and locational considerations (Figure 6.35).

CONCLUSION

There are two divergent views about the size of the city quarter. There is that view represented by Jacobs which stresses the political function of the quarter. This view emphasizes the need for a community occupying a given territory to be able to organize itself politically. The community must be big enough and powerful enough to defend the group's interests. Jacobs believes that this is only possible for communities with a population greater than 100 000. Such groups, it is argued, have the muscle or political clout to affect the behaviour of elected representatives. At another extreme Alexander argues that communal decision-making is only effective in small groups of 500 to 2000 people at the most. A small, cohesive group of this size can identify and agree communal goals then pursue those goals actively and efficiently.

Another view, held mainly by physical planners, relates the size of quarter to a comfortable walking distance from its centre to periphery. This viewpoint is a particularly important consideration when designing a sustainable quarter. This definition of the quarter is advocated eloquently, particularly with his drawings, by Leon Krier. The size of the quarter for Krier is about 12 000 people, that is, the number of people housed at moderate to high densities which can be accommodated within 10 to 15 minutes walk from a central place. This is a Continental European interpretation of the sustainable quarter and follows the tradition of the Continental city where street blocks of four and five storeys are common.

The British tradition straddles both views, that is, the North American and Continental European approaches, in an uneasy compromise. The culture of the British city results in a form which is dictated by a desire for low to medium density residential living conditions. The garden suburb comprising detached or semi-detached houses set in their own plots is still the ideal for most British people. The neighbourhood of about 5000 people which was a feature of the early post-war British new towns was designed for easy pedestrian movement. The size was limited to 5000 so that it was a comfortable walk from the periphery to the centre while accommodating the population at, by British standards, reasonable densities. Those early new towns grouped neighbourhoods to form a district of 18 000 to 24 000 people. This district with its centre is possibly the British equivalent to the Continental quarter. The gross density of the district in those early new towns was reduced still further by the introduction of landscaped areas between the neighbourhoods. This practice, while strengthening the physical identity of its component parts, increases the need for movement and makes walking less attractive. This tendency is further compounded by the provision of additional land to facilitate the motor car.

Clearly there are a number of terms which have been used to describe sections of a city: they are sector, district, quarter, neighbourhood, domain and community. The position is complicated further by the different definitions given to these terms by those working in the field of urban design and planning. In this chapter the term quarter is used to describe a large section of the city with a population of 20 000 to 100 000 people. Neighbourhood is used here for an area of the city which has a population of between 5000 and 12 000 people and the term local community is used to describe a few related streets with a population of 500 to 2 000 people. There is no ideal or fixed size for a quarter, neighbourhood or local community, nor is it essential for a city to be structured to include all these urban components. It is probably true to say that the size of these urban components will vary with the size of the city. For large metropolitan cities the quarter may be large with a population of 100 000, while for smaller cities a suitable size may be 20 000. In addition to city size and attitudes to high density living having an effect upon the form of a quarter, the arrangement and type of public transport facilities may also play a role in determining the size of the quarter.

The division of the city into quarters or districts, the name is unimportant, is essential for achieving sustainable development. This process of the division of the city into quarters is most effective in promoting sustainable development when these divisions of the city are legitimized politically and when their elected councils are given a remit to protect and enhance the quality of the local environment. The quarter has the potential to support further the process of sustainable development when their form is compatible with, and promotes, public transport.

THE URBAN STREET BLOCK

7

The degree to which a city is sustainable is affected both by the form of the urban street block and also by the composition of the activities it accommodates. The way in which the street blocks are designed and the land use mix within street blocks also affects the quality of the built environment. Current conventional wisdom adopted by those in the field of sustainable development rejects the cruder notions of land use zoning in favour of more subtle urban structuring based upon a mix of uses and activities. The traditional city with residential and office accommodation arranged over ground floor shopping streets is often cited as an ideal arrangement for a lifestyle which is not dependent upon high levels of mobility. It is also argued that a city with a fine grain of land use, rather than the homogeneous zones of residential commercial or industrial uses common in modern metropolitan areas, is more likely to reduce the need for travel, and, incidentally, also be more likely to create an interesting and liveable environment. There is little doubt that a city is judged by the quality of its public streets and squares: by their form, the façades which enclose them, the floor plane on which visitors tread, and the great sculptures and fountains which delight the eye. It is, however, the size, function and structure of the street block which gives form to public space and contributes to the vitality of those spaces. This chapter examines the various ideas about the form and function of the street block and its role in structuring the city, analysing, in particular, the street block in a sustainable city.

The street and street block of the traditional nineteenth century city received great criticism during the 1920s and 1930s from the leaders of the modern movement in architecture. Le Corbusier, for example, said of the street: 'Our streets no longer work. Streets are an obsolete notion. There ought not to be such a thing as streets; we have to create something to replace them' (Le Corbusier, 1967). Gropius was expressing similar sentiments: 'Instead of the ground-floor windows looking on to blank walls, or into cramped and sunless courtyards, they command a clear view of the sky over the broad expanse of grass and trees which separate the blocks and serve as playgrounds for the children' (Gropius, 1935). Projects of the time speak most clearly to this aim of destroying the traditional urban fabric of the city and replacing it with ranks of

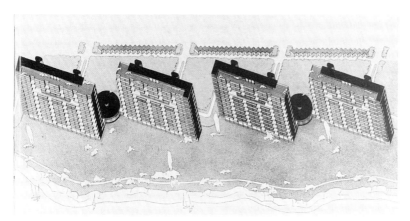

7.1

7.2

Figure 7.1 Project for a riverside or lakeside (Gropius, 1935)

Figure 7.2 Project for a group of ten-storey dwellings (Gropius, 1935)

unadorned blocks standing serenely in a field of green (Figures 7.1 and 7.2). Giedion, the apologist for the Modern movement in architecture is quite clear in his condemnation of the street block. Berlage's fine development in Amsterdam South is composed of streets and street blocks: for this and

other shortcomings, Giedion dismisses Berlage as an architect of the previous century: '... Berlage's schemes reflect the central difficulty at that date: the inability to arrive at new means of expression in the solutions offered for the problems peculiar to the times. In the 1902 plans particularly (and to some extent in the later version of 1915) we sense the struggle involved in Berlage's attempt to break with the formulae of previous decades ...' (Giedion, 1954). In contrast Giedion, in his discussion of the Cité Industrielle, commends Garnier for his arrangement of lots at right angles to the road and for his elimination of the street block: 'The closed blocks and light-wells of Hausmann's time are completely eliminated' (Giedion, 1954). It is time to reassess the value of the street and street block in the light of the new imperative of the green agenda for the city and in particular in the light of the need to reduce atmospheric pollution caused by the burning of fossil fuels. The green agenda for the city renders obsolete the critique of the street and street block by the masters of the Modern movement in architecture. It is necessary to turn for inspiration, once again, to the great traditions of city building: to interpret those traditions in today's context in order to develop a new and enlightened vision for the sustainable city.

In the design of street blocks there are three broad sets of considerations. The first is the socio-economic function of the block; the second is the visual or physical role of the block in the city structure; and the final set of considerations is concerned with making the block work in terms of technology and includes considerations such as the lighting, ventilation and heating of the buildings which comprise the block. When form was considered the product of function and technology then the street block varied in size according to function and to the limits set by technological feasibility. The result is all too obvious: cities with large blocks of single use disrupting the intricate network of public paths; a coarse-grained city dying at night, a fearful place for citizens unprotected by the comforting envelope of a fast-moving car (Figures 7.3 and 7.4). Most urban functions, however, can be accommodated reasonably in urban street blocks of similar shape and form (Turner, 1992). Street blocks or insulae in historic towns dating back many centuries have been modified a number of times as they have changed ownership or use. The following paragraphs, while addressing function and technology, will place greater emphasis on the visual and structuring role of the street block in the city. If a reasonable size and form for the street block can be determined from considerations of its structuring role within the urban fabric, then it is argued here that it will accommodate, with modification, most city needs.

While the theory of sustainable development points clearly towards a mix of land uses in the city, the quarter and the street block, neither the precise nature nor the degree of intricacy of land use mix is specified. Clearly the placing of buildings designed for large-scale noxious, noisy or dangerous activities next to family homes would be unacceptable to both professional and citizen alike. More difficult is the decision about the juxtaposition of homes where peace and quiet may be the expectations of some with pubs, 'takeaways' and other small-scale commercial activities which may cause noise, litter and other nuisance. Such activities in a city, however, add to its life and liveliness. To what degree, therefore, should land uses be mixed in the city? In particular, should the street block itself be of mixed use? These two questions are part of the debate in sustainable development. Theories can only give part answers; an examination of developing practice will provide the evidence for definitive answers.

Clearly there will be single-use street blocks in the city of the future; that is, street blocks given over to, or almost entirely to, residential, commercial, industrial or some other single land use. Where possible, large areas of the city devoted to such single use should, however, be avoided. As a guide, a city quarter of 20 000 to 100 000 people should contain within its boundaries a reasonable mix of city land uses. It should comprise a mix of uses to include opportunities for work, education, leisure, shopping and governance in addition to residential areas. The quarter is a town within a town and as such it should have a balance of land uses reflecting the balance in the city as a whole. It is the quarter and not the street block which is the main instrument for ensuring a balanced distribution of land uses throughout the city. The city street block, however, with great benefit for the environment, may house a mix of activities, including such uses as residential, shopping, office accommodation and a small nursery school. Many existing city centres would have remained safer and livelier places if the tradition of 'living over the shop' had survived. Some city councils are indeed pursuing a policy which aims at bringing unused accommodation over shops back into use as flats. It seems that in the sustainable city of the future there will be a range of city street blocks varying from single-use blocks to those of multi-use in varying proportions and with varying combinations of uses.

The size of an ideal urban street block cannot be established any more precisely than the size of a quarter or neighbourhood. As a rough guide Krier suggests that urban blocks should be: 'as small in length and width as is typologically viable; they should form as many well defined streets and squares as possible in the form of a multi-directional horizontal pattern of urban spaces' (Krier, 1984). The smallest street blocks are generally found in the centre of traditional cities. They represent a form of development which creates the maximum number of streets and therefore street frontages on a relatively small area: such a structure of street blocks maximizes commercial benefits. The high densities associated with this type of development stimulate intense cultural, social and economic activity, the lifeblood of city culture. The typical ground floor in this type of central city development has many doors and openings. The traditional European town centre has a quality of permeability: 'Only places which are accessible to people can offer them choice. The extent to which an environment allows people a choice of access through it, from place to place, is therefore a key measure of its responsiveness' (Bentley *et al.*, 1985). The street in the traditional centre facilitates distribution in addition to its role in economic exchange and social intercourse. In contrast, large modern street blocks have a few guarded entrances and most of the interchange takes place inside the building where internal corridors, private streets or splendid atria facilitate movement and distribution: the corridor replaces the street, which loses its primary function. The larger and more homogeneous the street block the greater will be its power to destroy the social, economic and physical networks of the city. The large-scale single-use, single-ownership street block is the instrument most influential in the decline of the city: its effect together with that of its partner the motor car are among the real causes of the death of the great city.

It may be difficult to be precise about the size of the ideal urban street block, but it is possible to eliminate the block which is too large. Such blocks covering extensive areas are out of scale in a democracy where power is vested in the people and not with the board of a conglomerate or council of a university. Street blocks in the early industrial cities increased in size towards the periphery of the urban

area where land values were low and where development could be expansive. As a city grew in both wealth and population, so too would its centre. The central city expanded and consequently land values increased at its former periphery, resulting in development pressures and large overdeveloped street blocks surrounded by fewer but usually wider roads. Building programmes have increased in size throughout this century with single owners or developers building large sections of the city. The large development in single or corporate ownership, however, is not entirely recent as a phenomenon. The medieval castle or the cathedral and its ancillary buildings have in the past dominated the city. Where this has happened such institutions have presented an alternative power structure independent of the city and its citizens. In this century these alternative sources of power have multiplied in the city. Large industrial complexes, hospitals, universities and not least the extensive shopping mall are common to most cities (Figures 7.3 and 7.4). These large-scale single-ownership street blocks, or in some cases city districts, may be convenient for those who manage or own the establishment but citizen rights are not paramount: this is private property and those with legal possession have great autonomy within their ownership boundary. There seems, however, no reason why for example a city university cannot be

Figure 7.3 Broadmarsh Shopping Centre, Nottingham
Figure 7.4 Victoria Shopping Centre, Nottingham

7.3

7.4

7.5

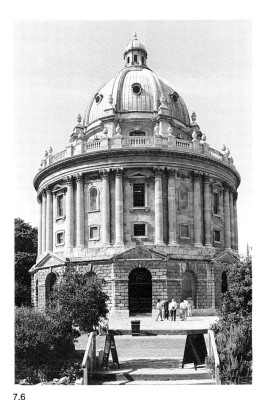

7.6

Figure 7.5 Oxford High Street. (Photograph by Bridie Neville)
Figure 7.6 The Radcliffe Camera, Oxford

designed to occupy small-scale city street blocks with buildings designed specifically for this purpose. A good example of such development is Oxford University with its rich mix of town and gown (Figures 7.5 and 7.6). The University of Liverpool in contrast followed a modernist approach to planning, destroying communities, the street pattern and also the rich grain of small-scale urban street blocks. In place of the rich nineteenth century urban structure there is a large district of the city which dies when students leave at night for the halls of residence and atrophies completely during vacation when they leave the campus for home (Figures 7.7 and 7.8).

The idea of the city as a 'growing whole' led Alexander to postulate a number of rules to achieve organic growth, the results of which he much admires, in traditional cities such as Venice (Figures 7.9 and 7.10). One of these rules of organic growth is that growth should be piecemeal: 'furthermore that *the idea of piecemeal growth be specified exactly enough so that we can guarantee a mixed flow of small, medium, and large projects in about equal quantities*' (Figure 7.11). In detail he specifies that no single increment should be too large and: '*There are equal numbers of large, medium and small projects*' (Alexander, 1987). The figure Alexander places on the upper limit for projects, based presumably on the North American experience, is 100 000 square feet. This figure represents a four-storey building block, without light

7.7a

7.8

7.7b

7.9

Figure 7.7 University
Buildings, Abercrombie
Square, Liverpool
Figure 7.8 University of
Liverpool, Bedford Street
North
Figure 7.9 Rialto Bridge,
Venice

wells, of just under an acre in extent. The upper limits set by Alexander may be too high for the British context where street blocks traditionally tend to be smaller than those in the USA. Sustainable development suggests an upper limit for development of three to four storeys, which also points to development units of smaller scale than those envisaged by Alexander. There seems to be a strong case for breaking down into discrete units of single street blocks those large-scale developments which have become increasingly more common in recent years. The street block developed to three and four storeys should be the determinant of project limitation. Using the notion of a correct distribution of project sizes, then for sustainable development, particularly in the British context, a majority of small and medium size developments should be the strategy for city planning and design and not the equal

7.10

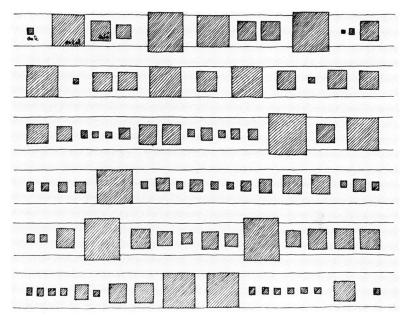

7.11

Figure 7.10 Rialto Bridge, Venice
Figure 7.11 Sequence and size of development projects (Alexander, 1987)

numbers of large, medium, and small projects suggested by Alexander.

There is of course a gain to the public purse in the building of megastructures which obliterate the finer grain of older city networks. With the megastructure the amount of public street is reduced, therefore there are savings to be made by the city in its maintenance. In addition, since circulation in the megastructure is along private streets the policing role can be privatized, so saving additional resources. One measure, however, of a civilized society is the degree to which its city streets and squares are public and open to all citizens to use freely and safely. This, civilized, society requires a city which meets Jacobs' criterion for self-policing rather than one depending for safety on the night-time closure

of whole sections of the city which are policed in daylight hours by security firms and made safe by the ubiquitous surveillance camera (Jacobs, 1965).

People live both public and private lives. Institutions, too, have a private face and public connections. These two personae, the public and private aspects of life, meet and are resolved in the façade of the building block. The friendly and responsive environment is one which maximizes choice of access through it from place to place, while privacy requires enclosure and controlled access. Maximizing choice of access has to be balanced against the privacy for individuals, groups and corporate bodies. The delicate balance between public and private space is maintained by the system of access adopted. In some cultures where family privacy is of profound importance there may be a whole system of semi-public and semi-private spaces linking the inner private world of the family and the public world of the street and market place (Moughtin, 1985). The richness of the environment, in part, is a reflection of the way in which these mutually conflicting requirements of privacy and access are resolved.

'Both physical and visual permeability depend on how the network of public spaces divides the environment into *blocks*: areas of land entirely surrounded by public routes' (Bentley *et al.*, 1985). A city with small street blocks gives to the pedestrian a great choice and variety of routes between any two points. The medieval European city is an extreme example of such a form: to the stranger the city may appear almost like a maze (Figure 7.12). Large street blocks on the other hand give less choice of routes and also produce an increased distance between paths. Smaller street blocks in cities increase the visibility of corners which announce the junction of paths and in consequence both the physical and visual permeability is increased. As a general principle the city street block should be as small as practicable. Where

street blocks since the 1950s have been enlarged for development, consideration should be given to the restoration of the traditional street pattern and block size if the opportunity presents itself.

The need for both contact and privacy in daily life leads inevitably to a built form which acts as a filter between these two opposing requirements. Until the advent of modernist thinking in city planning the traditional and sensible solution to this problem was a building form having a public face and a private rear. In Bath, designed by John Wood and his son (also John Wood), this principle of design is given eloquent testimony by the local people who describe the great civic spaces as having: '*a Queen Anne Front and a Mary Ann Backside*'. The design principle is quite simple: the front of the building should face onto the public street or square where all public activities including entrances occur, while the back of the building faces onto private space of an inner court screened from public view. When this principle is applied systematically to city development the result is a system of insulae or street blocks surrounded by buildings along their perimeters enclosing inner private courtyards. This type of development was anathema to Le Corbusier, Gropius and the avant-garde of the modern movements in architecture and planning. The case presented by designers like Le Corbusier is made difficult to refute when, as in Ireland in particular, with the notable exception of Westport, developments literally turned their backside onto the river, which was used as an open drain. All rivers, canals and waterways in the sustainable city should be lined by building frontages and be, in their own right, important landscape features of the city (Figures 7.13 and 7.14).

We have seen that the size of the street block should be as small as the form and the function of the buildings on its perimeter permit. In Britain the acre has a long tradition as a measure of land surface for costing purposes and as a recognized means of land sub-division. In the more rational systems of measurement adopted in continental

Figure 7.12 Bruges, Drawing from Sitte

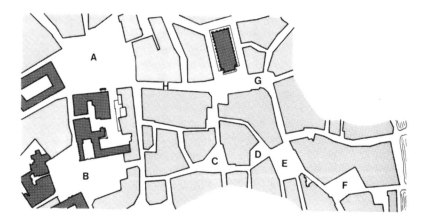

7.13   7.14

Europe the hectare serves the same purpose as the acre in this country. It seems reasonable to suggest that most street block functions could be accommodated in insulae varying from 70 by 70 to 100 by 100 metres. There is a relationship between the size of the perimeter block surrounding the insulae and the private activities carried on in the private courtyard. Bentley *et al.*, illustrate this relationship graphically for three main types of building use: non-residential use, flats and houses with gardens (Bentley *et al.*, 1985) (Figures 7.15 to 7.17). Applying the results of Martin and March's analysis of the Fresnel square it would appear that for any given size of street block a form where perimeter buildings abut the back of the pavement give the most effective relationship between building volume and usable open space (Martin and March, 1972). Applying the graphs in Bentley *et al.* (1985) to a street block of 70 by 70 metres a four-storey perimeter block of 50 square metre flats would surround a courtyard large enough to provide one car parking space per dwelling. Similarly a 70 by 70 metre street block with periphery development comprising two-storey, five-person terrace houses with 50 square metres of private garden would cater for one car

Figure 7.13 Westport, County Mayo, Ireland

Figure 7.14 Westport, County Mayo, Ireland

Figure 7.15 Relationship of parking standards and street block (Bentley *et al.*, 1985)

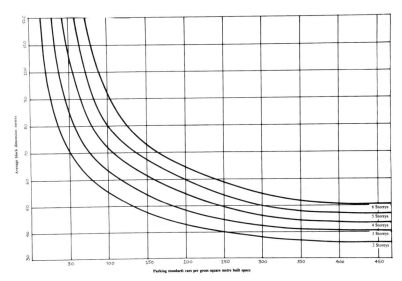

7.15

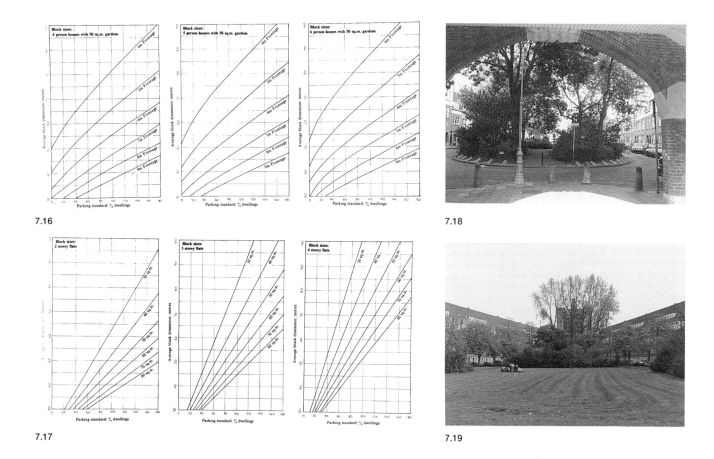

7.16

7.17

7.18

7.19

per dwelling provided the frontage of the house was less than five metres (Figures 7.18 and 7.19). The graphs illustrated in Bentley *et al.* were prepared before the current interest in sustainable development - spaces within the courts need not necessarily be allocated for car parking but could be given over to extra garden space or other use compatible with sustainable development.

Perimeter development in street blocks, however, is clearly the most effective method of allocating space in a sustainable city.

THE URBAN STREET BLOCK IN PRACTICE

HEMBRUGSTRAAT, SPAARNDAMMERBUURT, AMSTERDAM

This project was designed and built by de Klerk in 1921. It consists mainly of five-storey flats built for the *Eigen Haard* 'Own Hearth' housing association. Two terraces, the ends of street blocks, form a public square in this part of Amsterdam. The third part of the project is a triangular street block comprising flats, communal room, post office and school. The main part of the project is this small enclosed street block with perimeter development, and it is of exceptional architectural interest (Figures 7.20 to 7.24).

De Klerk died at the age of 39, two years after the project at Hembrugstraat was complete. He was the unofficial leader of the Amsterdam School, greatly revered by his associates. Piet Kramer, a member of the school and a close colleague, wrote of de Klerk: 'The power of conviction that radiates from his drawings gives us that curious, happy feeling of being closer to the Almighty' (Pehnt,

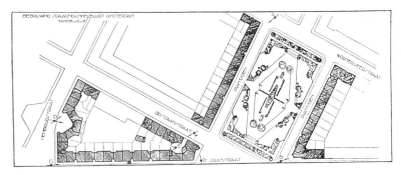

7.20

7.21

7.22

7.23

Figures 7.20 to **7.22**
Hembrugstraat by de Klerk
Figure 7.23 Hembrugstraat
by de Klerk, use of space
within the street block

Figure 7.24 Hembrugstraat by de Klerk, details

7.24a

7.24b

1973). De Klerk's vision was not infused with any notions of satisfying functional need; he was more interested in forms: forms with which to delight the user. In his search for personal expression he broke most rules of composition and most norms of structural propriety. De Klerk set bricks vertically in undulating courses and he clad upper floors in roof tiles, though this part of the building is structurally and visually part of the vertical wall plane. In places windows follow their own capricious external pattern with little regard for internal requirements. At the base of the triangular block is the most extravagant gesture, a tall tower, celebrating nothing more than two flats which sit beneath it and a small path within the block which leads to a small

community room. The street block nevertheless is intensely human in scale and delightfully individual in expression. The project at Hembrugstraat remains a fine model for the treatment of a street block in the sustainable city of the twenty-first century.

THE SUPERBLOCK: UNWIN

In an essay 'Nothing to be Gained by Overcrowding', Unwin demonstrated the mathematical truth that perimeter development is more cost-effective than the typical nineteenth century byelaw housing laid out in long parallel rows of streets (Unwin, 1967). In his article Unwin presents two diagrams for a 10 acre plot. One shows typical rows of terraced housing with streets between; the other

7.26

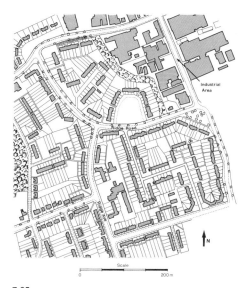

7.25

7.27

Figure 7.25 Letchworth, the superblock
Figure 7.26 Letchworth, use of space within the block
Figure 7.27 Letchworth, the Greens

places dwellings around the perimeter. The demonstration shows clearly that when all the items making up the cost of the development are considered, including savings on roads and service runs, the cost for the more open and less crowded perimeter scheme is less. Unwin used this idea of the perimeter block in some of his work in Letchworth, incorporating within the courtyard allotments for tenants while the house fronts faced onto public greens (Figures 7.25 to 7.27). In the USA, experiments in superblock design were conducted by architects such as Perry, Stein and Wright (see Figure 6.3). The result is Radburn housing which takes the ideal of perimeter planning and distorts it out of all recognition in order to service the motor car. In its purer forms the Radburn system offers little privacy and an unclear definition of front and back. The superblock, as visualized by Unwin and when small in extent or when broken by busy pathways, is still a useful concept for urban housing, particularly when perimeter development surrounds private gardens and/or allotments.

RICHMOND RIVERSIDE DEVELOPMENT, SURREY: ERITH AND TERRY

Quinlan Terry's redevelopment of Richmond Riverside, completed in 1988, is a major contribution to urban design and town planning. Opinion is divided about the architectural integrity of this attempt at Classical revival. The particular concern for those advocating an honest architecture and a unity between interior and exterior is the discrepancy between the highly mannered Classical façade and the functional interior. The comfortable office spaces are fitted with suspended ceilings which drop below the window head, air conditioning and strip lighting: they are little different from any similar office in a 'traditional 1960s' office block. The waterfront seen from the South

Figures 7.28 to 7.30
Richmond, Riverside
Development

bank of the river or from the bridge is a mixture of new, restored and remodelled Georgian houses, which are used for commercial purposes or as civic buildings. It is difficult for the lay person to see where the new begins and the old ends. It is also obvious that this is a popular part of

Richmond. From this populist viewpoint alone the development is highly successful. Terry has completed the street block and riverside frontage with buildings of mixed use and which have a clear front and back. The perimeter development encloses a pleasant court of classical proportions which provides semi-private space for circulation, light and air. This development, in terms of urban design, is an elegant solution to the problem of a city block in an historically sensitive area. It is also a magnificent setting for a popular parade (Figures 7.28 to 7.30).

7.28

7.29

7.30

ALBAN GATE, LONDON WALL, TERRY FARRELL PARTNERSHIP

Alban Gate is a giant, twin-towered office block straddling London Wall. It replaces one of the slab-like curtain-walled office towers dating from the 1950s that sit along the London Wall. This lump of a building in an extravagant American Post Modernism style compares unfavourably with the nearby Barbican, a currently underrated example of Modernism (Figures 7.31 and 7.32). The Barbican, despite its faults, has a variety of uses, lavishly landscaped public spaces, water gardens and good quality residential accommodation. It is a good attempt to create an urban environment with enclosed and sheltered public spaces (Figures 7.33 and 7.34). In contrast Alban Gate is a large building standing alone and depending for effect on its three-dimensional qualities: it creates no public space of consequence. In simple terms, the Barbican is a work of urban design, Alban Gate is not. This project illustrates very clearly the dilemma facing the architect working at the scale of urban design. The commercial pressures of the market place and an architectural profession which at times appears to be in collusion with those forces determines an urban architecture of single-use free-standing buildings which maximize floorspace at the expense of public space. The architect's role, if he or she accepts it, is to clothe the building mass in the latest fashionable style. The comprehensive planning of the 1950s and 1960s did often result in dreary city redevelopments but it also offered the opportunity of urban design incorporating the street block: admittedly this opportunity was rarely taken.

Figures 7.31 and **7.32** Alban Gate, London
Figures 7.33 and **7.34** The Barbican, London

7.31

7.32

7.34

Figure 7.35 Horselydown
Square (Glancey, 1989)
Figure 7.36 Horselydown
Square

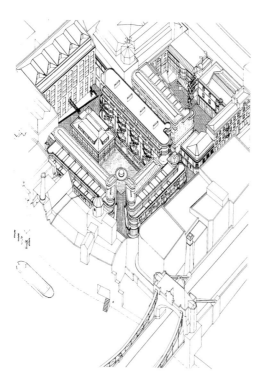

7.35

7.36a

7.36b

7.36c

HORSELYDOWN SQUARE: JULYAN WICKHAM
Horselydown Square by Julyan Wickham, begun in
1987, occupies a site close to Tower Bridge (Figures
7.35 and 7.36). The project is of mixed development comprising housing, commercial and retail
space. The architecture, according to Glancey, is
cheerful but 'owes precious little to mainstream
architectural fads' (Glancey, 1989). The development completes an urban street block and in doing
so creates pleasant, enclosed and protected courts:
it is an area of calm amidst the bustle and noise of
the surrounding streets. The street block, which is
five and six storeys, has a lively and decorative
roofline in keeping with its riverside location.
Possibly because it owes nothing to current architectural fashion, Horselydown Square is the type of

development which in both form and function encapsulates many of the principles expected of sustainable development in a busy city urban street block.

INLAND REVENUE BUILDING, NOTTINGHAM: RICHARD ROGERS

This is not simply a single building on one plot - Rogers has developed the site as a group of island street blocks surrounded by streets (Figures 7.37 to 7.39). The building is the result of a competition won by Rogers. It occupies once derelict and under-used land. This is how Rogers describes the scheme:

7.38

7.37

7.39

Figures 7.37 to **7.39** Inland Revenue Building, Nottingham

'We set out to investigate all the practical means in nature to produce a tempered environment. As so often in city developments, two sides of the site were polluted and noisy. However, one side bordered a quiet canal. We pushed the buildings to the edge of the roads and opened up a public garden beside the canal. Since opening windows on all façades was not possible, we divided the building in two - basic administration at the back, and social functions and communal facilities nestling around the new garden. Between the two buildings, we created a central landscaped courtyard - a type of small ravine. Around this gently curving landscape, the two lines of buildings were linked by glazed bridges' (Rogers, 1995b).

The streets within the development are tree-lined to give protection and shade from the summer heat and to help purify the air in this part of Nottingham. The building pattern adopted for the development by breaking up the mass into strips of slimmer accommodation permits more of the occupants to be near a window, so reducing the need for artificial lighting while giving them a pleasant view of the landscaped courts. The Inland Revenue building in Nottingham has a number of innovative features for reducing the energy used in running the buildings, and is also sited on 'brown land' rather than a green field site. As urban design the complex enlivens the canal while the organization of the programme into a number of semi-autonomous units has enabled a breakdown of the accommodation into blocks of small scale. This is, however, a large development of single use which is dead in 'out of office' hours, and the development does little to revive the architecture of the city centre. The developers, perhaps, should have considered the conversion of some of the unused office space in the city before embarking on a prestige building on the canal site. Despite these criticisms, the Inland Revenue building in Nottingham is a great work of architecture which will give delight to visitors and particularly those viewing the development from the canal. Being a major employer, the Inland Revenue building will bring extra business to the city and possibly stimulate the redevelopment of worn-out properties in the city centre.

APARTMENT BLOCKS, KREUZBERG, BERLIN

The area of Kreuzberg close to the site of the Berlin Wall consists of city blocks of high-density housing. The blocks are four- and five-storey apartment blocks built over shops and arranged around the perimeter of the block. In addition there is a mix of apartments, workshops and small-scale industries grouped around courtyards. The area, run down and ripe for redevelopment, is typical of inner city areas in large European cities. The intention for many years was to demolish the properties and rebuild de novo on the cleared site: this was the typical reaction to run-down areas by most European city authorities in the 1950s and 1960s. After a reversal of policy and with the residents' support it was decided to rehabilitate the area but without causing disruption to the existing community. Buildings were made structurally sound, weatherproofed, well insulated and the accommodation was upgraded by adding new bathrooms and kitchens. The refurbishment had energy savings: '... since the apartments have relatively few external surfaces from which to lose heat' (Vale and Vale, 1991).

One block is of particular interest, having been designed as an ecological showpiece. Solar energy systems have been installed, waste water filtered through the roots of reed beds and methods of water economies introduced. Where flats and other buildings have been demolished the spaces have been intensively planted. The rehabilitation of Kreuzberg with the active participation of the residents has set a pattern and model for the sustainable rehabilitation of inner city areas. The treatment of street blocks is of particular interest: this development has proved to be an effective method of urban regeneration (Figure 7.40).

7.40a

7.40b

7.40c

Figure 7.40 Block 103, Kreuzberg, Berlin. (Photographs by June Greenaway)

BERLIN GOVERNMENT CENTRE: LEON AND ROB KRIER

Leon and Rob Krier see a project like this for the Berlin Government Centre not only as a unique opportunity to create a governmental quarter but also as a possibility to integrate these functions with an urban fabric of mixed use: 'Over 100 000 square metres of three/four storey high residential blocks with commercial ground floors are thus spread in a checkerboard fashion throughout the new government district. The central symbolic buildings, the Parliament (the old Reichstag building), Bundesstat and Chancellery, are grouped around a vast artificial lake which will become the largest public space in Berlin' (Krier and Krier, 1993). This is a project which illustrates clearly the thinking of both Leon and Rob Krier: it is also in the mainstream of current urban design theory. Like their project for the new quarter for Venta-Berri in San Sebastian, the arrangement of medium-rise street blocks with mixed uses arranged as perimeter development is a model many urbanists would advocate for city development (Figures 7.41 and 7.42).

POTSDAMER PLATZ – LEIPZIGER PLATZ: HILMER AND SATTLER

The planning of the area around Potsdamer Platz was the subject of a competition. The district was

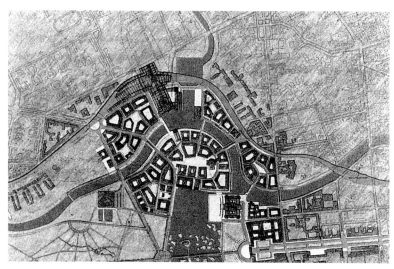

7.42

Figure 7.41 The Berlin Government Centre (Architectural Design, 1993)
Figure 7.42 The Berlin Government Centre (Architectural Design, 1993)

badly damaged during the Second World War and by the time of the competition in 1991 the area was an empty tract of land. The aim of the development is to rejuvenate the district so that it becomes a busy part of the city once again. The area was designed to contain a mix of uses, offices, hotels, shopping, restaurants and also residential accommodation. The plan by Hilmer and Sattler defines public spaces, squares, streets and boulevards, together with the density of development and the general building height of 35 metres. The scheme deals with general massing only: 'Our concept ... is not based on the globally-accepted American model of an agglomeration of high-rise buildings at the core of the city, but rather on the idea of the compact, spatially complex European town. It is our view that urban life should not develop within the interiors of large-scale building complexes like glass-covered atriums and megastructures, but in squares, boulevards, parks and streets' (Sattler, 1993). Despite this reference to the compact and complex European town the drawings of street blocks have the appearance of buildings standing as solid volumes in rows along a wide street. Richard Reid, in his discussion with Sattler, articulated this view: 'When I look at the plans of your urban blocks, and in particular the diagrams, they are all a series of enclosed private spaces off the main urban grid. And in a sense that seems to be more like the American rather than the European model' (Architectural Design, 1993). The formality of this project for the Potsdamer Platz district of Berlin and its overwhelming scale has none of the subtlety found in the work of Leon and Rob Krier for the same city (Figures 7.44 and 7. 45).

CONCLUSION

The main ornaments of the city are its streets and squares (Sitte, 1901). It is, however, the street block or insulae which forms the boundaries of public space. The street block is also at the interface

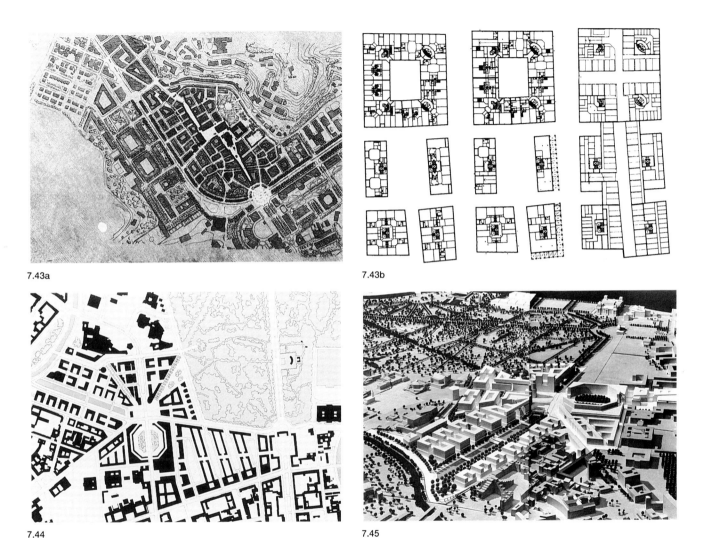

7.43a

7.43b

7.44

7.45

between the public world of the street and the inner life of the courtyard and its surrounding buildings. Perimeter development is clearly the most effective way of arranging buildings to act as a filter between the public façade and the private activities which are pursued within the block. There is general agreement that street blocks of mixed uses result in a more vital and interesting city. There also appears to be wide agreement that street blocks should be as small as is reasonably possible in order to maximize the 'permeability' of city districts. An alternative view sees the need for street blocks to be large enough to accommodate single large schemes (Bruges, 1992). It would seem, however, that large single users, such as the

Figure 7.43 The new quarter of Venta-Berri in San Sebastian

Figures 7.44 and **7.45** Potsdamer Platz by Hilmer and Sattler (Architectural Design, 1993)

Inland Revenue in Nottingham, can be accommodated within a number of small street blocks. In this case the result is a fine piece of urban architecture and a canal scene of great quality.

The conclusions derived from the debate on sustainable development support the idea of small-scale city street blocks composed of compatible mixed activities or mixed land uses, surrounded by a perimeter block of two, three or four storeys. Sustainable forms of this type also provide a framework for the development of a city with vitality but with a friendly human scale: that is, with a scale normally associated with the morphology of a traditional European city (Krier, L., 1984).

CONCLUSION

8

INTRODUCTION

There is a great danger that 'sustainable development' may become the latest fashionable panacea
for the solution to all mankind's problems: it could
degenerate into a 'buzz word' without meaning. It
would be unfortunate if this movement aimed at
achieving an environment of quality in harmony
with nature, were to be 'yesterday's developmental
hope'. Fine sentiments and convincing rhetoric are
not enough. The previous chapters have demonstrated that there are a number of national and international documents which identify a specific set of
requirements for sustainable development. There are
also a number of successful experiments in sustainable development at a local level both in land
use/transport planning and in architecture and the
built environment. Clearly it is necessary to develop
a method and sets of policies for sustainable development which are easily implemented and effective.
The results of such methods and policies should be
immediately apparent and quantifiable. This chapter
will concentrate on the practical steps which can be
taken immediately to achieve a more sustainable
urban environment and in particular it will outline
those concepts useful in the process of urban
design.

Sustainable development is concerned with
improving the quality of life of human beings while
living within the carrying capacity of the global
ecosystem. For those concerned with urban design
it is the meaning and application of this definition
for the city and its region which is important. No
city, region or even nation state can be completely
self-sufficient, economically, socially or environmentally. Sustainable development, however, does imply
that at all of these levels the aim should be development which does not export pollution and does not
import resources which adversely affect the global
ecosystem or negatively affect sustainable development in other territories. Local sustainable development is concerned with improving the quality of life
of the local community and where practicable living
within the carrying capacity of the local environment. The aim, therefore, is for a high degree of
local self-sufficiency. Sustainability planning is far
easier if the planning units are natural domains such
as river catchment areas. If the planning unit is too
large it will be far from the people it serves; and if
it is too small it cannot influence and coordinate all
the relevant factors. The city and its region seems to
be the natural unit for many decisions affecting local
sustainability. For example, sustainable transport
may best be planned for 'travel to work' areas. So,

too, the management of waste disposal may be most effectively organized at a local city regional scale:

> This is also the most appropriate level for reconciling conflicting demands. Windmills can be scenically intrusive; conifer plantations and short-rotation coppice are better for energy forestry than traditional mixed woodlands; new housing will often generate less extra traffic if it encroaches on a green belt than if it is built the far side of it ... Communities will rarely be unanimous about this kind of issue ... sustainable development is a social goal which can only be arrived at through processes of consultation, shared responsibility and partnership. Democratically elected local government and the planning system are the means by which such choices and decisions are made openly and democratically. (Local Government Management Board, 1993)

POLITICAL FRAMEWORK

A key concept in sustainable development is participation. For citizen participation to be other than gesture, manipulation or tokenism, the structure of government must be reorganized so that the political process itself becomes more participatory. Our current political structures emphasize decision-making by elected representatives and by those to whom they delegate power. In Europe much is written and spoken about 'subsidiarity' while at the same time in Britain, local authorities are being emasculated, decision-making and power being concentrated at the centre or delegated to a clutch of non-elected Quangos. Some form of regional government is necessary for structured public participation in sustainable development. The precise nature of regional government best suited for implementing sustainable development is unclear, with much room for debate. The city and its regional hinterland has much to commend it with powerful arguments in its favour, though a division of England, in particular, into fewer 'natural' ecological

and cultural regions likewise is attractive. A combination of a system which has the city region as the basic elected local authority, supported by regional councils for about twelve major cultural areas of England, may be the type of compromise which will be acceptable in this country. Scotland, Wales and Northern Ireland presumably will have their own assemblies at some point in the future. Below the level of the city there is a need for elected authorities having limited powers, particularly associated with issues affecting local sustainable development. It is at the level of the city quarter that public participation in urban policy formulation is most appropriate (Moughtin, 1992).

TRANSPORT–LAND USE INTERFACE

A key variable which will affect the rate at which society moves towards sustainable development is the transport system operating within the city and throughout its region. Clearly there are powerful trends towards a decentralized city form dependent upon the car. These trends are complemented by lifestyle pressures and cultural preferences, reinforced by a persuasive and aggressive market. The rhetoric of sustainability is strong but practice in the field of transport until quite recently has been the reverse. There are, however, hopeful signs that in Britain the movement towards sustainable development is gaining momentum. The Government has produced *Sustainable Development: The UK Strategy* (Department of the Environment, 1994d) while the Local Agenda 21 initiative has been running in this country since 1993. This initiative encourages local authorities to seek consensus for the design of policies for sustainable development. The most promising of all recent developments is the Report of the Royal Commission on Environmental Pollution: it sets tough pollution targets and amongst its clear and precise conclusions is a planning process for roads which should identify the 'best practicable environmental option'. The

Report also recommends far-reaching restructuring of the Department of Transport: 'from Ministerial level downwards, to reflect the fundamentally different approach which a sustainable transport policy will involve' (Royal Commission on Environmental Pollution, 1994). The Report also recommended that all road construction proposals, including trunk roads, should be subject to environmental assessment. The Royal Commission's recommendations are already affecting policy-making. SACTRA (Standing Advisory Committee on Trunk Road Assessment) is reconsidering and reassessing its road building programme, including bypass proposals. While conceding that this may be a simple cost-saving operation, it still indicates a major shift in public roads policy and a move towards recognizing the importance of sustainable development.

Most encouraging is the inclusion of concepts of sustainable development in Planning Policy Guidance Notes produced by The Department of the Environment. Of particular importance are PPG6, PPG12 and PPG13. PPG6, *Town Centres and Retail Developments* (Department of the Environment, 1993c), is currently being revised. The July 1995 draft amendments emphasize the importance of the vitality and viability of town centres. One of the government's objectives according to PPG6 is: 'To maximise the opportunity of shoppers and other town centre users to use means of transport other than the car.' The draft of PPG6 states quite clearly that: 'Town centres should, wherever possible, be the preferred locations for developments that attract many trips,' and goes on to advise local authorities to adopt policies to locate major generators of travel in existing centres; to strengthen existing centres; to maintain and improve choice for people to walk, cycle or use public transport for journeys to and from the town centre; and to ensure an appropriate supply of attractive, convenient and safe parking for shopping and leisure trips to the centre but to limit commuter parking to a level necessary only for the functioning of the town centre. PPG12 (Department of the Environment, 1992c) requires local authorities

to adopt a 'plan-led' development process which takes account of the environment in all its aspects both global and local. PPG13, *Transport* (Department of the Environment, 1994c), translates the concern for pollution and global climatic concern into practical advice on land use/transport planning. The advice from the DoE raises hope that sustainability arguments will be given greater prominence in plan enquiries, appeals and development control decisions. PPG13, for example, advises local planning authorities to consider carefully: 'the impacts on travel demand of all new development before planning permission is granted. Well considered locational policies in plans, designed to reduce the need for travel, can be undermined by development control decisions which fail to reflect those policies.' Further on, PPG13 advises local authorities in their structure plan policies for industry and commerce to: 'focus the opportunities for development of travel intensive uses (such as offices) in urban areas in locations well served, or with a clear potential to be well served, by public transport.' The advice coming from the Department of the Environment is clearly moving in the direction of planning for a sustainable future.

It is in the field of transport that the planning system can exert the greatest influence on sustainability. Transportation and land use patterns are closely linked and it is here that planning has its most important role. This planning role can have a great influence upon the form of cities, an influence which may be stimulating or restrictive and regressive. Clearly those interested in urban design in all its many aspects should be making certain that the planning system takes into account the principles of sustainable urban design. The planning system is going through a major and welcome change. The ideas of the designer should be at the centre of those changes to counterbalance the politically more powerful voice and disabling myopic vision of the roads transport industry.

Trips in the motor car have tended to get longer over the last few decades. This is partly because of the low fuel costs but also because of the changes in land use patterns and the development of road infrastructure. Planning policies should therefore avoid perpetuating this situation by avoiding road investment where possible and by supporting land use policies which emphasize both non-motorized travel and the longer journeys by public transport. The planning policies to achieve these objectives would: maximize self-sufficiency in cities and their quarters in terms of jobs, services and facilities; plan compact rather than dispersed cities; plan for higher densities; dispose development along public transport corridors; and develop clear viable centres with vitality.

Most journeys made in cities are still short with walking as the main mode of movement; cycling has great potential but is inhibited by a lack of safe routes in many cities. Planning should aim to increase the use of walking and cycling as a means of movement in cities, while reducing the need for longer journeys. This policy means, in practical terms, that schools, shops, health facilities and work places should be close to the home, that is, in centres serving a residential catchment area of 500 metres radius. Achieving these planning aims presupposes priority being given to walking in both centres and in residential areas, including the development of a safe and attractive network of pedestrian priority routes. A similarly effective system of cycle routes like those in some parts of Nottingham is also a necessary objective of environmental planning. The policy presupposes average net residential densities of 100 people per hectare or 40-50 dwellings to the hectare, with buildings being arranged in street blocks of one acre to one hectare with perimeter development defining a clear and permeable system of streets and paths. A mix of land uses in city areas is more likely to result in a safer, vibrant and more sustainable city than one sub-divided into large single-use zones. At the heart of the pedestrian zone or neighbourhood should be the centre composed of the facilities required by the community for daily living.

The achievement of an energy-efficient city transport system where priority is given to public transport, walking and cycling depends ultimately upon a reversal of trends in the economy and in life-styles. In particular it means a more general acceptance of public transport and the rejection of the long-standing and deep love affair the British people have with the motor car. For urban form it will mean the concentration of development along public transport corridors where high density suburbs based on concepts similar to those of Soria y Mata may prove useful in restructuring cities. It will also mean the promotion of development at points of public interchange, encouraging walking and cycling to such points rather than park and ride schemes which in some instances promote the use of the car. Other interesting ideas for car restraint are being proposed in Amsterdam. In 1991 there was a change in planning philosophy in Amsterdam which since then insists that new urban developments of high density occur within or on the periphery of existing cities, thus reducing the need for mobility: the aim is the compact city. The new attitude to development involves classifying all proposed developments and redevelopments according to their transport mobility needs and their accessibility characteristics. The policy is specifically designed for urban areas and the location of the main generators of journeys, offices, shops, services, entertainment, recreation and cultural facilities, schools and health facilities. Developments are then steered to appropriate sites. Locations are given accessibility profiles and developments mobility profiles. The aim of the planning process is to match the profile of the developments' needs and the locations' qualities. Existing and potential urban sites are given one of three classifications:

Class A locations are served mainly by public transport, centred on a main railway station and served by a frequent inter-city service to other towns and cities. Stringent car parking standards are applied with the aim that no more than 10-20 per cent of commuters travel by car. The area should be pleasant and easy to use by pedestrians, cyclists, the disabled and those with special needs: it should also be well served by other means of public transport.

- Class B locations are reasonably well served by good public transport and have good accessibility by road and motorway interchanges. These areas may be centred on a suburban rail station, a major metro station, a Sneltram (Light Rail) stop or the hub of bus services in a small town. Parking is mainly restricted to the needs of businesses which are moderately dependent on the car for their work.
- Class C locations are sited close to motorway interchanges with no plans or requirements for public transport but collective transport such as car and van pooling is encouraged. These locations are intended for business and other activities with low work intensity but dependent on road freight.

The Amsterdam policies are of great interest for their attempt to distribute activities throughout the urban area on a rational analysis of their mobility requirements and also for the thorough way in which public transport is prioritized (Sturt, 1993).

There are two broad views about the type of urban form which best facilitates sustainable development. There are those who emphasize high density development: they would argue that high densities encourage and support walking, cycling and public transport. High densities are also associated with terrace development and therefore with energy-efficient buildings, and also with economies in the provision of infrastructure such as sewers, drain and water mains. High densities also have advantages for the installation of combined heat and power schemes. High density urban development is usually associated with the rich townscapes of medieval European cities like Venice, Florence or Montepulciano. With such a pedigree the high density model for sustainable urban form is

endowed with a clear aesthetic appeal. This model of sustainable development, in general terms, is being strongly advocated in Continental Europe where it has a long and distinguished cultural history. In Britain there are those who stress garden city or garden suburban forms. This group point out that low densities have advantages for solar heating in homes, for extensive vegetable gardens and allotments for the recycling of domestic waste. There is a third compromise solution which aims to combine the best features of both schools of thought: good accessibility without town cramming. This suggestion relies on high net densities as applied to specific street blocks while gross densities are low enough to include the neighbourhood parks, allotments, shelter belts and wild life refuges. The net densities being advocated are 100 persons to the hectare (Barton *et al.*, 1995). The type of four-storey development in Elkin *et al.* (1991a) (Figure 8.1) would be compatible with densities of 100 persons per hectare or higher. While this may be the ideal

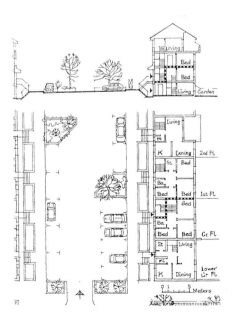

Figure 8.1 Four-storey development (Sherlock, 1990 from Elkin *et al.*, 1991)

built form for the sustainable city and could result in a fine urban landscape, it does little to counter the preference of the British for the detached or semi-detached villa in a leafy suburb. Sustainable city planning must come to terms with the vast suburban sprawl enveloping most towns and cities which will survive for many decades. It will also be helping to form the housing preferences for the next generation. In this country any move towards higher net densities will be slow if the views of the British people are to be considered.

Open green space in and around cities is important for a number of reasons. These reasons include: the function of soil and its vegetation as a carbon sink; the function of the tree cover as an 'atmospheric scrubber' removing particulate pollution; the function of green areas as protectors of flora and fauna and the maintenance of biodiversity. In addition to these environmental functions the green areas associated with cities provide areas for recreation, food production and economic tree cropping. The reasons to protect the countryside and enhance the landscaping in and around cities are manifold. The byproduct of care for the natural landscape is the great aesthetic pleasure it affords the citizen. With such great benefits to mankind there should be no problem with conservation of the landscape in and around cities, as Barton *et al.* (1995) point out: 'Nature conservation is not contentious in principle, but when "balanced" against need for development, tends to be marginalized in reality. *Sustainable development* takes more account of the intrinsic value of the natural capital, and requires that any proposed development – once justified in terms of actual human need – respects the natural environment as the context within which it should fit.'

The star-shaped city is an urban form which may prove to be useful for the spatial organization of small to moderately sized cities (Blumenfeld, 1949). It offers the prospect for the development of high density urban corridors based on a public transport spine alternating with continuous landscape features

connecting the innermost parts of the urban areas with the working countryside. Green corridors permit the movement of wildlife within cities and if formed of indigenous vegetation they provide a rich habitat for a diversity of flora and fauna. A number of cities, Leicester for example, are developing this idea of the green corridor as a tool both for the protection of biodiversity and to provide a sense of continuity between town and country. Other features of the city's landscape plan would include the protection of large-scale *refuges* for the management of areas of ecological interest. Where it is not possible to connect refuges and other landscape features into corridors, small stepping stones or areas of vegetation can be used to provide shelter for local wildlife in transit between them: areas of private open space such as networks of rear gardens, green building façades and roof gardens complete a system of havens for small creatures.

The quarter is the main component of urban design. It is also fundamental for sustainable development, particularly when the idea of a physical area of homogeneous architectural character is linked with the notion of the quarter as a political unit within the city. Effective sustainable development is linked with the idea of public participation in decision-making and with people taking responsibility for the environment. For example, the catch phrase; 'think globally act locally' is linked with the Local Agenda 21 movement which exhorts people to become involved with the concerns for their immediate environment. Local action built on public participation requires the legitimacy of a political structure and a population or power base big enough to challenge the views of the city authority but small enough to encourage high levels of participation. The population of a quarter is also, in part, determined by the area it occupies and the density of occupation. There is a growing consensus which would limit the area of a quarter to one which is determined by the comfortable walking distance from the perimeter to its centre, a distance of about a half mile at the most. There is no absolute or perfect population size for the quarter. Ideas vary from Jacobs who suggests 100 000 to the British 1950s new town neighbourhood of 5 000 people. The size of the quarter may vary with the size of the city, the densities acceptable in the locality or the general culture of community which exists in the city. Most cities, however, are sub-divided into traditional quarters which can be named and recognized by the inhabitants of the city. It is these traditional quarters which should be the starting point for the definition of the political unit for purposes of participation. More important than size is delegated political power in the form of an elected body with a recognized role. Anything short of a political structure is the emasculation of the idea of the quarter for purposes of local action for sustainable development: the quarter in these circumstances is little more than a device for developing areas with distinctive visual identity but without social *raison d'être*. Leicester, with its fine tradition in the field of sustainable development and sensitive approach to the environment, seems to have adopted this superficial approach to the definition of *Quartier* for the City Centre (Leicester City Council, 1995).

The street block of between an acre and hectare in extent surrounded by three- or four-storey perimeter development appears to be the basic urban form which is being advocated for city infill by a growing consensus of designers. It also appears that this form of urban insulae, when it is occupied by a mix of uses, has advantages for the purposes of sustainable development. City centres where large street blocks were formed when redevelopment occurred have resulted in the destruction of the original fine grain of the traditional city. Large street blocks occupied by single uses, often in single ownership, destroy the vigour and vitality of the city, particularly if the sections of the city they occupy die at night or at the weekend. It is an attempt to arrest and reverse this process which is one of the reasons for the current preoccupation with the design of small-scale insulae or street

blocks. Where street blocks are designed primarily for residential use the backs of the properties can face onto shared external semi-private space: 'A small area of external space can be directly related to each housing group, dedicated to shared activities and uses ... The distribution of open spaces relating directly to small housing groups may result in a more economical use of space, of higher quality, with better maintenance, than the specification of a single large area of public open space' (Barton *et al.*, 1995). There is a fine model at Letchworth designed by Unwin for this method of siting small groups of housing. The homes arranged around the perimeter of the block have individual gardens and, in some cases, there is also a communal vegetable garden or allotments in the internal court (Figures 7.26 to 7.27). The traditional morphology of the medieval European town on which Unwin based many of his own writings is still today a sound basis for developing a form of insulae suited to the needs of the sustainable city.

There are two types of energy used in buildings (Vale and Vale, 1993). The first is the energy used to construct the building, which becomes the energy capital analogous to the capital value of the completed property. The second is energy revenue or energy used to service, operate and maintain the building. In any decision to demolish, rebuild or refurbish a building both types of energy consumption in each option should be assessed and, in theory, the decision should favour the development which is most economic in the expenditure of energy, particularly from non-renewable energy sources.

There are a number of design principles which help in this delicate balancing act and which assist in achieving energy conservation in buildings. The first principle of sustainable building is a preference for and a presumption in favour of the conservation of buildings and their adaptation to new uses. An extension of this principle is a strong preference for the reuse and recycling of building materials and components in the construction of new buildings and infrastructure as opposed to the use of new materials and components straight from the factory or quarry. The second principle requires the use of local or regional materials where possible and particularly where those materials require low energy inputs in fabrication, transportation to the site and in the construction process itself. In Weobley, for example, new developments have been carefully crafted from local materials, using local structural systems. Weobley is a fine example of a half-timbered medieval village and the infill is particularly sensitive but the cost of the new properties would probably be beyond the means of most rural workers. Another example of recent buildings using traditional materials are the groups of delightful thatched cottages in many Irish small towns which provide much-needed self-catering holiday accommodation (Figures 8.2 to 8.7). The third principle is to avoid those materials which cause environmental damage such as the destruction of the tropical rain forest or leave behind scars on the landscape. The fourth principle is to relate buildings to the local environment and particularly to the local climate: for example, in a cold climate to insulate the building effectively; to reduce to a minimum the amount

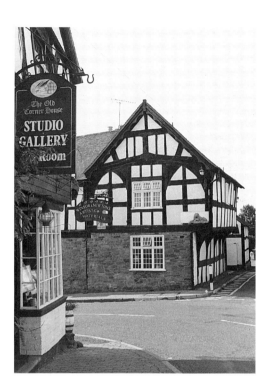

Figures 8.2 to 8.4
Weobley

8.2

8.4

8.5

8.6

8.7

of external wall surface; to orientate the building towards the sun; to provide a buffer on the cold north face and to build conservatories on the sunny façades. The fifth principle is to design robust and flexible buildings which will stand up to the test of time. Buildings should be designed so that a mix of uses can be accommodated beneath the same roof and so that floor plans can be adapted for different uses during its lifetime. Finally, new buildings should be located on public transport routes and with close connections to other parts of the urban infrastructure. Wherever possible, buildings should be erected on urban infill sites, that is, they should fit into the street block as perimeter development where they should complement the street scene being three to four storeys high and without lifts.

The requirements of sustainable development closely mirror the current agenda in urban design. The reactions to modern architecture and planning have led to a new appreciation of the traditional European city and its urban form. The current preoccupations of urban designers with the form of urban space, the vitality and identity of urban areas, qualities of urbanity, respect for tradition and the preferences for developments of human scale can all be encompassed within the schema of sustainable development. The two movements - Sustainable Development and Post Modern Urban Design - are mutually supportive. Post Modern Urban Design gives form to the menu of ideas subsumed under the title of Sustainable Development; in return, it is given functional legitimacy. Without this functional legitimacy and the discipline it imposes on the design process Post Modern Urban Design may develop into just another esoteric aesthetic. The foundation of urban design is rooted in social necessity: society is faced with an environmental crisis of global proportions and it is coming to terms with the effects of this crisis on the world's cities which gives purpose and meaning to urban design.

Figure 8.5 Weobley, new property. Well-mannered architecture or pastiche? Sustainable development or expensive building construction for the wealthy?

Figure 8.6 Self-catering holiday accommodation, Ireland

BIBLIOGRAPHY

Abercrombie, P. (1945) *Greater London Plan*,London: HMSO.

Alberti, L.B. (1955) *Ten Books on Architecture* (trns. Cosimo Bartoli into Italian and James Leoni into English),London: Tiranti.

Alexander, C. (1965) 'A City is not a Tree', *Architectural Forum*, April pp. 58-62, May pp. 58-61.

Alexander, C. (1979) *The Oregon Experiment*, Oxford: Oxford University Press.

Alexander, C. (1979) *A Timeless Way of Building*, New York: Oxford University Press.

Alexander, C. *et al.* (1977) *A Pattern Language*, New York: Oxford University Press.

Alexander, C. *et al.* (1987) *A New Theory of Urban Design*, Oxford: Oxford University Press.

Amourgis, S. (ed.) (1991) *Critical Regionalism*, California: University of Pomona.

Architectural Design (1993) *New Practice in Urban Design*, London: Academy Editions.

Aristotle (1981) *The Politics* (trans. T.A. Sinclair, revised by T.J. Saunders), Harmondsworth: Penguin.

Barton, H. *et al.* (1995) *Sustainable Settlements*, Luton: L.G.M.B.

Bennett, H. *et al.* (1961) *The Planning of a New Town*, London: HMSO.

Bentley, I. *et al.* (1985) *Responsive Environments*, Oxford: Butterworths.

Beresford, M. (1967) *New Towns of the Middle Ages*, London: Lutterworth Press.

Blowers, A. (ed.) 1993) *Planning for a Sustainable Environment*, London: Earthscan.

Blumenfeld, H. (1949) 'Theory of City Form: Past and Present', *Journal of the Society of Architectural Historians*, Vol. 8, July.

Boyd, A. (1962) *Chinese Architecture and Town Planning*, London: Tiranti.

Boyd, C. *et al.* (1945) *Homes for the People*, London: HMSO.

Breheny, M. and Rookwood, R. (1993) 'Planning the Sustainable Region', in *Planning for a Sustainable Environment*, ed. A. Blowers, London: Earthscan.

Bruges, J. (1992) 'Changing Attitudes to the City', *Urban Design Quarterly*, July, Issue 43, pp. 23-5.

Buchanan, C.D. (1963) *Traffic in Towns*, London: HMSO.

Buchanan, C.D. (1963) *Traffic in Towns: The Specially Shortened edition of the Buchanan Report*, Harmondsworth: Penguin.

Buchanan, C.D. *et al.* (1966) *South Hampshire Study*, London: HMSO.

Calthorpe, P. (1993) *The Next American Metropolis*, New York: Princetown Architectural Press.

Camblin, G. (1951) *The Town in Ulster*, Belfast: Mullan.

Capra, F. (1985) *The Turning Point*, London: Flamingo.

Carpenter, R. (1970) *The Architects of the Parthenon*, Harmondsworth: Penguin.

Carson, R. (1962) *Silent Spring*, Harmondsworth: Penguin.

Chadwick, G.F. (1966) 'A Systems View of Planning', *Journal of the Town Planning Institute*, Vol. 52, pp. 184-6.

Christaller, W. (1933) *Die zentrallen Orte in Suddeutschland*, Jena: Gustav Fischer.

Christaller, W. (1966) *Central Places in Southern Germany* (trns. C.W. Baskin), Englewood Cliffs, New Jersey: Prentice Hall.

Clifton-Taylor, A. (1972) *The Pattern of English Building*, London: Faber and Faber.

Colvin, B. (1948) *Land and Landscape*, London: John Murray

Commission of the European Communities (1990) *Green Paper on the Urban Environment*, Luxembourg: CEC

Commission of the EC (1992) *Towards Sustainability: A European Community Programme of Policy and Action in relation to the Environment and Sustainable Development*, Official Publication of the EC (Cm (92) 23/11 Final).

Cullen, G. (1961) *Townscape*, London: Architectural Press.

de Bono, E. (1977) *Lateral Thinking*, Harmondsworth: Penguin.

Denyer, G. (1978) *African Traditional Architecture*, London: Heinemann.

Department of the Environment (1969) *Committee on Public Participation: The Skeffington Report*, London: HMSO.

Department of the Environment (1990) *This Common Inheritance, Britain's Environmental Strategy*, CM 1200, London: HMSO.

Department of the Environment (1992a) *Development Plans, A Good Practice Guide*, London: HMSO.

Department of the Environment (1992b) *Planning, Pollution and Waste Management*, London: HMSO.

Department of the Environment (1992c) *Planning Policy Guidance: PPG12, Development Plans and Regional Planning Guidance*, London: HMSO.

Department of the Environment (1993) *Planning Policy Guidance: PPG6, Town Centres and Retail Development (Revised)*, London: HMSO.

Department of the Environment (1993a) *Reducing Transport Emissions Through Planning*, London: HMSO.

Department of the Environment (1993b) *Environmental Appraisal of Development*, London: HMSO.

Department of the Environment (1993c) *Planning Policy Guidance, Town Centres and Retail Developments, PPG6 (Revised)*, London: HMSO.

Department of the Environment (1994a) *Climate Change, The UK Programme*, London: HMSO.

Department of the Environment (1994b) *Biodiversity: The UK Action Plan*, London: HMSO.

Department of the Environment (1994c) *Sustainable Forestry: The UK Programme*, London: HMSO.

Department of the Environment (1994d) *Sustainable Development: The UK Strategy*, London: HMSO.

Department of the Environment (1994e) *Planning Policy Guidance, Transport, PPG13*, London: HMSO.

Dethier, J. (1981) *Down to Earth* (trns. Ruth Eaton), London: Thames and Hudson.

Dobson, A. (1990) *Green Political Thought*, London: Harper Collins Academic.

Dobson, A. (1991) *The Green Reader*, London: Andre Deutsch.

Doxiadis, C.A. (1968) *Ekistics*, London: Hutchinson.

Dutt, B.B. (1925) *Town Planning in Ancient India*, Calcutta: Thacker, Soink. (Reprint 1977, Delhi: Nai Sarak.)

Elkin, T. *et al.* (1991a) *Reviving the City*, London: Friends of the Earth.

Elkin, T., *et al.* (1991b) *Towards Sustainable Urban Development*, London: Friends of the Earth.

European Conference of Ministers of Transport (ECMT) (1993) *Transport Policy and Global Warming*, Paris: OECD.

Fairman, H.W. (1949) 'Town Planning in Pharaonic Egypt', *Town Planning Review*, April, pp. 32-51.

Fawcett, C.B. (1961) *Provinces of England*, revised edition, London: Hutchinson.

Fox, A. and Murrell, R. (1989) *Green Design*, London: Architectural Design and Technology Press.

Frankfort, H. (1954) *The Art and Architecture of the Ancient Orient*, Harmondsworth: Penguin.

Futagawa, Y. (ed) (1974) *Le Corbusier - Chandigarh, the New Capital of Punjab, India 1951*, Tokyo: A.D.A Edita.

Geddes, P. (1949) *Cities in Evolution*, London: Williams and Norgate.

Ghazi, P. (1995) 'Motorists to Face Blitz on Pollution', *The Observer*, 12 February, p.2.

Gibberd, F. (1955) *Town Design*, London: Architectural Press.

Gibson, T. (1979) *People Power*, Harmondsworth: Penguin.

Giedion, S. (1954) *Space, Time and Architecture*, 3rd edition, enlarged 1956, Cambridge, Massachusetts: Harvard University Press.

Glancey, J. (1989) *New British Architecture*, London: Thames and Hudson.

Glasson, J. (1978) *An Introduction to Regional Planning*, second edition, London: Hutchinsons.

Gordon, W.J.J. (1961) *Synectics: the Development of Creative Capacity*, New York: Harper Row.

Gosling, D., and Maitland, B. (1984) *Concepts of Urban Design*, London: Academy Editions.

Gropius, W. (1935) *New Architecture and the Bauhaus* (trns. P.M. Shand and F. Pick), London: Faber and Faber.

Guidoni, E. (1975) *Primitive Architecture*, London: Faber and Faber.

HRH The Prince of Wales (1989) *A Vision of Britain*, London: Doubleday.

Hardin, G. (1977) 'The Tragedy of the Commons', in *Managing the Commons*, eds G. Hardin and J. Baden, San Francisco: Freeman and Co..

Harvey, D. (1973) *Social Justice and the City*, London: Edward Arnold.

Herbertson, A.J. (1905) 'The Major Natural Regions', *Geographical Journal*, Vol. 25.

Horton, R. (1971) 'Stateless Societies in the History of West Africa,' *History of West Africa, Vol. 1*, ed. J.F.A. Ajayi and M. Crowder, London: Longmans.

Houghton-Evans, W. (1975) *Planning Cities: Legacy and Portent*, London: Lawrence and Wishart.

Howard, E. (1965) *Garden Cities of Tomorrow*, London: Faber and Faber.

Hugo-Brunt, M. (1972) *The History of City Planning*, Montreal: Harvest House.

Irving, R.G. (1981) *Indian Summer*, New Haven: Yale University Press.

Jacobs, J. (1965) *The Death and Life of Great American Cities*, Harmondsworth: Penguin.

Koenigsberger, O.H. *et al.* (1973) *Manual of Tropical Housing, Part 1, Climate Design*, London: Longman.

Kopp, A. (1970) *Town and Revolution* (trns. Burton), London: Thames and Hudson.

Korn, A., and Samuelly, F.J. (1942) 'A Master Plan for London', *Architectural Review*, No 546, June, pp. 143-50.

Krier, R. (1979) *Urban Space*, London: Academy Editions.

Krier, L. (1978) *Rational Architecture*, Brussels. Archives d'Architecture Moderne.

Krier, L. (1984) *Houses, Palaces and Cities*, ed. D. Porphyrios, London: Academy Editions.

Krier, L., and Krier R. (1993) 'Berlin Government Centre', in *Architectural Design, New Practice in Urban Design*, London: Academy Editions.

Le Corbusier (1946) *Towards a New Architecture*, London: Architectural Press.

Le Corbusier (1947) *Concerning Town Planning*, London: Architectural Press.

Le Corbusier (1967) *The Radiant City*, London: Faber and Faber.

Le Corbusier (1971) *The City of Tomorrow*, London: Architectural Press.

Le Courbusier and de Pierrefeu F. (1948) *The Home of Man*, London: The Architectural Press.

Leicester City Council (1989) *Leicester Ecology Strategy, Part One*, Leicester: Leicester City Council.

Leicester City Council (1995) *A City Centre for People (Draft)*, Leicester: Leicester City Council.

Ling, A. (1967) *Runcorn New Town Master Plan*, Runcorn: Runcorn Development Corporation.

Lip, E. (1989) *Feng Shiu for Business*, Singapore: Times Editions.

Llewellyn-Davies, R. (1966) *Washington New Town Master Plan*, Washington: Washington Development Corporation.

Llewellyn-Davies, R. (1970) *The Plan for Milton Keynes*, Bletchley: Milton Keynes Development Corporation.

Lloyd Wright, F. (1957) *A Testament*, New York: Horizon Press.

Lloyd Wright, F. (1958) *The Living City*, New York: Mentor Books.

Local Government Management Board (1993) *A Framework for Local Sustainability*, Luton: LGMB.

Lynch, K. (1960) *The Image of the City*, Cambridge, Massachusetts: MIT Press.

Lynch, K. (1981) *A Theory of Good City Form*, Cambridge, Massachusetts: MIT Press.

March, L. (1974) 'Homes beyond the fringe', in *The Future of Cities*, ed. A. Blowers, London: Hutchinson, pp. 167-78.

Martin, L. (1974) 'The Grid as Generator', in *The Future of Cities*, ed. A. Blowers, London: Hutchinson, pp. 179-89.

Martin, L., and March L., (eds) (1972) *Urban Space and Structures*, London: Cambridge University Press.

Matthew, R. (1967) *Central Lancashire: Study for a City*, London: HMSO.

Macdonald, R. (1989) 'The European Healthy Cities Project', *Urban Design Quarterly*, April, pp. 4-7.

McKei, R. (1974) 'Cellular Renewal', *Town Planning Review*, Vol. 45, pp. 274-90.

McLaughlin, J.B. (1969) *Urban and Regional Planning: A Systems Approach*, London: Faber.

Meadows, D.H., *et al.* (1972) *The Limits to Growth*, London: Earth Island.

Meadows, D.H., *et al.* (1992) *Beyond the Limits*, London: Earthscan.

Miliutin, N.A. (1973) *Sotsgorod: The Problem of Building Socialist Cities*, eds G.R. Collins and W. Alex (trns. A Sprague), Cambridge, Massachusetts: MIT Press.

Millon, R. (1973) *Urbanization at Tetihuacan, Mexico*, Austin: University of Texas Press.

Morris, A.E.J. (1972) *History of Urban Form*, London: George Godwin.

Moughtin, J.C. (1985) *Hausa Architecture*, London: Ethnographica.

Moughtin, J.C. (ed.)(1988) *The Work of Z.R. Dmochoski, Nigerian Traditional Architecture*, London: Ethnographica.

Moughtin, J.C. (1992) *Urban Design: Street and Square*, Oxford: Butterworth.

Moughtin, J.C., Oc, T. and Tiesdell, S.A. (1995) *Urban Design: Ornament and Decoration*, Oxford: Butterworth.

Moughtin, J.C., and Simpson, A. (1978) 'Do it yourself planning in Raleigh Street', *New Society*, 19 October, pp. 136-7.

Mumford, L. (1938) *The Culture of Cities*, London: Secker and Warburg.

Mumford, L. (1946a) *City Development*, London: Secker and Warburg.

Mumford, L. (1946b) *Technics and Civilization*, London: George Routledge.

Mumford, L. (1961) *The City in History*, Harmondsworth: Penguin.

Nicolas, G. (1966) 'Essai sur les structures fondamentales de l'espace dans la cosmologie hausa', *Journal de societie des Africanistes*, Vol. 36, pp. 65-107.

Norberg-Schulz, C. (1971) *Existence, Space and Architecture*, London: Studio Vista.

Ons Amsterdam (1973) *Amsterdamse School*, Amsterdam.

Osborn, F.J., and Whittick, A. (1977) *New Towns*, London: Leonard Hill.

Owens, S. (1991) *Energy Concious Planning*, London: CPRE.

Pateman, C. (1970) *Participation and Democratic Theory*, Cambridge: Cambridge University Press.

Pearce, D., *et al.* (1989) *Blueprint for a Green Economy*, London: Earthscan.

Pearce, D., *et al.* (1993) *Blueprint 3, Measuring Sustainable Development*, London: Earthscan.

Pehnt, W. (1973) *Expressionist Architecture*, London: Thames and Hudson.

Perry, C. (1929) *The Neighbourhood Unit, The Regional Plan of New York and its Environs, Vol. 7*, New York: Regional Plan Association.

Plato (1975) *The Laws* (trns. T.J. Saunders), Harmondsworth: Penguin.

Platt, C. (1976) *The English Medieval Town*, London: Martin Secker and Warburg.

Public Works Department, Amsterdam (1975) *Amsterdam, Planning and Development*, Amsterdam: The Town Planning Section, Public Works Department.

Rogers, R. (1995a) 'Looking Forward to Compact City, Second Reith Lecture,' *The Independent*, 20 February.

Rogers, R. (1995b) 'The Imperfect Form of the New: Third Reith Lecture,' *The Guardian*, 21 February.

Rose, R. (1971) *Governing without Consensus*, London: Faber and Faber.

Rosenau, H. (1974) *The Ideal City*, London: Studio Vista.

Royal Commission on Environmental Pollution (1974) *Fourth Report, Pollution Control, Progress and Problems*, Cmnd 5780, London: HMSO.

Royal Commission on Environmental Pollution (1994) *Eighteenth Report, Transport and the Environment*, Cmnd 2674, London: HMSO.

Rowland, B. (1953) *The Art and Architecture of India*, Harmondsworth: Penguin.

Sanders, W.S. (1905) *Municipalisation by Provinces*, London: Fabian Society.

Sattler, C. (1993) 'Posdamer Platz - Leipziger Platz,' in *Architectural Design, New Practice in Urban Design*, London: Academy Editions, pp. 86-91.

Schumacher, E.F. (1974) *Small is Beautiful*, London: Abacus.

Senior, D. (1965) 'The City Region as an Administrative Unit', *Political Quarterly*, Vol. 36.

Sherlock, H. (1990) *Cities are Good for Us*, London: Transport 2000.

Shukla, D.N. (1960) *Vastu-Sastra: The Hindu Science of Architecture, Vol. 1*, Lucknow: Vastu-Vanmaya-Praksana-Sala.

Sitte, C. (1901) *Der Stadt-bau*, Wien: Carl Graeser.

Spreiregen, P.D. (1965) *Urban Design: The Architecture of Towns and Cities*, New York: McGraw-Hill.

Stamp, L.D., and Beaver, S. H. (1933) *The British Isles, A Geographic and Economic Survey*, (6th edn 1971), London: Longmans.

Stevenson Smith, W. (1958) *The Art and Architecture of Ancient Egypt*, Harmondsworth: Penguin

Stroud, D. (1950) *Capability Brown*, London: Country Life.

Sturt, A. (1993) 'Putting Broad Accessibility Principles into Planning Practice', *Town and Country Planning*, October.

Svensson, O. (1981) *Danish Town Planning: Guide*, Copenhagen: Ministry of the Environment.

Toffler, A. (1973) *Future Shock*, London: Pan Books.

Toffler, A. (1980) *The Third Wave*, London: Collins.

Turner, T. (1992) 'Wilderness and Plenty: Construction and Deconstruction,' *Urban Design Quarterly*, September, Issue 44, pp. 20-1.

United Nations. (1992) *Conference on Environment and Development*, New York: UN.

Unstead, J.F. (1916) 'A Synthetic Method of Determining Geographical Regions', *Geographical Journal*, Vol. 48.

Unstead, J.F. (1935) *The British Isles: Systematic Regional Geography*, (5th edn 1960), London: London University Press.

Unwin, R. (1909) *Town Planning in Practice*, London.

Unwin, R. (1967) 'Nothing to be Gained by Overcrowding', in *The Legacy of Raymond Unwin: A Human Pattern of Planning*, ed. W.L. Crease, Cambridge, Massachusetts: MIT Press.

Vale, B., and Vale R. (1991) *Green Architecture*, London: Thames and Hudson.

Vale, B., and Vale, R. (1993) 'Building the Sustainable Environment', in *Planning for a Sustainable Environment*, ed. A Blowers, London: Earthscan Publications.

Vidal de la Blanche, P. (1931) *Principles of Human Geography*, ed. E. de Martonne (trns. M.T. Bingham), New York: Holt.

Walker, D. (1981) *The Architecture and Planning of Milton Keynes*, London: The Architectural Press.

Webber, M.M. (1964) 'The Urban Place and the Non Place Urban Realm', in *Explorations of Urban Structure*, eds M. Webber *et al.*, London: Oxford University Press.

Wheatley, P. (1971) *The Pivot of the Four Quarters*, Edinburgh: Edinburgh University Press.

Wiebenson, D. (undated) *Tony Garnier: The Cité Industrielle*, London: Studio Vista.

Williams-Ellis, C., *et al.* (1947) *Building in Cob, Pise, and Stabilized Earth*, London: Country Life Ltd.

Wilson L.H. (1958) *Cumbernauld New Town*, London: HMSO.

Wilson, L.H. (1959) *Cumbernauld New Town, 1st Addendum Report*, London: HMSO.

Wilson, L.H., *et al.* (1965) *Report on Northampton, Bedford and North Buckinghamshire Study*, London: HMSO.

World Commission on Environment and Development (1987) *Our Common Future: The Brundtland Report*, Oxford: Oxford University Press.

Wotton, H. (1969) *The Elements of Architecture*, London: Gregg.

FIGURE SOURCES

Table 1.1	World Commission on Environment and Development (1987) *Our Common Future: The Brundtland Report*, Oxford: Oxford University Press.
Tables 2.1 and 2.2	Vale, B. and Vale, R. (1991) *Green Architecture*, London: Thames and Hudson.
Fig. 3.3	Stamp, L.D. and Beaver, S.H. (1933) *The British Isles, A Geographic and Economic Survey* (6th Edn 1971), London: Longmans.
Fig. 3.4	Geddes, P. (1949) *Cities in Evolution*, London: Williams and Norgate. (Drawn by Peter Whitehouse.)
Fig. 3.5	Christaller, W. (1966) *Central Places in Southern Germany* (trans. C.W. Baskin), New Jersey: Englewood Cliffs. (Drawn by Peter Whitehouse.)
Fig. 3.6	Blowers, A. (Ed) (1993) *Planning for a Sustainable Environment*, London: Earthscan. (Drawn by Peter Whitehouse.)
Fig 3.7	Glasson, J. (1978) *An Introduction to Regional Planning* (2nd Edn), London: Hutchinsons. (Drawn by Peter Whitehouse.)
Figs 4.1 and 4.3	Stevenson Smith, W. (1958) *The Art and Architecture of Ancient Egypt*, Harmondsworth: Penguin.
Figs 4.2 and 4.30	Fairman, H.W. (1949) Town Planning in Pharaonic Egypt, *Town Planning Review*, April, pp. 32-51.
Figs 4.4 and 4.5	Frankfort, H. (1954), *The Art and Architecture of the Ancient Orient*, Harmondsworth: Penguin.
Fig. 4.6	Boyd, A. (1962) *Chinese Architecture and Town Planning*, London: Tiranti.
Fig. 4.7	Millon, R. (1973) *Urbanization at Tetihuacan, Mexico*, Austin: University of Texas Press.
Fig. 4.11	Morris, A.E.J. (1972) *History of Urban Form*, London: George Godwin.
Figs 4.12, 5.2, 5.25, 5.39, 5.59 and 6.2	Lynch, K. (1981) *A Theory of Good City Form*, Cambridge, Massachusetts: MIT Press. (Figures 4.12, 5.25, 5.39 and 5.59 drawn by Peter Whitehouse).
Fig. 4.16	Drawn by Peter Whitehouse.

Fig. 4.22	Photograph by Neil Leach.
Fig. 4.24	Drawn by Peter Whitehouse.
Fig. 4.25	Le Corbusier (1967) *The Radiant City*, London: Faber and Faber. (Drawn by Peter Whitehouse.)
Fig. 4.26	Drawn by Peter Whitehouse.
Figs 4.27, 5.4 and 5.5	Wiebenson, D. (undated) *Tony Garnier: The Cité Industrielle*, London: Studio Vista. (Drawn by Peter Whitehouse.)
Fig. 4.29	Le Corbusier (1967) *The Radiant City*, London: Faber and Faber.
Fig. 4.31	Wycherley, R.E. (1962) *How the Greeks Built Cities*, London: W.W. Norton.
Figs 4.32, 4.33, and 4.34	Ward Perkins, J.B. (1955) Early Roman Towns in Italy, *Town Planning Review*, October, pp.126-154.
Figs 4.35 and 5.3	Beresford, M. (1967) *New Towns of the Middle Ages*, London: Lutterworth Press. (Drawn by Peter Whitehouse.)
Fig. 4.36	Drawn by Peter Whitehouse.
Fig. 4.39	Camblin, G. (1951) *The Town in Ulster*, Belfast: Mullan.
Figs 4.40 and 4.41	Lloyd Wright, F. (1957) *A Testament*, New York: Horizon Press.
Figs 4.45 and 4.46	Gibberd, F. (1955) *Town Design*, London: Architectural Press. (Drawn by Peter Whitehouse.)
Fig. 5.1	Drawn by Peter Whitehouse.
Figs 5.6 and 5.7	Kopp, A. (1970) *Town and Revolution*, (trans. Burton), London: Thames and Hudson. (Drawn by Peter Whitehouse.)
Fig. 5.8	Drawn by Peter Whitehouse.
Figs 5.9, 5.15, 5.16, 5.54, 6.3, 6.4, 6.5 and 6.6	Houghton-Evans, W. (1975) *Planning Cities: Legacy and Portent*, London: Lawrence and Wishart. (Figures 5.9, 5.16, 5.54, 6.5 and 6.6 drawn by Peter Whitehouse.)
Fig. 5.10	Matthew, R. (1967) *Central Lancashire Study for a City*, London: HMSO. (Drawn by Peter Whitehouse.)
Fig. 5.11	Drawn by Peter Whitehouse.
Figs 5.17, 5.19, 5.20, 5.21 and 5.22	March, L. (1974) Homes beyond the fringe, in *The Future of Cities*, Ed. A. Blowers, London: Hutchinson, pp. 167-78. (Drawn by Peter Whitehouse.)
Fig. 5.18	Drawn by Peter Whitehouse.
Figs 5.23a and 5.23b	Drawings by Z.R. Dmochowski, in Moughtin, J.C. (ed.) (1988) *The Work of Z.R. Dmochowski: Nigerian Traditional Architecture*, London: Ethnographica.
Fig. 5.24	Lloyd Wright, F. (1958) *The Living City*, New York: Mentor Books.
Fig. 5.26	Buchanan, C.D. (1963) *Traffic in Towns: The Specially Shortened Edition of the Buchanan Report*, Harmondsworth: Penguin.
Figs 5.27, 5.28, 5.29 and 5.30	Drawings by Peter Whitehouse.
Figs 5.31, 5.32, 5.33, 5.34 and 5.37	Buchanan, C.D. *et al.* (1966) *South Hampshire Study*, London: HMSO. (Drawn by Peter Whitehouse.)
Fig. 5.35	Futagawa, Y. (Ed), (1974) *Le Corbusier - Chandigarh, The New Capital of Punjab, India 1951-*, Tokio: ADA EDITA. (Drawn by Peter Whitehouse.)
Fig. 5.36	Drawn by Peter Whitehouse.

Figs 5.49, 5.50 and 5.51	Howard, E. (1965) *Garden Cities of Tomorrow*, London: Faber and Faber.
Figs 5.57a, 5.58a, 5.58b, 7.41, 7.42, 7.43a, 7.43b, 7.44 and 7.45	Architectural Design (1993) *New Practice in Urban Design*, London: Academy Editions.
Fig. 5.60	Svensson, O. (1981) *Danish Town Planning: Guide*, Copenhagen: Ministry of the Environment.
Fig. 5.61	Stroud, D. (1950) *Capability Brown*. London: Country Life.
Fig. 6.1	Drawn by Peter Whitehouse.
Figs 6.7a, 6.7b and 6.7c	Photographs by Pat Braniff.
Figs 6.14, 6.15, 6.19 and 6.20	Giedion, S. (1954) *Space Time and Architecture*, Cambridge, Massachusetts: Harvard University Press.
Figs 6.16, 6.17 and 6.18	Public Works Department, Amsterdam (1975) *Amsterdam, Planning and Development*, Amsterdam: The Town Planning Section, Public Works Department.
Fig. 6.21	Doxiadis, C.A. (1968) *Ekistics*, London: Hutchinson.
Figs 6.31, 6.32 and 6.33	Krier, L. (1984) *Houses, Palaces and Cities*, Ed. D. Porphyrios, London: Academy Editions.
Figs 6.34 and 6.35	Calthorpe, P. (1993) *The Next American Metropolis*, New York: Princetown Architectural Press.
Figs 7.1 and 7.2	Gropius, W. (1935) *New Architecture and the Bauhaus* (trans. P.M. Shand and F. Pick), London: Faber and Faber.
Fig. 7.5	Photograph by Bridie Neville.
Fig. 7.11	Alexander, C. (1987) *A New Theory of Urban Design*, Oxford: Oxford University Press.
Fig. 7.12	Drawn by Peter Whitehouse.
Figs 7.15, 7.16 and 7.17	Bentley, I., *et al* (1985) *Responsive Environments*, Oxford: Butterworths.
Fig. 7.25	Drawing by Peter Whitehouse.
Fig. 7.20	Pehut, W. (1973) *Expressionist Architecture*, London: Thames and Hudson.
Fig. 7.35	Drawing by Julyan Wickham.
Figs 7.40a, 7.40b and 7.40c	Photographs by June Greenaway.
Fig. 8.1	Sherlock, H. (1990) *Cities Are Good For Us*, London: Transport 2000.

INDEX